THE ELEMENTARY ATARI

THE ELEMENTARY ATARI

By

William B. Sanders, Ph.D.
San Diego State University

Illustrations by
Martin Cannon

DATAMOST INC
8943 Fullbright Avenue
Chatsworth, CA 91311-2750
(818) 709-1202

DATAMOST

ISBN 0-88190-117-2

ACKNOWLEDGEMENTS

Several people helped directly or indirectly in the creation of ELEMENTARY ATARI. First and foremost, I owe a great deal to Eric Goez. Eric taught me more about programming than anyone else; especially about the importance of good algorithms in programming. Having only 16K of RAM memory in the standard ATARI 4ØØ, a good algorithm is indeed worth a thousand bytes of memory! Secondly, Bill Parker got across the point of structured programming to me better than anyone else ever has. Finally, the many users of the ATARI, especially those in the local ATARI club, the San Diego Atari Computer Enthusiasts (ACE), provided me with a number of hints and tips that I would have been unable to accumulate without their help and knowledge.

Dave Gordon of DATAMOST INC. provided a world of support for the book's production. Marcia Carrozzo edited the manuscript for style and consistency, making the work a good deal clearer. She also had to learn about using the ATARI to make sure that what was in the manuscript worked on the computer. Also, Marcia's strong background in math was very helpful for improving many of the programs. Hal Glicksman debugged the programs where the inevitable typos crept in. This will save beginner's from the frustrations of little errors that have disastrous results. Martin Cannon did the art work in a way that communicated ideas creatively and visually. He gave life to the notion that a picture is worth a thousand words. The rest of the staff at DATAMOST were equally helpful and friendly.

Finally, my wife Eli and sons Billy and David, and even our dog Cassiopeia, put up with the inconvenience of a writer in the house. To every one of these people I owe a debt of gratitude, but as in all such efforts, if anything goes wrong, it is only the author who is to blame. Therefore, while I happily give those who assisted credit, any of the book's shortcomings are the sole responsibility of the author.

ACKNOWLEDGEMENTS

TABLE OF CONTENTS

PREFACE

My first formal introduction to the workings of a computer was in 1966. At that time our wise mentor told us that if we learned the lowest level operations of a computer, we would be set for life. As a result of this philosophy, we were taught how to do everything from counting in binary and conversion to octal to the essentials of FORTRAN. The problem was that we never really sat down and programmed at a terminal. So while we had a terrific theoretical understanding of the workings of computers, we did not learn very much about actual programming.

Since that time, both computers and the people who use them have changed. To learn how to use a computer, it is unnecessary to learn everything about how they work or the theory behind their operation. It is true that by having a detailed understanding of the theory and operation of computers one can do more with them, but it is something that does not have to be done at the outset. One can learn how to program, and at a later date learn the more technical details of a computer's operation. After all, most people learn to drive without knowing the intricacies of the internal combustion engine of their automobile.

Another major change in computers has been the transition from "mainframes" and "terminals" to small individual computers. Your ATARI is not merely a terminal. It is a whole computer. Therefore, you are not dependent on using a piece of a larger computer, but you get the whole thing all to yourself. As a result, you are not subject to a set of policies and regulations for getting "on line" or paying for the time you use. You make your own policies and are the captain of your own computer ship. Therefore, it is unnecessary to spend a lot of time discussing the organizational aspects of accessing the CPU (Central Processing Unit), time-sharing, and so forth. We will go right to the heart of the matter, programming YOUR computer.

The purpose of this book is primarily to teach you how to work your computer and program in the language called BASIC. It is ELEMENTARY. So, while you will learn a lot, don't expect to learn everything about working with your ATARI. Once you are finished with this book, you will realize how much more you can do with your computer, and the more you learn, the more you will find to learn. However, by following the instructions and keying in the examples, you will learn how to write programs with most of the instructions in the version of BASIC on your ATARI. Since ATARI now has several different models — 4ØØ, 6ØØXL, 8ØØ, 8ØØXL, 12ØØXL, 14ØØXL, 145ØXL — it was important to have programs that work with all of these computers. Therefore, the STANDARD ATARI BASIC was used for all programs, and works with the BASIC that comes on all new models.

As a final note, don't expect to learn everything right away. Be patient with yourself and your computer, and you will be amazed at how much you will learn. If you do not understand a command or a procedure, you can always come back to it later. Try different things and play with your programs. Think up different projects you would like your computer to do and then try writing a program to do what you want. By all means, though, do not be afraid to make an attempt. With each step or attempt you will make some progress. While it may be slow at times, the accumulated knowledge will eventually lead to understanding.

CHAPTER 1

Introduction

This book is intended to help you operate your new ATARI computer, get started programming and make life easier with your computer. It is not for professional programmers or more advanced applications. It is only the first step, and it is for BEGINNERS on the ATARI computer. This book is intended for the ATARI 400, 600, 800, 800XL, 1200XL, 1400XL and 1450XL computers. There are some differences among the

machines, but the materials in this book apply to all. Where significant differences exist, they will be noted. Since this book is intended to teach you how to program your computer in BASIC, you will need the ATARI BASIC COMPUTING LANGUAGE cartridge for the 4ØØ/8ØØ (not XL) models. *Note: Our examples will be with ATARI BASIC (CXL4ØØ2). ATARI also sells ATARI Microsoft BASIC (CX8126) on diskettes. The Microsoft version is different in many respects; so to avoid confusion, use the ATARI BASIC.* Everything will be kept on an introductory level but, by the time you are finished, you should be able to write and use programs. (Really!)

To best use ELEMENTARY ATARI it is suggested that you start at the beginning and work your way through step-by-step. I have tried to arrange the book so that each part and section logically follows the one preceding it. Skipping around might result in your not understanding some important aspect of the computer's operation. The only exception to this rule is the last chapter where I have put a number of suggestions for programs you might want to buy in order to help you write programs (called UTILITY PROGRAMS). Also, there are descriptions of programs for doing other things such as business, word processing and so forth. When you're finished with this chapter, it would be a good idea to take a quick peek at some of the programs described in the last chapter to see if any of them fit your needs while you're learning about your ATARI. You don't have to purchase any of them but, depending on your interests and needs, you will find some of them very useful.

The first thing to learn about your computer is that it will not "bite" you. It requires a certain amount of care. There are ways you can destroy diskettes, tapes, and information but, by following a few simple rules, you should be all right. All of us have used sophisticated electronic equipment, such as our stereos, televisions, and video-tape recorders; and there is a certain amount of care they require. Otherwise, there is no need to fear them. Likewise, your computer is electronic. If you pour water or other liquids on the computer while the power is off or on, you're likely to damage it. Using reasonable care, go ahead and put it to use. Remember, it is virtually impossible to write a program which will harm the hardware (or electronic circuits) in your machine. At worst, one of your programs might erase the information on a tape or diskette. Throughout this book there will be tips about how to do things the right and wrong way but, in general, treat your computer as you would your microwave oven, garage door opener or radio — with care but without fear.

At this stage of the game it is unnecessary to learn a lot of computer jargon, but some of this terminology is necessary to help you understand how your computer operates. As we go on, more new terms will be introduced but, for the most part the text will be in plain English. Nevertheless, you should know the following just to get started:

Hardware

Hardware refers to the machine and all of its electronic parts. Basically, everything from the keyboard to the wires and little black chips in your computer is considered "hardware." You will also hear the term, "firmware." This is another type of hardware on which programs are written. Called "proms" or "eproms", these chips have information stored in them just as tapes and disks do. Firmware is either inside your computer or in cartridges or boards you plug in the top of your ATARI. A biological analogy of hardware is the physical body, most importantly the brain, and firmware is a like "inherent" intelligence or "transplanted" intelligence.

Software

Software consists of the programs which tell the computer to do different things. Whatever goes into the computer's memory is software. It is analogous to the mind or ideas. Treating the hardware as the brain, any idea which goes into the hardware is the software. Software is to computers as records are to stereos. Software operates either in Random Access Memory (RAM) or Read Only Memory (ROM). (Firmware is hardware with "burned in" software.)

RAM You may hear people talk about expanding their RAM. This is the part of the computer's memory into which you can enter information in the form of data and programs. The more memory you have, the larger the program and more data you can enter. Think of RAM as a warehouse. When you first turn on your computer, the warehouse is just about empty, but as you run programs and enter information, the warehouse begins filling up. The larger the warehouse the more information you can store there, and when it is full, you have to stop. ATARI's come with different amounts of RAM. The 8ØØXL, 12ØØXL, 14ØØXL and 145ØXL have 64K; the 8ØØ, 48K (some older models come with less); and the 4ØØ and 6ØØXL, 16K. The "K" for computerists refers to kilobytes or thousands-of-bytes, but the actual number is 1Ø24 bytes. (The new disk storage systems are measured in megabytes or millions-of-bytes — 1Ø24ØØ bytes to be precise. The next time you're at a cocktail party, mention megabytes and you'll really impress everyone.) For now, all you need to know about bytes is that they are a measure of storage in computers. The more bytes, the more room you have. Think of them in the same way you would gallons, inches or meters — simply a unit of measure. Up to 48K RAM can be added to the 8ØØ model with RAM cartridges, but you will need to take your 4ØØ to a service center to have additional memory added.

ROM A second type of computer memory is ROM meaning "Read Only Memory." This type of memory is "locked" into your computer's chips. Your ATARI's programming language, called BASIC, is stored in ROM. The difference between ROM and RAM is that whenever you turn off your computer, all information in RAM evaporates, but ROM keeps all of its information. Don't worry, though, you can save whatever is in RAM on diskettes and tape and get it back. We'll see how that is done later.

Now that you know a few terms and enough not fear your computer, let's get it cranked up and running. If you already have your computer all hooked up and working properly, you can skip the next section and go directly to the "Power On!" section of this chapter.

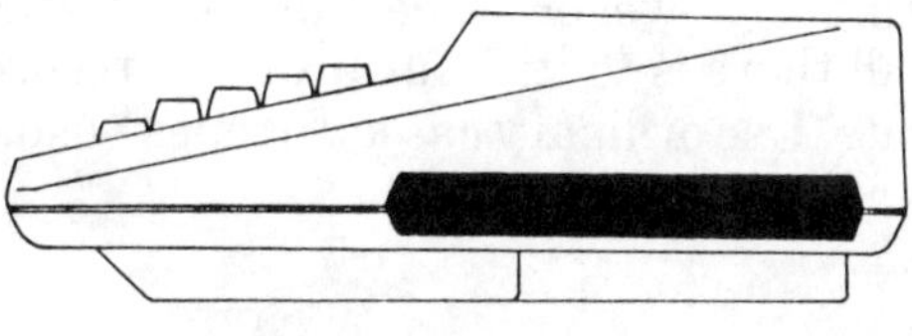

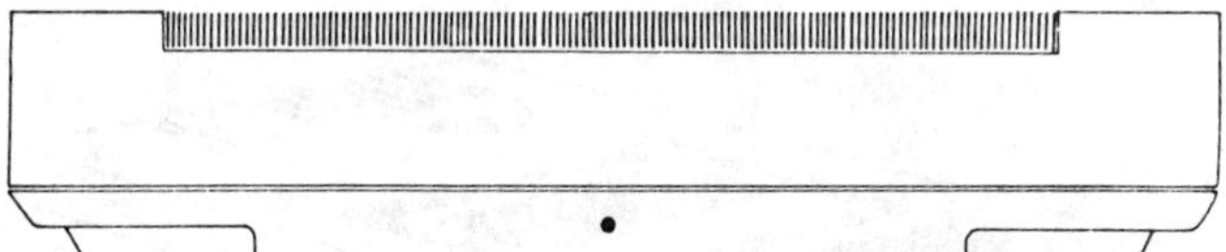

Hooking Up Your Atari and Peripheral Equipment

The LAST thing you should do after reading this section is plug in your ATARI and turn it on. Everything else should be done first. If you bought your computer without a tape recorder or disk drive, it will work fine, but you will need an Atari 41Ø or 1Ø1Ø Program Recorder or an Atari 81Ø or 1Ø5Ø Disk Drive to save information. If you have just the computer, skip to the section on hooking up your TV set to the computer.

Program Recorder

(Skip this section if you have only a disk drive.) If you are using a program recorder, either with or without a disk operating system, hooking it up is quite simple. On your Atari 41Ø or 1Ø1Ø Program Recorder is a cable to connect it to the computer. Take the cable and insert it into the slot labeled "PERIPHERAL" on the right side of your computer. (It's the biggest slot on the side.) Make sure that it is lined up correctly with the "teeth" in the slot, and do not use excessive force when connecting it; however, be certain that it goes in all the way. That is all there is to it! Your program recorder is now ready to operate. Use ordinary cassette tapes - usually 5 or 1Ø minute tapes are the best.

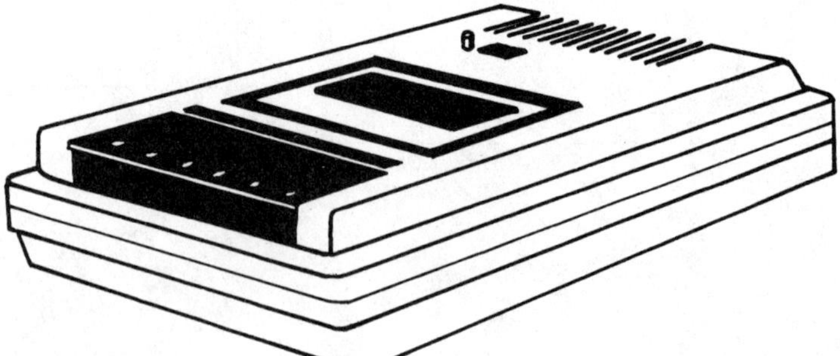

Disk Drive

With the ATARI you should use the ATARI 81Ø or 1Ø5Ø disk drive or other Atari compatible drives. We will be using examples from the 81Ø disk drive system. The 1Ø5Ø and new DOS are compatible with the 81Ø, but they have added features you will find in your disk manual. To connect your disk drive, insert one end of the disk cable into the socket marked "PERIPHERAL" on the *right* side of your computer (the largest socket on that side) and the other end to the socket in the back of your disk drive, in one of the sockets labeled "I/O CONNECTORS." Now plug the power cord for your disk drive into the socket labeled "PWR." (There are two round holes near the "PWR." label. Use the smaller of the two, directly above where it is marked "PWR.") When everything else is connected, you can plug your disk power cord into a wall socket and flip the switch located on the front of your drive to ON. If everything is connected correctly, both the red lights on the front of your computer will come on. The head in your drive will spin for a while and then stop and the light labeled "BUSY" will go off. If that happens, everything is connected correctly. *Note: If you are using a program recorder and a disk drive, connect the recorder to the disk drive through the "I/O CONNECTORS" port in the back of the disk drive. This combination is handy since you can make "back-ups" of your programs on cassette tapes, which are are good deal cheaper than diskettes.*

TV or Monitor

In order to see what's going on in your computer, you need a TV set. On some computers it is necessary to purchase an RF modulator, but your ATARI comes with a built-in RF modulator. It is the cable extending from the back of your computer. Attach the disconnected end into the box that you attach to your TV. The box is attached to the antenna leads marked "VHF" on the back of your TV set, and the switch on the box is flipped to "computer." Finally, there is a switch marked "2-CHAN.-3" on the right side of your computer right next to where you connect the disk drive or program recorder cable. Switch it to channel 2 or 3 depending on what channel is "free" in your area. If it is switched to the back (relative to facing the front of your keyboard), it is set for channel 3, and for channel 2 if switched to the front. Then set your TV dial to channel 2 or channel 3. Once that's done you are all set.

Another option you can use with your ATARI is a monitor instead of a TV set. Basically, a monitor is the same as a TV except it has higher resolution, and it is quite useful if you're doing a lot of word processing. To connect to a monitor, you will have to purchase a special cable that will fit the socket marked "MONITOR" located on the right side of your computer. The other end should go into the monitor itself. The CX82 Monitor Cable (for black & white and green screen) or CX89 Monitor Cable (color monitor) required for monitors is available from your Atari dealer. Connecting a monitor to the TV cable leading from the back of your computer will not work! The following descriptions of monitors and TV sets are the range of video devices you can use with your ATARI.

Types of TV Sets

TVs come in a jillion different shapes, sizes, etc.; either a color or black and white will work fine. BE CAREFUL in the selection of the TV set you buy! Not all televisions work well with your ATARI; so ask first before you buy. When I bought my TV set, a color one for the graphics, I simply looked at the color TVs being used on the computers in the stores and bought the same make and model at an "El Cheapo" discount house. An inexpensive way to get clear text is to purchase a black and white set. It has better resolution than a color set, is less expensive, and is good for word processing. Best of all, though, you can get one for as little as $5Ø and used ones for even less. Whatever the case, check to make sure that the TV set you purchase will work with your ATARI.

Types of Monitors

Green screen This type of monitor gives a green or amber on black display and can be bought for between $1ØØ and $2ØØ. The green and black display is quite good for people doing a lot of word processing and non-graphic programming since it is easy on the eyes. However, since this display presents only green and black, it is not too good for color graphics. Monitors also come with amber or blue screens, but the green screens are the most popular. Amber is good if you have florescent lights in your room.

Black and white This monitor is essentially the same as the green screen, but is in black and white instead of black and green. However, it is more expensive than a black and white TV set, and while it gives better resolution than a television set, the extra cost may not be worth the difference. If you are considering the purchase of a black and white monitor, compare the resolution with a black and white TV set first to see if the extra cost is justified.

Color This type of monitor is the most expensive, but for people who work a lot with graphics, it is probably worth the added cost. It provides the high resolution for seeing graphics in detail. The very best color monitors require a special interface. Make sure you can get one for your ATARI before buying.

Printers

This section simply tells you how to hook up your printer and a little about the different kinds of printers. If your printer is already hooked up and working, take a look at Chapter 9 for tips on maximizing your printer's use.

Types of Printers

There are three basic kinds of printers - dot matrix, letter quality and thermal. However, for specialized use, there are also devices called plotters, ink-jet printers, line printers, laser printers and drum rotate printers. For heavy business use or specialized applications, you may want to ask your dealer about these other ones not described below.

Dot Matrix First, the most popular kind of printer is the "dot matrix" printer. This printer has a number of little pins which are fired to form little dots that print out as text or graphics. The advantage of dot matrix printers is their relatively low cost and the fact that many of them can do both text and graphics. The improved quality of text printing of dot matrix printers gives an almost letter quality product, and usually can give you several different type faces. In Chapter 9 there are several examples of different printing modes on dot matrix printers. The ATARI 850 Interface Module, or similar interface made for the Atari, is required to connect most of the popular dot matrix printers on the market. On the XL series computers, interfaces are built in the computer. The ATARI 1025 is the standard ATARI dot matrix printer.

Letter Quality Second, for people whose major use of their computer is to do word processing, there are letter quality printers. Most of these are daisy wheel printers and type characters in much the same way as a typewriter does. Each symbol has a molded image as on typewriter heads. These printers are not good for graphics, but for the user who wants top notch looking letters, manuscripts, reports and other written documents, this type of printer is the best. They tend to be relatively expensive, however, and for most written materials, dot matrix printers are fine. The ATARI 1027 printer is an exception to an expensive letter quality printer - it sells for less than $300! It is relatively slow, but if you are looking into letter quality printing, the 1027 is a good buy. The thing to do before you buy is compare. Special interfaces may be needed to connect a letter quality printer to your ATARI; so make sure you get a demonstration with the correct interface before buying a printer. Since the ATARI 400/800 have serial ports (instead of a parallel port), you will probably want to get a printer that is serial compatible. The XL series models have parallel ports making it simple to plug in parallel printers.

Thermal Third, for those people who are really on a budget, there are thermal printers. These printers work with a special kind of paper, usually on a roll, and make a picture of what is on the computer screen. They can easily handle both text and graphics, but the quality of output is relatively low and the paper is very expensive. The best feature of these printers is their small size and light weight, and for people who travel with their computers and need print-outs, they can be handy. The ATARI 822 printer is a 40 column thermal printer that hooks directly into the serial port of your computer. Other thermal printers are available, but before purchasing one, make sure you can interface it to your ATARI.

FREE ADVICE

Before you buy a printer, decide what you will need it for and then look at the features of the different kinds before buying!!! And by all means, ask to see a demonstration on an ATARI. Never let a salesperson convince you a certain printer will work without seeing a demonstration. Even a salesperson with the best intentions (e.g., he/she thinks a certain printer is the best for your needs) may not realize that the model cannot be interfaced to your machine. Only a demonstration is sufficient to remove all doubts!

If you purchase an ATARI 822 or ATARI 82Ø or similar printer, connecting it is very simple. Just plug it into the serial port, "PERIPHERALS" or "I/O CONNECTORS" on your disk drive. If you have a parallel printer, such as the ATARI 825 or 1Ø25, connect the printer cable to the ATARI 85Ø Interface Module. The interface module is connected either directly into the "PERIPHERAL" slot, or one of the "I/O CONNECTORS" slot in the back of your disk drive. This is called "daisy chaining" the printer to the computer through the interface module and disk drive. With the XL models, just connect parallel printers to the parallel port on the computer.

CAUTION

NEVER insert or remove cables or interfaces to your computer while the POWER IS ON! Even if you are rich and can afford to buy new chips every time you blow them by messing with the hardware on your ATARI while the power is on, you might give yourself the SHOCK of a lifetime by doing so.

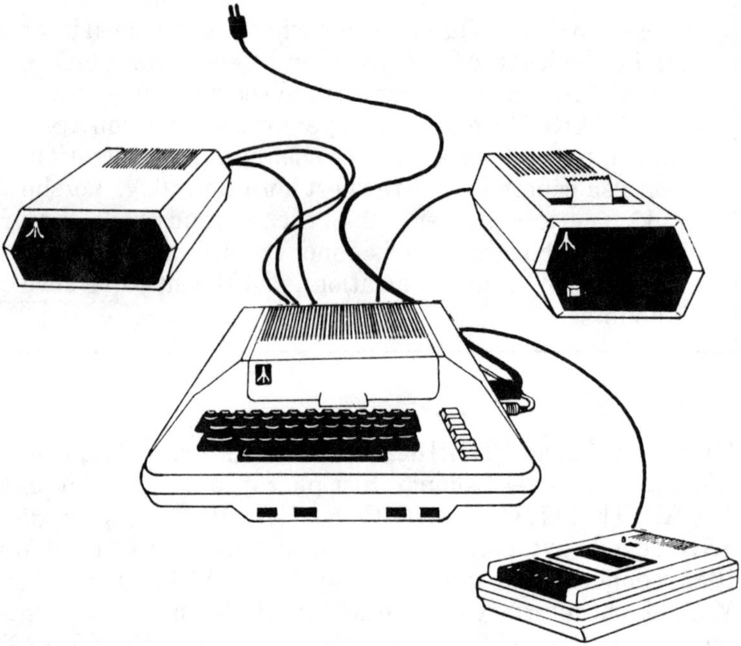

Other Gadgets

Besides the disk drive, TV/monitor, and printer, most new users do not have anything else to hook up at this point, so you can skip on to the next section. However, if you plan on expanding your ATARI or have other gadgets you bought with your system, you had better read the following section.

Many Ports of Call

The nicest feature of the ATARI is its expandability and adaptability. The various ports and slots on your computer can be used to add many different devices to enhance your system.

Modem A MODEM is a device which allows your computer to communicate with other computers over telephone lines. These devices usually require that you hook up your telephone to a part of the modem, or place the phone in an acoustic sender/receiver. The ATARI 83Ø Acoustic modem can be used with your computer by connecting it to your ATARI 85Ø Interface Module or the ATARI 835 or 1Ø3Ø Direct Connect modem through your serial port. The ATARI TeleLink I cartridge provides the communication software needed to "talk" to other systems. Not only can the modem be used to call up computer bulletin boards, but you can access such information centers as "The Source" to get everything from weather reports to airline tickets!

More Wonderful Gadgets There are numerous other cartridges and interfaces to make the ATARI into a multifaceted machine. Special interfaces will allow you to access and use a variety of peripherals such as various disk drive systems, printers and other devices. So while the ATARI is a terrific microcomputer all by itself, it is fully expandable to make it even better.

POWER ON!

SYSTEM CHECK-OUT

Now that you have your ATARI all set to go, you simply plug it in, along with your TV or monitor, program recorder, disk drive and printer, turn on the power and let her rip! Before you start, make sure the ATARI BASIC CARTRIDGE is in place on ATARI 4ØØ/8ØØ models. (On all the XL series computers, BASIC is built-in.) On the ATARI 4ØØ, it is placed in the slot on the top of the computer; on the 8ØØ, it goes in the top *left* slot.

If you have a color TV, the letters will be in light blue against a dark blue background surrounded by a black border. Directly below the READY message is a little square. It is called the "cursor," indicating your computer is waiting for you to press some keys and tell it what to do. Press the RETURN key several times and the cursor will move down the side of the screen. The READY message will scroll off the top of your screen. Your cursor is now at the bottom of the screen. To get it to the top, press the key marked CLEAR/< in the upper right hand corner of your keyboard and the SHIFT key. Now the cursor will pop to the upper left hand corner. That done, you know your keyboard and computer are all set. We will return to the keyboard in a bit, but first let's check out your printer, disk drive and/or program tape recorder. (You may skip the sections dealing with the printer, disk drive and program recorder if you do not have these peripherals.)

Printer Check

To see if your printer is working correctly, put in the following program EXACTLY as it appears below: First write in the word NEW and press RETURN. (<RETURN> means press the button marked "RETURN.")

```
1Ø OPEN #2,8,Ø,"P:"
2Ø PRINT #2; "MY PRINTER IS WORKING!"
3Ø CLOSE #2
```

Make certain you have written the program EXACTLY as it appears above. If there are even minor differences, change it so that it is precisely the same. Put the ribbon and some paper into your printer. Now, turn on your printer, making sure it is "On Line", and write in the word RUN on your computer and <RETURN>. If your printer is attached properly, it will print out the message, MY PRINTER IS WORKING! If an ERROR- 133 AT LINE 20 or some other error message jumps on the screen, it means that you wrote the little test program improperly; so go back and do it again. If the system hangs up - the screen goes blank and nothing happens - check to make sure the printer is turned on and all of your connections are correctly installed. If it still doesn't work, turn off the power on the printer and computer and review the steps for hooking up your printer and try again.

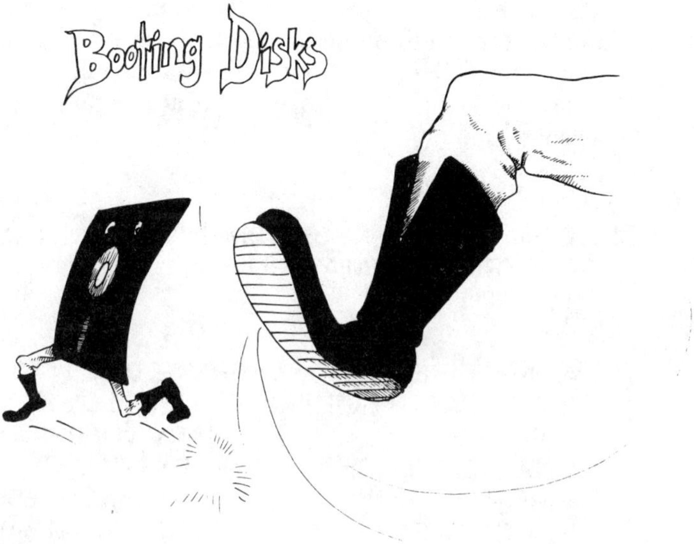

Booting Disks

Assuming your system is working correctly, let's "boot" a diskette on your ATARI 81Ø disk drive. (If you have another type of disk system, see the manual that comes with your disk drive.) This will get your Disk Operating System (DOS - pronounced "DAS") operating. Here's how:

1. Turn your computer *off*.

2. Turn on your disk drive by flipping the switch located in the front of the drive to the ON position. The red lights will light and some noises will come out for a few seconds and then the top red light will go off.

3. At this point insert your MASTER DISKETTE II in the drive with the label facing upwards, oriented toward the right side of the disk drive door. Put it in all the way. Now close the door on the disk drive until it clicks shut. Turn your computer *on*.

4. After the READY prompt appears on your screen and the top red light on the disk drive is out, type in DOS <RETURN>. Your disk drive will make some noise and soon the following will appear on your screen:

```
DISK OPERATING SYSTEM II VERSION 2.ØS
COPYRIGHT 198Ø ATARI

A. DISK DIRECTORY       I. FORMAT DISK
B. RUN CARTRIDGE        J. DUPLICATE DISK
C. COPY FILE            K. BINARY SAVE
D. DELETE FILE(S)       L. BINARY LOAD
E. RENAME FILE          M. RUN AT ADDRESS
F. LOCK FILE            N. CREATE MEM.SAV
G. UNLOCK FILE          O. DUPLICATE FILE
H. WRITE DOS FILES

SELECT ITEM OR (RETURN) FOR MENU
```

Note: On ATARI 815 and 1Ø5Ø Dual Disk systems, you will have VERSION 2.ØD instead of 2.ØS. I'll bet that the "D" means "double density" and the "S" is for "single density." What do you think?

At this point, your DOS is all set. However, in order to save information to a diskette, it is necessary to have a "formatted" diskette. To format a diskette, you will need a single-density diskette for your ATARI 810 drive. (If you have an ATARI 815 Dual Disk Drive, you need a "*double* density" diskette. When you purchase diskettes make sure to specify single or double density.) The "write protect notch" must be "open" on the diskette. (That means there should be no write-protect tab over the little square notch on your diskette.)

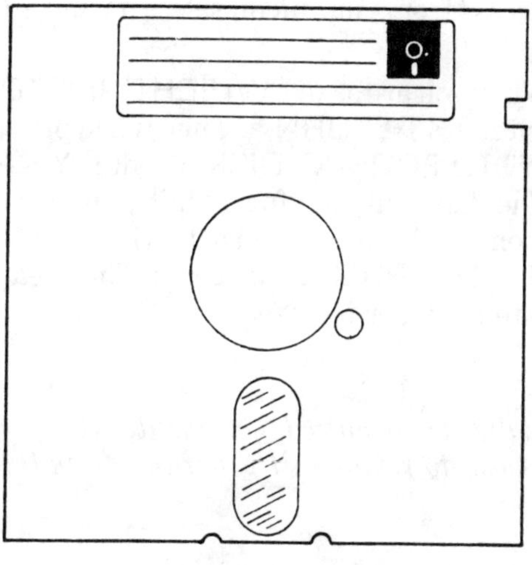

To format your disk, follow these steps:

1. Remove your MASTER DISKETTE from the drive, but do not turn off the disk drive or computer and do not remove the DOS Menu from the screen.

2. Insert your blank diskette in the disk drive with the write protect notch oriented toward the left side of the drive door and close the door. (If you have multiple drives, put it in "Drive 1" as described in your disk operating manual.)

3. Press I from your menu selection and <RETURN>.

4. When you are asked, WHICH DRIVE TO FORMAT? enter 1 <RETURN>. Then when prompted, TYPE "Y" TO FORMAT DISK 1, enter Y <RETURN>. The disk will spin for a while, and then stop. Your menu will then return to the prompt, SELECT ITEM OR PRESS RETURN. This means your diskette is all set for use.

Note: Once a disk is formatted, you should NOT format it again unless you want to remove all programs from the diskette.

Now that you have a formatted diskette, you will have to decide whether or not you want DOS on the diskette. The advantage of having DOS on your disk is that whenever you enter DOS from your keyboard, you will get the DOS menu and functions. This means less swapping back and forth between the disk you are using and your MASTER DISKETTE. The disadvantage is that having DOS takes up space on your diskette. To see this, enter A from your menu and press RETURN twice. You will see that your newly formatted diskette has 7Ø7 FREE SECTORS. Now let's put DOS on your diskette to see how it's done and how many sectors of disk space are used. Here's how:

1. Insert a formatted diskette. (Leave in the one you just formatted.)

2. Choose H from the DOS Menu and <RETURN>.

3. Enter 1 <RETURN> for the drive and Y <RETURN>. WRITING NEW DOS FILES will appear, and when the DOS files are written the SELECT ITEM OR PRESS RETURN prompt will appear. Now you have DOS on your diskette.

To see how many sectors you used, enter A and <RETURN> twice. Now you will see that you have only 626 FREE SECTORS, and:

```
DOS SYS Ø39
DUP SYS Ø42
```

This means that files named DOS and DUP are written to your disk. Both are "system files" indicated by the SYS and one takes up 39 sectors and the other 42 sectors. (Add 39 and 42 and subtract that sum from 7Ø7. You will get 626, the new number of free sectors on your formatted disk.)

To get back to BASIC, enter B, the RUN CARTRIDGE choice, from the menu and <RETURN>. To see if everything is working correctly, enter the following once you get your READY prompt:

```
DOS <RETURN>
```

Now you should see your DOS Menu. Press A and <RETURN> twice and there are your two system files, DOS and DUP. In Chapter 2, we will see how to save and retrieve programs from disks, so keep your formatted diskette handy. Whenever you wish to see the directory for any diskette, choose A. This is how you access the "directory" of your diskette. (See Chapter 9 for more details on using your disk system.)

WARNING!!

When you buy commerical programs on diskette, they are already formatted. If you format them, you will destory all the programs you have bought. In fact, any programs on a diskette, whether commercial or ones you wrote yourself, will be clobbered if you attempt to format them. (It's really miserable, though, when you spend $49.95 for a really neat program and then blow it into silicon heaven by formatting it.) The best way to protect yourself against accidental re-formatting is to put a "write protect" tab on your diskette over the write protect notch. In this way you will know not to try to format that disk. You can always remove the write protect tab if you want to save programs to the disk or re-format it to have a blank diskette.

LOADing and RUNning Programs From Tape

The procedure for loading and running programs from tape is quite simple. The following steps show you how:

STEP 1 Make sure your tape recorder is connected and rewind it to the beginning. If you have a tape with programs on it, use it to test loading. (A game cassette, *not cartridge*, will work fine.) If you do not have a tape with a program on it, enter the following program:

```
NEW <RETURN>
10 PRINT "<YOUR NAME>" <RETURN>
20 END <RETURN>
```

Press REC and PLAY on your recorder and enter

```
CSAVE <RETURN> <RETURN>
```

After the first <RETURN> your computer will "beep" a couple times, and after the second <RETURN> the Program Recorder will begin saving your program. (The beep is to remind you to press REC and PLAY, so if you already have them on, just press RETURN a second time.) When the READY prompt comes on your TV screen, press STOP/EJ. on your recorder and rewind your tape. To make sure there is nothing in memory, turn off your computer.

STEP 2 Turn on your computer. When you get the READY prompt and cursor, press PLAY on your recorder and write in the following:

```
CLOAD <RETURN> <RETURN>
```

STEP 3 When the program is loaded, you will get the READY prompt and cursor. At this point your program is all loaded and ready to go. Enter the word RUN, and your program will then execute. If you used our example program, your name will simply be printed on the screen. Rewind your tape now so that it will be ready for the next time. Do *not* forget to reset the program counter. That makes it a lot easier to find your programs later. In fact, a good habit is to write down the beginning and ending locations of your tape programs in a log book. Later, to find your programs stored on tape, simply press the ADVANCE key on your recorder to set it to the beginning of the program you want. Each time you CSAVE a program, it erases whatever is on the portion of the tape you are using. Therefore, programs should be save sequentially.

TAPE TO DISK TRANSFER

If you have both a tape and disk system and you don't want to wait for the longer loading time of tapes every time you run it (especially when you start accumulating several programs on tape), why not transfer your tape files to disk? Just boot your DOS, put a formatted disk into the drive, and then load your program on tape. Once your tape program is loaded, simply write in SAVE "D1: <name of file>", and now your tape program is on disk! Makes life simpler.

Cartridge Programs

When you purchase cartridge programs for your computer, simply insert the cartridge into the cartridge port and turn on your computer. It will automatically run the program for you.

The ATARI Keyboard

Almost Like a Typewriter: The Familiar Keys

If you are familiar with a typewriter keyboard, you will see most of the same keys on your ATARI. For the most part, they do almost the same thing as your typewriter keys. If you type in the word COMPUTER, hitting the same keys you would on a typewriter, the word COMPUTER appears on the screen just as it would on paper in a typewriter. However, the upper-case (capital letters) and lower-case letters do not work exactly the same as a typewriter. On the ATARI, you have to shift into the "upper/lower-case" mode by pressing the "CAPS/LOWR Key" (the little one in the lower right hand corner above the SHIFT key). When you do that, your keys will work more like a typewriter. When you want upper-case, simply press the SHIFT key and a letter to get upper-case as you would on a typewriter. Also, the screen has only 38 columns instead of 80 like most typewriters. Of course, you cannot type just anything on the screen. If you start typing away, you'll get a ERROR- every time you press RETURN unless you put in the proper commands. Otherwise, think of your keyboard as you would a typewriter keyboard. Pressing the SHIFT key and CAPS/LOWR key simultaneously will return all keys to upper case. *Note: In most of the programming examples, we will be using upper-case only. This is because your computer recognizes commands only in upper case. If you enter* run *instead of* RUN *you will get an* ERROR-. *However, you can output lower case messages.*

```
10 REM HIT THE "SHIFT" KEY AND THE "CAPS LOWR"
   KEY AT THE SAME TIME FOR ALL UPPER CASE
20 REM hit just the "caps lowr" key for lower case
30 REM USE THE  KEY TO TOGGLE BETWEEN
   NORMAL AND INVERSE VIDEO
```

Keys You Won't See on a Typewriter

While most of the keys on your ATARI look like those on a typewriter, many do not, and they are important to understand. The following keys are peculiar to your computer; you will soon get used to them even though they will be a bit mysterious at first:

ATARI KEY This key, located in the lower right hand corner of your keyboard, is used for shifting between normal and inverse video. It toggles between the two displays. Press it and type in some letters. They will be inverse. Press it again, and they will return to normal. The inverse mode is used to highlight messages on your screen. On the 4ØØ/8ØØ computer it has the ATARI logo, and on the XL models it is a little square with a diagonal slash.

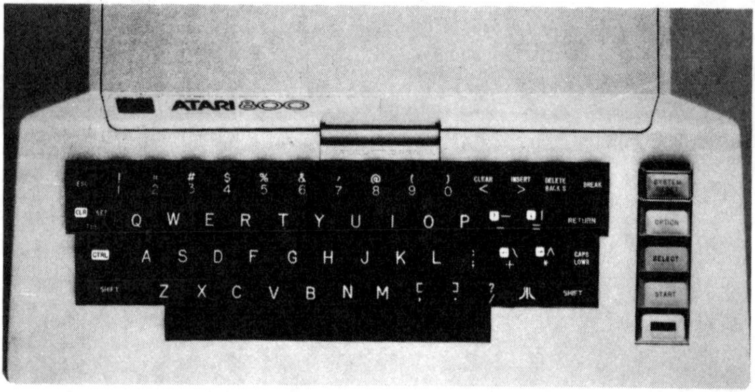

CTRL (control) On the far left side of your keyboard is the CTRL key, called the "control key." By pressing the CTRL key and one of the alphabetic keys, you will be presented with graphics on your screen instead of letters. Try holding down the CTRL key and pressing letters of the alphabet. The CTRL key is also used in editing programs, as we will see in the next chapter.

ESC (escape) In programming, this key allows the user to include certain features that delay execution until the program is RUN. For example, if you want a program to clear the screen when it is first executed, by pressing the ESC key and CLEAR key within quotation marks in a PRINT statement, your screen will be cleared at the program's beginning. In combination with other keys, the ESC key allows access to various graphic characters as well.

BREAK This key will stop a program in the middle of execution and listings. It is very handy when you have long programs and want to examine the middle of the listing.

CLEAR (clear home) In the upper right hand corner is a very important key, the CLEAR key. In computer talk, HOME refers to placing the cursor in the upper left hand corner of the screen, and CLEAR means to erase the screen. To test this key, write anything on your screen and press the RETURN key several times so that the cursor is at the bottom of the screen. Now press the SHIFT and CLEAR key, and the cursor will pop to the top of the screen and everything you entered will disappear.

INSERT This key is handy for editing programs. The SHIFT-INSERT will enter an additional line, and CTRL-INSERT will place a single space between letters. By moving the arrow keys (see below), and using the INSERT key, editing programs is made very simple.

ARROW (cursor) KEYS In the middle right hand side of your keyboard are the four cursor keys - arrows set on inverse backgrounds. They are used to move the cursor around the screen without affecting anything on the screen. The arrows on the keys indicate the direction they will move when they are pressed with the CTRL key. To get used to using them, here's a little exercise. Press SHIFT-CLEAR and then place the cursor right in the middle of the screen using only the cursor keys. If you can do that, you can use the keys correctly. When the cursor keys are used within quotation marks in PRINT statements, using the ESC key, funny things begin to happen. Your computer is reading the cursor as though an invisible hand were moving the cursor. *Note: In the following example, first press* ESC *and then the* CTRL *key and the arrow keys simultaneously.*

```
PRINT "[ESC CTRL-DOWN-ARROW 1Ø TIMES]
HELLO" <RETURN>
```

You will get a series of down pointing arrows, and when you press RETURN the message HELLO will be spaced 1Ø places below the line on which you entered the command.

RETURN The RETURN key is something like the carriage return on a typewriter. In fact, you may see it referred to as a "Carriage Return" or "CR" in computer articles. It works in an analogous manner to a typewriter's carriage return, because the cursor bounces back to the left-hand side of the display screen after you press it. However, there are other uses for the RETURN key which will be discovered as you get into programming.

CARAT keys Under the CLEAR and INSERT keys, and on the right arrow key are little "horns" or "carats." The left and right carats are used in comparative formulas to indicate "less than" or "greater than," and together (<>) to indicate "not equal to." The vertical carat key is used for exponentials of numbers. For example, enter PRINT2 ^ 2 and <RETURN>. Your screen will print 3.99999996, the value of 2 to the second power. (Actually, the value is "4", but this little quirk of your computer is because it is attempting precision to 8 decimal point positions. Enter PRINT 2 * 2 <RETURN> for the exact right answer!)

DELETE/BACKS (delete back space) This key is an "editing key" to backspace and delete characters. Enter ABCDEFGHIJK and then hit the key several times and watch the backspace gobble up your characters. (A do-it-yourself PAC-MAN.) If you press the CTRL key and DELETE key simultaneously, the character at the cursor will be deleted. In editing, the DELETE/BACK S key is used in combination with the INSERT key to edit programs.

CLR/SET/TAB (tab set and clear) This key is like the tab set and clear on a typewriter. The default setting on the key is 8 columns across the screen, except from the far left side, when it is 6. (That's because the screen prints out 38 columns. The first two columns are used as margins. Thus, 6+8+8+8+8=38.) Press the key several times and watch the cursor jump across the tab stops. Using the space bar, place the cursor two spaces from the left side and press SHIFT-CLR/SET/TAB. This will set a tab at the second column. Thus, whenever you press SHIFT-CLR/SET/TAB, you set a tab at the cursor. Now, go back to where you set the tab and press CTRL-CLR/SET/TAB. This clears the tab stop. If you clear all the tab stops, the cursor will jump one vertical line whenever you press the TAB key.

SPECIAL KEYS On the far right side of your keyboard on the ATARI 400/800 and at the top of the ATARI 1200s are keys used for special applications. About the only key you will be using in beginning programming is the SYSTEM RESET key (RESET on the 1200, located on the top left side above the keyboard.) This is a "panic button" that will reset everything if your computer "freezes up" on you. Both beginning and experienced programmers will enter information that will tie up the normal operation of your computer. Even the BREAK key will not "release" the computer back to your control, so by pressing the RESET key, you can restore operations to normal. Even your program in memory will not be affected. Therefore, do not be afraid to use this key if you run into problems. On the XL series, the HELP key is useful for beginners since it will show you various instructions on certain programs. The OPTION, SELECT and START keys are explained in Chapter 10. Finally, on the XL series ATARIs, the "function keys", numbered from F1 to F4 are for special applications also discussed in Chapter 10.

Some New Meanings For Old Keys

Some of the familiar keys have different meanings for the computer than we usually associate with the key symbols. Many are math symbols you may or may not recognize. In the next chapter, we will illustrate how these keys can be operated and discuss them in detail. For now let's just take a quick look at the math symbols.

Symbol	**Meaning**
+	Add
–	Subtract
*	Multiply (different from conventional)
/	Divide (different from conventional)
^	Exponentiation

In addition to some of the new representations for math symbols, other keys will be used in a manner to which you are not accustomed. As we go on, we will explain the meanings of these keys, but just to get used to the idea that your ATARI has some special meanings for keys, we'll show you some more here which will have special meanings later.

Symbol	**Meaning**
$	Used to indicate a string variable and hexadecimal value.
:	Used to indicate "end of statement" in program.
?	Can be used as PRINT command.

Don't worry about understanding what all of these symbols do for the time being. Simply be prepared to think in "computer talk" about symbols. As you become familiar with the keyboard and the uses and meanings of these symbols, you will be able to handle them easily, but the first step is to be aware that the different meanings exist.

SUMMARY

This first chapter has been an overview of your new machine. You should now know how to hook up the different parts of your ATARI and get it running. Also, you should be able to boot and format a disk, view the contents (directory) of a disk, and run a program from disk or tape. You should know some of the basic DOS commands for manipulating files on your diskette. Finally, you should be familiar with the keyboard and know what the cursor means. At this point there is still much to learn, so don't feel badly if you don't understand everything. As we go along, you will pick up more and more, and what may be confusing now, later will become clear. Have faith in yourself and in no time, you will be able to do things you never thought possible.

The next chapter will get you started in learning how to program your ATARI. It is vitally important that you key in and run the sample programs. Also, it is recommended you make changes in them after you have first tried them out to see if you can make them do slightly different things. Both practical and fun (and crazy!) programs are included so that you can see the purpose behind what you will be doing and enjoy it at the same time.

CHAPTER 2

Ladies and Gentlemen, Start Your Engines

Introduction

This chapter will introduce you to writing programs in the language known as BASIC. ATARI BASIC is different from some other versions of the language, and if you are already familiar with BASIC, you will find these differences. However, if you are new to the language, then you will find programming in BASIC very simple. To get ready, turn on your computer. When the "READY" sign comes up on your TV, you are all set to begin programming. If something else is on your screen, press SHIFT-CLEAR and key in the word NEW to clear memory.

Your Very First Command! PRINT

Probably the most often used command in BASIC is PRINT. Words enclosed in quotation marks following the PRINT command will be printed to your screen, and numbers and variables will be printed if they are preceded by a PRINT command. It is used to command your computer to print output to the screen from within a program or in the Immediate mode. You may well ask what the difference is between the Immediate and Program modes. Let's take a look.

Immediate Mode The Immediate mode executes a command as soon as you press RETURN. For example, try the following:

```
PRINT "THIS IS THE IMMEDIATE MODE"
<RETURN>
```

If everything is working correctly, your screen should look like this:

```
READY
PRINT "THIS IS THE IMMEDIATE MODE"
THIS IS THE IMMEDIATE MODE

READY
```

See how easy that was? Now try PRINTing some numbers, but don't put in the quote marks. Try the following:

```
PRINT 6 <RETURN>
PRINT 54321 <RETURN>
```

As you can see, numbers can be entered without having to use quote marks, but as we will see later, the actual value of the number is placed in memory rather than a "picture" of it.

PROGRAM MODE This mode "delays" the execution of the commands until your program is "RUN". All commands which begin with numbers on the left side will be treated as part of a program. Try the following:

```
10 PRINT "THIS IS THE PROGRAM MODE"
<RETURN> -
```

nothing happens, right? Enter the RUN command and your screen should look like this:

```
READY
10 PRINT "THIS IS THE PROGRAM MODE"
RUN
THIS IS THE PROGRAM MODE
```

Your Very First Program! Clearing the Screen and Writing Your Name

Let's write a program and learn two new commands. First, the new commands are CLEAR and END. The CLEAR command clears the screen and places the cursor in the upper left hand corner. The CLEAR command is a one key command made by pressing the SHIFT key and CLEAR keys at the same time. In the Program Mode, the CLEAR appears as a little bent arrow on your TV from within a program, entered as PRINT "{ESC-SHIFT-CLEAR}". It is important to remember to *first* press the ESC key when entering CLEAR in a program. If you don't, your screen will immediately be cleared. The END command tells the computer to stop executing commands. From the Immediate mode write in the CLEAR command to see what happens. Now, let's write a program using {ESC-SHIFT-CLEAR}, END and PRINT. From now on, press the RETURN key at the end of each line. Throughout the rest of the book, I will no longer be putting in <RETURN> except in reference to entries in the Immediate mode.

```
READY
10 PRINT "{ESC-SHIFT-CLEAR}" : REM A LITTLE
    BENT ARROW WILL APPEAR ON YOUR SCREEN
20 PRINT "<YOUR NAME>".
30 END
RUN <RETURN>
```

All you should see on the screen is your name, READY and the cursor. Now, we're going to introduce two shortcuts which will save you time in programming and in memory. First, instead of entering new line numbers, it is possible to put multiple commands on the same line by using a colon ":" between commands. Also, instead of typing in PRINT, you can key in a question mark "?". Try the following program to see how this works.

```
10 ? "{ESC-SHIFT-CLEAR}"
20 ? "<YOUR NAME>" : END
RUN <RETURN>
```

It did exactly the same thing, but you did not have to put in as many lines or write out the word PRINT. Neat, huh? Now, as a rule of thumb, ALWAYS begin your programs with PRINT "{ESC-SHIFT-CLEAR}". This will help you get into a habit which will pay off later when you're running all kinds of different programs. There will be exceptions to the rule but, for the most part, by beginning your programs with {ESC-SHIFT-CLEAR}, you will start off with a nice clear screen rather than a cluttered one.

While we're just getting started, it will probably be a good idea to use the colon sparingly. This is because it is easier to understand a program with a minimum number of commands in a single line. Later, when you become more adept at writing programs, and want to figure out ways to save memory and speed up program execution, you will probably want to use the colon a good deal more. Also, we want to make liberal use of the REM statement. After the computer sees a REM statement in a line, it goes on to the next line number, executing nothing until it comes to a command that can be executed. The REM statement works as a REMark in your program lines so that others will know what you are doing and as a reminder to yourself what you have done. Just to see how it works, let's put it into our little program.

```
10 PRINT "{ESC-SHIFT-CLEAR}" : REM THIS
   CLEARS THE SCREEN
20 PRINT "<YOUR NAME>" : END
30 REM THIS MAGNIFICENT PROGRAM WAS
   CREATED BY <YOUR NAME>
```

Now RUN the program and you will see that the REM statements did not affect it at all! However, it is much clearer as to what your program is doing since you can read what the commands do in the program listing.

Setting Up a Program

Using Line Numbers

Now that we've written a little program, let's take a look at using line numbers. In your first program, we used the line numbers 1Ø, 2Ø and 3Ø. We could have used line numbers 1, 2 and 3 or Ø, 1 and 2 or even 1ØØØ, 2ØØØ and 3ØØØ. In fact, there is no need at all to have regular intervals between numbers, and line numbers 1, 32 and 1543 would have worked just fine.

However, we usually want to number our programs by 1Ø's, starting at 1Ø. You may well ask, "Wouldn't it be easier to number them 1, 2, 3, 4, 5, etc.?" In some ways maybe it would, but overall, it definitely would not! Here's why. Type in the word LIST <RETURN>, and if your program is still in memory it will appear on the screen. Suppose you want to insert a line between lines 2Ø and 3Ø that prints your home address. Rather than re-writing the entire program, just enter a line number with a value between 2Ø and 3Ø (such as 25) and enter the line. Let's try it, but *first remove* the END command in line 2Ø.

```
25 PRINT "<YOUR ADDRESS>"
RUN <RETURN>
```

Aha! You now have your name and address printed on the screen, and all you had to do was to write in one line instead of retyping the whole program. Now if we had numbered the program by 1's instead of 1Ø's you would not have been able to do that since there would be no room between lines numbered 2 and 3 as there was between 2Ø and 3Ø. You would have to rewrite the whole program. Now with a small program, this would not be much of a problem, but when you start getting into 1ØØ and 1ØØØ line programs, you'll be glad you have space between line numbers!

LISTING YOUR PROGRAM

As we just saw, using the word LIST gives us a listing of our program. To make it neat, type in (SHIFT) CLEAR and LIST <RETURN>, and you'll get a listing on a clear screen. However, once you start writing longer programs, you won't want to list everything, but only portions. Let's examine the options available with the LIST command.

What You Write	What You Get
LIST	Lists entire program
L.	Shortcut for LIST.
LIST 2Ø	Only line 2Ø is listed (or any line number you choose.)
LIST 2Ø,3Ø	All lines from 2Ø to 3Ø inclusive are listed (or any other range of lines you choose).

Try listing different portions of your program with the options available to see what you get. The following commands will give you some examples of the different options:

```
L.
LIST 25
LIST 25,3Ø
```

MY SCREEN IS FREAKING OUT!

If you leave your screen on while working with this book, as you should be doing, you might notice that all of a sudden it starts turning different colors. (If you have a black and white TV it will turn different shades of gray.) No, your computer has not been gobbling Morning Glory seeds, but rather it is keeping your screen from becoming "etched" with lines from the text on your screen. This is an important feature of ATARI computers, and very good for your TV screen. As soon as you press any key, it will return to normal. ATARI 12ØØXLs will go blank instead bursting into different colors. Again, it's just trying to save your TV or monitor screen.

Saving Your Program

Suppose you write a program, get it working perfectly and then turn off your computer. Since the program is stored in the RAM memory, it will go to Never-Never Land, and you will have to write it in again if you want to use it. Fortunately, it is a simple matter to SAVE a program to your diskette. Let's use our program for an example of SAVEing a program to disk. Make sure your program is still in memory by LISTing it, and if it is not, rewrite it. Make sure a formatted disk is in the drive and write in the following: (If you are not certain about disk formatting, review the section covering those items in Chapter 1.)

```
SAVE "D1:PROG1.BAS"
```

The disk will start whirling and both red lights will glow on the disk drive. This means the disk drive is writing your program to disk. When the top red light goes out, write in DOS; when the DOS menu appears enter A <RETURN> RETURN>. You will be presented with a directory of the disk, and if you see:

```
PROG1 BAS 001
```

in the directory, that means your program has been successfully saved to disk.

Saving Programs on Tape

To save a program to tape, put a blank cassette into your tape recorder and rewind it. Press the REC button and the PLAY button together on your tape recorder and write in CSAVE <RETURN> <RETURN>. The tape recorder will start spinning. When it is done, the READY prompt will reappear on the screen Your program is now SAVEd to tape. Unlike SAVEing to disk, you do not have to enter a device number (e.g., D1:) since the ATARI defaults to the cassette drive with the CSAVE command.

Saving your Program

Retrieving Your Programs

The best way to make sure you have SAVEd a program to disk or tape is to completely turn off your ATARI, and then turn it on again. Go ahead and do it. Call up DOS and view your disk directory. You should be able to see your program, (PROG1.BAS) in the directory. Now return to BASIC, choosing B from the DOS menu. Enter LOAD D:PROG1.BAS. The disk drive will whirl for a while, and then your program will be loaded and the READY prompt will reappear. LIST and RUN your program to made sure it's the same one you SAVEd. If it is the same, you know you have successfully SAVEd it to disk.

If you have a tape cassette, press the PLAY button on your recorder and enter CLOAD. The tape will whirl looking for the program, and then load it, responding with a READY when completed. LIST and RUN it to make sure it's the correct one.

Now that you have SAVEd and LOADed programs, let's look at another neat trick. Remembering you SAVEd your file under the name PROG1.BAS, let's change the contents of that file. First, add the following line and then LIST your program:

```
27 PRINT "<YOUR CITY, STATE & ZIP>"
```

Your program is now different from the program you SAVEd in the file PROG1.BAS since you have added line 27. Now write in

```
SAVE "D1:PROG1.BAS" <RETURN>
```

Clear memory with NEW, LOAD the file PROG1.BAS and LIST it. As you can see, line 27 is now part of PROG1.BAS. All you have to do to update a program is to LOAD it, make any changes you want, and then SAVE it under the same file name. However, BE CAREFUL. No matter what program is in memory, that program will be SAVEd when you enter the SAVE command; therefore, if your disk has PROGRAM A and you write PROGRAM B, and then SAVE it under the title PROGRAM A, it will destroy PROGRAM A and the SAVEd program will actually be PROGRAM B. Also, if you have a really important program, it is a good idea to make a "back-up" file. For example, if you saved your current program under the file names, PROG1.BAS and PROG1.BKU, it would have two files with exactly the same program. To really play it safe, save the program on two different diskettes.

I TOLD YOU SO DEPT.

Sooner or later the following will happen to you: You will have several disks or tapes, one of which you want to format or save programs on. You will pick up the wrong diskette or cassette, one with valuable programs on it. There will be no write protect tab on the diskette or cassette, and after you format it or overwrite programs on it and blow away everything you wanted to keep, you will realize your mistake and say, "!&$#"!%&", and kick your dog. You cannot prevent that from happening at least once, believe me. Therefore, to insure that such a mistake is not irreversible, do the following: MAKE BACK-UPs. Take your ORIGINAL and put it somewhere out of reach, so when you accidentally erase a disk or tape, you can make another copy. Remember, if you fail to follow this advice, your dog will have sore ribs. Be kind to your dog.

FILE NAMES

Naming your files is very important, for as you begin collecting more and more programs, names like PROG1 are not very useful. How do you know what's on PROG1 and PROG25? Rather than having to write down all program names and starting locations as you do with programs saved on tapes, it is better to make the names descriptive. For example, instead of PROG1, we could have called it NAMEADDR or any other name that will tell us something about the program we saved. The only limitation is in the size of the file name, which is limited to eight characters.

Extenders It is possible to use three character extenders after programs on your ATARI. These extenders can be used to tell you the kind of program you have saved. For example, BAS can be used for BASIC programs and BKU can be used to indicate a "Back-up." To add an extender, simply enter a period and the three-character extender to your program as we did in our examples. Later we will see how to save programs using the LIST command; programs saved this way require a different loading technique. Therefore, it is a good idea to differentiate a program saved with SAVE and one with LIST. However, since most of the time we will be saving programs in BASIC, we can SAVE them without any extenders, assuming that programs in the directory with no extenders are SAVEd in BASIC. Everything else will have extenders, including back-ups.

On The Run

If you want to RUN your program as soon as it's loaded, you do not have to go through a two step process of first LOADing or CLOADing it and then RUNning it. From disk enter

```
RUN "D1:PROG1.BAS" <RETURN>
```

and from tape press PLAY and enter

```
RUN "C:" <RETURN> <RETURN>
```

This method of getting up your programs is handy if you simply want to RUN them instead of editing or adding program lines to them.

Using Your Editor: Fixing Mistakes on the Run

The Error Messages and Repairing Them

By now you probably entered something and got an ERROR-ABC, ERROR- 9 AT LINE 3Ø, referring to error type 9 line 3Ø or any other line where an error is detected. This occurs in the Immediate mode as soon as you hit RETURN and in the Program mode either when you enter the error or as soon as you RUN your program. Depending on the error, you will get a different type of message. As we go along, we will see different messages depending on the operation. For now, we will concentrate on how to fix errors in program lines rather than the nature of the errors themselves. This process is referred to as "editing" programs. (See APPENDIX A for a complete list of error messages. It would be a good idea to make a copy of those error messages on a separate sheet and paste them on cardboard. In this way you will have a handy reference with you as you program.)

Deleting Lines

The simplest type of editing involves inserting and deleting lines. Let's write a program with an error in it and fix it up.

```
NEW <RETURN>
10 PRINT "{ESC-SHIFT-CLEAR}"
20 PRINT " AS LONG AS SOMETHING CAN"
30 PRINT A$ : REM LINE WITH ERROR
```

```
4Ø PRINT "IT WILL"
5Ø END
RUN <RETURN>
```

If the program is written exactly as depicted above, when you RUN it you will get ERROR- 9 AT LINE 3Ø. Now, write in

```
3Ø <RETURN>
LIST <RETURN>
```

What happened to line 3Ø?! You just learned about deleting a line. Whenever you enter a line number and nothing else, you delete the line. We already learned how to insert a line; so to fix the program enter the following:

```
3Ø PRINT "GO WRONG"
```

Now run the program. It should work fine. The error was PRINTing the A$. (Later we will see that PRINTing A$ is not an error as long as we set it up properly.) Another way you could have fixed the program was simply to re-enter line 3Ø correctly without first deleting it, but I wanted to show you how to delete a line by entering the line number.

Using the ATARI Editor

Within your ATARI is a trusty editor. To see how to work with your editor, we'll write another bad program and fix it. OK, write the following program and RUN it.

```
NEW
1Ø PRINT "{ESC-SHIFT-CLEAR}"
2Ø PRINT "IF I CAN GOOF UP A PROGRAM "
3Ø PRINT "I CAN" : FIX IT: REM BAD LINE
4Ø END
RUN <RETURN>
```

All right, you got

```
3Ø ERROR- PRINT "I CAN" : FIX [I]T :
   REM BAD LINE
```

as soon as you pressed RETURN after entering line 3Ø. To repair it, instead of rewriting line 3Ø do the following:

STEP 1. LIST your program.

STEP 2. Press CTRL and the UP-ARROW and "walk" the cursor to line 3Ø.

STEP 3. Now using the CTRL key and RIGHT-ARROW key "walk" the cursor to the "E" in ERROR-

STEP 4. Press the CTRL and DELETE keys until you have erased "ERROR-".

STEP 5. The cursor should now be over the "P" in PRINT in line 3Ø. Using the CTRL and RIGHT-ARROW keys, walk the cursor to the second quote mark at the end of the word "CAN" and delete the quotation mark and the colon using the CTRL and DELETE keys together.

STEP 6. Now, walk the cursor to the inverse "I" in the word "IT" and change it to a normal "I" simply by pressing "I".

STEP 7. All that's left is to insert a quotation mark between the word "IT" and the colon before the REM statement. Walk the cursor so that it is directly over the colon and press the CTRL and INSERT keys simultaneously. The colon will move over, so now enter a quotation mark in the space. You are all finished!

LIST the program again. Line 3Ø should now be correct. RUN the program. You should see the statement, IF I CAN GOOF UP A PROGRAM I CAN FIX IT. Let's learn more about the editor. Put in the following program: (Remember, in ATARI

BASIC, we can use question marks to replace PRINT statements. So when you see the question marks where you would normally expect to see a PRINT statement, don't be surprised.)

```
NEW
1Ø ? "{ESC-SHIFT-CLEAR}"
2Ø ? "SOMETIMES I LIKE TO WRITE LONG, LONG,
   LONG, LONG LINES" : WHEW!
3Ø ? "AND SOMETIMES I LIKE SHORT LINES"
4Ø END
LIST <RETURN>
RUN <RETURN>
```

OK, after you entered line 2Ø the program went El Bombo. The problem was that we stuck in that WHEW! without a PRINT statement or quote marks after the colon had terminated the line, or, alternatively, we left out a REM statement before WHEW!. To repair it, LIST the program, "walk" the cursor up to line 2Ø using the CTRL and UP-ARROW keys and starting at line 2Ø put the cursor over the E in ERROR- and press the CTRL and DELETE/BACK S keys at the same time until ERROR- disappears. To make it simple, remove the second quote mark, leaving the colon in place, and add a quote mark after the word WHEW!. Since the colon is now inside the quote marks, it will be printed as part of the PRINT statement and be ignored as a line termination statement. Press RETURN and RUN the program.

Now let's take a look at a feature of the ATARI editor that might cause some problems. Enter the following BUT DO NOT HIT RETURN!!!!:

```
NEW
2Ø PRINT "I LIKE TO COMPUUUUUUT
```

Whoops! There's a mistake, but you haven't finished the line. No sweat. Just press DELETE BACK S and back the cursor over the multiple "U's" and re-enter it correctly. That's a lot easier than having to go back once the error has been entered with RETURN!

WATCH OUT FOR 'RUNDY'

After editing with the ATARI, I have often entered RUN over the READY prompt, ending up with RUNDY. Of course, instead of having the program RUN, it gives an ERROR-. On some computers, as soon as you press RETURN, the remaining characters on the line are forgotten if the cursor has not been passed over them. Therefore, if you are used to other kinds of computers, watch out for RUNDY!

More Editing

Let's do a few more things with your editor before going on. We'll practice some more with inserting characters and numbers, but we will also see how to edit groups of characters. So, let's see how we can use the editor to do more with "insertions." Try the following little program:

```
NEW
10 PRINT "{ESC-SHIFT-CLEAR}"
20 PRINT "NOW IS THE TIME FOR ALL
   GOOD MEN";
30 PRINT "TO COME TO THE AID OF
   THEIR COUNTRY"
40 END
```

So far so good, but you meant to include women as well as men in line 2Ø. You could retype the entire line, but all you really need to add is AND WOMEN after MEN. Also, it's really boring to have everything in upper case. Let's change the line to include women and make it both upper and lower case:

STEP 1. Press the CAPS-LOWR key and every non-shifted alphabetic character you enter will now be in lower case.

STEP 2. "Walk" the cursor up to the beginning of line 3Ø using the CTRL and ARROW keys and then place the cursor to the right of the first quotation mark.

STEP 3. Press the CTRL and INSERT keys to make enough spaces to include "and women", and enter and women.

STEP 4. To make the sentence look better, overwrite the line with lower case characters where appropriate. *REMEMBER* that all the commands must be in upper case; so leave them as they are.

After these repairs, you now have upper and lower case, and when you RUN your program it should read

```
Now is the time for all good men and women to come to
the aid of their country.
```

You will save yourself a great deal of time if you use the editor rather than retyping every mistake you make. Therefore, to practice with it, there are several pairs of lines below to repair. The first line shows the wrong way and the second line in the pair shows the correct way. Since "little" things can make a big difference, there are a number of changes to be made. However, as you will soon see, those little mistakes are the ones we are most likely to get snagged on. Practice on these examples until you feel comfortable with the editor — time spent now will save you a great deal later.

EDITOR PRACTICE

```
50 PRINT TIS BETTER TO HAVE LOVE AND LOST
   THAN TO HAVE NEVER LOVED AT ALL"
50 PRINT "TIS BETTER TO HAVE LOVE AND LOST
   THAN TO HAVE NEVER LOVED AT ALL"

10 PRINT {ESC-SHIFT-CLEAR}
10 PRINT "{ESC-SHIFT-CLEAR}"

80 PRINT "A GOOD MAN IS HARD TO FIND"
80 PRINT "A GOOD PERSON IS HARD TO FIND"

40 PRINT "{ESC-SHIFT-CLEAR}" PRINT "WE'RE OFF!
40 PRINT "{ESC-SHIFT-CLEAR}" :
   PRINT "WE'RE OFF!"
```

If you fixed all of those lines, you can repair just about anything. Once you get the hang of it, it's quite simple.

ELEMENTARY MATH OPERATIONS

So far all we've done is to PRINT out a lot of text, but that isn't too different from having a fancy typewriter. Now let's do some simple math operations to show you your computer can compute! Enter the following:

```
{SHIFT-CLEAR}
PRINT 2 + 2 <RETURN>
```

This is what your screen should look like now:

```
PRINT 2 + 2
4
```

Big deal, so the computer can add - so can my $5 calculator and my 8 year old kid. Who said computers are smart? The programmer (you) is who is smart. OK, so let's give it a little tougher problem.

```
{SHIFT-CLEAR}
PRINT 7.87 * 123.65 <RETURN>
973.1255
```

Still nothing your calculator can't do, but it'd be a little rough on the 8 year old.

As we progress, we can include more and more aspects of mathematical problems. In the next chapter, we will see how we can store values in variables and a lot of things that would choke your calculator. For now, though, all we'll do is to introduce the format of mathematical manipulations. The "+" and "–" signs work just as they do in regular math, and the "x" is replaced by "*" (asterisk) for multiplication and "÷" is replaced by the "/" (slash) for division.

As we begin dealing with more complex math, we will need to observe a certain order in which problems are executed. This is called "precedence." Depending on the operations we use, and the results we are attempting to obtain, we will use one order or another. For example, let's suppose we want to multiply the sum of two numbers by a third number — say the sum of 15 and 2Ø multiplied by 3. If you entered

```
3 * 15 + 2Ø
```

you would get 3 multiplied by 15 with 2Ø added on. That's not what you wanted. The reason for that is precedence — multiplication precedes addition. To help you remember the precedence, let's write a little program you can run and then play with some math problems in the Immediate mode to see the results and refer to your "Precedence Chart" on the screen. (This little program is quite handy, so save it to disk or tape to be used later.)

```
1Ø {ESC-SHIFT-CLEAR}
2Ø PRINT "1. - (MINUS SIGNS FOR NEGATIVE
   NUMBERS - NOT SUBTRACTION)"
3Ø PRINT "2.  ^  (EXPONENTIATION)"
4Ø PRINT "3. * / (MULTIPLICATION AND DIVISION)"
5Ø PRINT "4. + - (ADDITIONS
   AND SUBTRACTIONS)"
6Ø PRINT "NOTE: ALL OTHER PRECEDENCE
   BEING EQUAL PRECEDENCE IS FROM
   LEFT TO RIGHT"
7Ø PRINT "YOUR COMPUTER FIRST EXECUTES
   THE NUMBERS IN PARENTHESES, WORKING
   ITS WAY FROM THE INSIDE OUT IN
   MULTIPLE PARENTHESES."
```

Try some different problems and see if you can get what you want. *Note: In Chapter 4, we will be dealing with "Relationals." All string relationals have a higher precedence than negative designations(–), and all numeric relationals have lower precedence than plus and minus (+, –). For now, don't worry about it, though.*

Re-ordering Precedence

Once you get the knack of the order in which math operations work, there is a way to simplify organizing math problems. By placing two or more numbers in PARENTHESES, it is possible to move them up in priority. Let's go back to our example of adding 15 and 2Ø and then multiplying by 3, but this time we will use parentheses.

```
PRINT 3 * (15 + 2Ø)
```

Now since the multiplication sign has precedence over the addition sign, without the parentheses we would have gotten 3 times 15 plus 2Ø. However, since all operations inside parentheses are executed first, your computer FIRST added 15 and 2Ø and then multiplied the sum by 3. If more than a single set of parentheses is used in an equation, then the innermost is executed first, working its way out.

THE PARENTHESES DUNGEON

To help you remember the order in which math operations are executed within parentheses, think of the operations as being locked up in a multi-layer dungeon. Each cell represents the innermost operation, and the cells are lined up from left to right. Each "prisoner" is an operation surrounded by walls of parentheses. To escape the dungeon, the prisoner must first get out of the innermost cell, go to his right and release any other prisoners in their cells. Then they break out of the "cell-block" and finally out into the open. Unfortunately, since operations are "executed," this is a lethal analogy for our poor escaping "prisoners." Do some of the examples and see if you can come up with a better analogy.

The following examples show you some operations with parentheses.

```
PRINT 2Ø + 1Ø * (8 - 4)
PRINT (12.43 + 92) / 3 ^ (11 - 3)
PRINT (22 - 3.1415) * (22 + 3.1415)
PRINT ((16 - 4) + (3 + 5)) / 18
PRINT 19 + 2 * (51 + 3) - (1ØØ - 14)
```

Now try some of these problems in the proper format expected by your computer:

> Multiply the sum of 4 , 9 and 2Ø by 15
>
> Add up the charges on your long distance calls and divide the sum by the number of calls you made. This will give you the average expense of your calls. Remember, though, you have to do this in one set of statements in a single line. Do the same thing with your checkbook for a month to see the average (mean) amount for your checks.

SUMMARY

This chapter has covered the most basic aspects of programming. At this point you should be able to use the editor in your ATARI and write commands in the Immediate and Program (deferred) modes. Also, you should be able to manipulate basic math operations. However, we have only just begun to uncover the power of your computer, and at this stage, we are treating it more as a glorified calculator than a computer. Nevertheless, what we have covered in this chapter is extremely important to understand, because it is the foundation upon which your understanding of programming is to be built. If there are parts you do not understand, review them before continuing. If you still do not understand certain operations after a review, don't worry. You will be able to pick them up later, but it is still important that you try and get everything to do what it is supposed to do and what you want it to do.

The next chapter will take us into the realm of computer programming and increase your understanding of your ATARI considerably. If you take it one step at a time, you will be amazed at the power you have at your fingertips and how easy it is to program. Also, we will be leaving the realm of calculator-like commands and getting down to some honest-to-goodness computer work. This is where the fun really begins.

CHAPTER 3

Moving Along

Introduction

In the last chapter, we saw how to get started in executing commands in both the Immediate and Program modes. From now on we will concentrate our efforts on building from the foundation set in Chapter 2 in the Program mode, tying various commands together in a program. We will, however, use the Immediate mode to provide simple examples and to give you an idea of how a certain command works. Also, as we learn more and more commands, it would be a good idea if you started saving the example programs on your disk or cassette so that they can be used for review and a quick "look-up" of examples.

On disk, use file names that you can recognize, such as VARS1 or GOSUB3 and REMEMBER each file has to have a different name; so be sure to number example file names (e.g., ARRAYS1, ARRAYS2, etc.). For programs CSAVEd on tape, use more descriptive names in a log, and be sure to write down the beginning counter position for each program saved.

VARIABLES

Perhaps the single most important computer function is in variable commands. Basically, a variable is a symbol that can have more than a single value. If we say, for example, X = 1Ø, we assign the value of 1Ø to the variable we call "X". Try the following:

```
X = 1Ø <RETURN>
READY
PRINT X <RETURN>
```

Note: You can define variables using LET (e.g., LET X = 1Ø), but it is unnecessary to use LET; so we won't.

Your computer responded

```
10
```

Now type in

```
X=55.7 <RETURN>
READY
PRINT X <RETURN>
```

This time you got

```
55.7
```

Each time you assign a value to a variable, it will respond with the last assigned value when you PRINT that variable. Now try the following:

```
X = 10 <RETURN>
Y = 15 <RETURN>
PRINT X + Y <RETURN>
```

And your ATARI responded with

```
25
```

As you can see, variables can be treated in the same way as math problems using numbers. However, instead of using the numbers, you use the variables. Now let's try a little program using variables to calculate the area of a circle.

```
10 PRINT "{ESC-SHIFT-CLEAR}"
20 PI = 3.14159265: REM THIS IS THE VALUE
   OF PI FROM YOUR GEOMETRY CLASS.
30 R = 15 : REM R IS THE RADIUS OF OUR CIRCLE
40 PRINT PI * (R * R) : REM THIS GIVES US PI
   TIMES THE RADIUS SQUARED.
50 END
```

When you RUN the program, you will get the area of a circle with a radius of 15. If you change the value of "R" in line 30, it is a simple matter to quickly calculate the area of any circle you want! Since our example "squares" a result, why don't we use our exponential sign " ^ ". Change line 40 to read

```
40 PRINT PI * (R ^ 2)
```

That saves typing, doesn't it. RUN the program again and see if you get the same results. You don't, but they're close. That's because " ^ " drops some decimal points on the end. Also, change the value of R to see the areas of different circles.

Variable Names

When you name a variable, the computer looks at all the characters in a variable name. For example, if you name a variable NUMBER, your computer will differentiate it from NU. Since many computers use only the first two characters of a variable, you should be aware of this difference. Try the following:

```
NUMBER = 63
NU = 999
PRINT NUMBER
PRINT NU
```

You got 63 for NUMBER and 99 for NU.

Now it may seem the best thing to do is to use variable names with as few characters as possible to save time, but as you get into more and more sophisticated programs, it helps to use variable names that are descriptive. For example, the following program uses MEAN as a descriptive variable name:

```
10 PRINT "{ESC-SHIFT-CLEAR}"
20 A = 15 : B = 23 : C = 38
30 MEAN = (A + B + C) / 3
40 PRINT MEAN
50 END
```

If the above program were a hundred or more lines long, you would know what the variable MEAN does — it calculates a "mean." This makes it a lot easier to understand what the variable does.

Other considerations in naming variables include not using "reserved words" (i.e., programming commands). In fact, if the first characters of a variable have a reserved word in it, it will be invalid. Let's look at some examples of what is and what is not a valid variable name:

PRINT=987 (Invalid name since PRINT is a reserved word.)

R1 = 321 (Valid name since first character is a letter.)

1R = 55 (Invalid since first character is not a letter.)

FORT = 222 (Invalid since variable name begins with reserved word FOR.)

TFOR = 8910 (Valid since variable does not begin with reserved word FOR.)

PR = 99 (Valid name, for even though reserved word PRINT begins with PR, only part of the reserved word is used in variable name.)

IF = 99999999 (Invalid since IF is a reserved word.)

ADFETDCVRRWRDAAF = 10 (Valid name, but really dumb.)

It is also possible to give values to variables with other variables or a combination of variables and numbers. In our example with the variable MEAN we defined it with other variables. Here are some more examples:

```
T = A * (B + C)
N = N + 1
SUM = X + Y + Z
```

Types of Variables

Real Variables

So far we've used only "real" or "floating point" variables in our examples. Any variable that begins with a capital letter and does not end with a dollar sign ($) is a real variable. The value for a real variable can be from – to + 9.99999999E+97. The "E" is the scientific notation for very big numbers. For the time being, don't worry about it, but if you get a result with such a letter in a numeric result, get in touch with a math instructor. At this juncture, figure you can enter numbers in their standard format with 9 significant digits. (If your checkbook debit or income tax payments have a scientific notation in them, leave the country.) Think of real variables as being able to hold just about any number you would need along with the decimal fractions.

String Variables

String variables are extremely useful in formatting what you will see on the screen, and like real variables, they are sent to the screen by the PRINT statement. However, rather than printing only numbers, string variables send all kinds of characters, called "strings," to the screen. String variables are indicated by a dollar sign ($) on the end of a variable. For example, A$, BAD$, G$, and PULL$ are all legitimate string variables. (In computer parlance, we use the term "string" for the dollar sign. Thus, our examples would be called "A string", "BAD string", etc.) String variables are defined by placing the "string" in quotation marks, just as we did with other messages we printed out.

Before we can use string variables, we must first "dimension" them using the DIM statement. The DIM statement sets the maximum length of the string. For example, if you wanted your string to be CAT you would have to DIMension it to 3. To set the DIMension of a string, enter

```
DIM A$(9)
```

or any other string name or size. In our example, we want a string for CAT to be "3" since there are 3 characters in the word CAT. We will use the variable name C$; thus, we would enter

```
DIM C$(3)
```

Let's try out a few examples from the Immediate mode:

```
DIM ABC$(3) : ABC$ = "ABC" : PRINT ABC$
    <RETURN>
DIM G$(9) : G$ = "BURLESQUE" : PRINT G$
    <RETURN>
DIM DOG$(3) : DOG$ ="DOG" : PRINT DOG$
    <RETURN>
DIM NUMBER$(7) : NUMBER$ = "1234567" :
    PRINT NUMBER$ <RETURN>
DIM B1$(11) : B1$ = "5 + 10 + 20" :
    PRINT B1$ <RETURN>
```

Note: B1$ *was* DIM*ensioned to be 11 instead of 7. That's because spaces* count *as characters.*

In the same way as real variables, a string variable must begin with a letter and use non-reserved words. More importantly, you probably noticed in our examples that numbers in string variables are not treated as numbers, but rather as "words" or "messages." For example, you may have noticed that when you PRINTed B1$, instead of printing out "35" (the sum of 5, 1∅ and 2∅), B1$ printed out exactly what you put in quotes, 5 + 1∅ + 2∅. Do not attempt to do math with string variables. (In later chapters, we'll see some tricks to convert string variables to numeric -real or integer- variables, but for now just treat them as messages.)

Now let's put all of our accumulated knowledge together and write a program that uses variables. We will start a little program which will allow you to subtract a check from your checkbook and print the amount. This program will be the beginning of something we will later develop to give you a handy little program with which to do checkbook balancing.

```
 10 PRINT "{ESC-SHIFT-CLEAR}"
 20 BALANCE = 571.88 : REM ANY FIGURE WILL
    DO. BALANCE IS A REAL VARIABLE
 30 CHECK = 29.95 : REM WHAT YOU LAST
    SPENT IN THE COMPUTER STORE. CHECK
    IS A REAL VARIABLE.
 40 DIM B$(28) : B$ = "YOUR BEGINNING
    BALANCE IS $"
 50 DIM C$(19) : C$ = "YOUR CHECK IS FOR $"
 60 DIM NB$(21) : NB$ = "YOUR NEW BALANCE
    IS $": REM B$, C$ AND NB$ ARE
    STRING VARIABLES
 70 PRINT B$;BALANCE
 80 PRINT C$;CHECK
 90 N = BALANCE - CHECK
100 PRINT NB$; N
110 END
```

Since this is a fairly long program for this stage of the game, make sure you put in everything correctly. For the computer, it is critical that you distinguish between commas, semicolons, periods, etc. Also, save it to disk or tape. To play with it, change the values in lines 2Ø and 3Ø.

Let's quickly review what we have done.

STEP 1. First we defined the real variables BALANCE and CHECK.

STEP 2. Then we dimensioned and defined string variables B$, C$, and NB$ to use as labels in screen formatting.

STEP 3. Finally, we printed out all of our information using our variables, with one new variable, N, defined as the difference between BALANCE and CHECK.

Note how we formatted the "output" (what you see on your screen) of our PRINT statements. The semi-colon ";" between the variables accomplished two things: (1) it told the computer where one variable ended and the next began, and (2) it told the computer to PRINT the second variable right after the first one. Thus, it took the string variable NB$

```
YOUR NEW BALANCE IS $#
```

and stuck the value of the real variable N right after the dollar sign (exactly where we placed the hatch #). Later we will go more into the formatting of output, but for now let's take a quick look at using punctuation in formatting text. We will use the comma "," and semicolon ";" and "new line" to illustrate basic formatting. Put in the following little program:

```
NEW <RETURN>
  10 PRINT "{ESC-SHIFT-CLEAR}"
  20 DIM A$(4), B$ (5), C$ (5), D$ (4)
```

```
 30 REM NOTE HOW ALL STRINGS
    WERE DIMENSIONED
 40 REM USING A SINGLE 'DIM' STATEMENT
 50 A$ = "HERE" : B$ = "THERE" :
    C$ = "WHERE" : D$ = "DERE"
 60 PRINT A$; : PRINT B$; : PRINT C$; :
    PRINT D$; : REM SEMI-COLONS
 70 PRINT
 80 PRINT A$, : PRINT B$, : PRINT C$,:
    PRINT D$, : REM COMMAS
 90 PRINT : REM A 'PRINT' BY ITSELF GIVES
    A VERTICAL 'SPACE' IN FORMATTING
100 PRINT A$ : PRINT B$ : PRINT C$ : PRINT D$:
    REM 'NEW LINES'
110 END
```

Now RUN the program. As you should see, the little differences in lines 60, 80, and 100 made big differences on the screen. The first set is all crammed together, the second set is spaced evenly across the screen, and the third set is stacked one on top of the other. As we saw in the previous program, semicolons put numbers and strings right next to one another. However, using commas after a PRINTed variable will space output in groups of four across the screen, and using "new lines" in the form of colons or new line numbers will make the output start on a new line. A PRINT statement all by itself will put a vertical "linefeed" between statements. Try the following little program to see how PRINT statements all by themselves can be used.

```
NEW <RETURN>
10 PRINT "{ESC-SHIFT-CLEAR}"
20 PRINT "WHENEVER YOU PUT IN A PRINT
   STATEMENT"; : REM NOTE PLACEMENT
   OF SEMI-COLON
30 PRINT " ALL BY ITSELF, IT GIVES A 'LINEFEED'."
40 PRINT
50 PRINT "SEE WHAT I MEAN?"
60 END
```

Play with commas, semicolons, and "new lines" with variables and string variables until you get the hang of it. They are very important and are the source of program "bugs."

your program may have BUGS

BUGS and BOMBS

We've mentioned "bugs" and "bombs" in programs but never really explained what they meant. "Bugs" are simply errors in programs that either create ?SYNTAX ERRORs or prevent your program from doing what you want it to do. "Debugging" is the process of removing "bugs." "Bombing" is what your program does when it encounters a "bug." This is all computer lingo, and if you use it in your conversations, people will think you really know a lot about computers or have a bug in your personality.

Programs can BOMB

Input and Output (I/O)

Input and output, often referred to as I/O, are ways of putting things into your computer and getting it out. Usually we put IN information from the keyboard, save it to disk or tape, and then later put it in from the disk drive or cassette recorder. When we want information OUT of the computer, we want it to go to our screen or printer. This is what I/O means. So far, we have entered information IN the computer from the keyboard either in the Program or in the Immediate mode. Using the PRINT statement, we have sent information OUT to the screen. However, there are other ways we can INPUT information with a combination of programming and keyboard commands. Let's look at some of these ways and make our CHECKBOOK program a lot simpler to use.

Input

The INPUT command is placed in a program and expects some kind of response from the keyboard and then a RETURN. (A RETURN alone will also work, but the response is read as " ".) Let's look at a simple example:

```
NEW <RETURN>
1Ø PRINT "{ESC-SHIFT-CLEAR}"
2Ø INPUT X : REM 'X' IS A NUMERIC VARIABLE SO
   ENTER A NUMBER
3Ø PRINT X
4Ø END
```

RUN the program and your screen will go blank and a "?" along with a blinking cursor will sit there until you enter a number and then the computer will PRINT the number you just entered. Really interesting, huh?

Let's try INPUTing the same information using a slightly different format. Look at the following program:

```
NEW <RETURN>
1Ø PRINT "{ESC-SHIFT-CLEAR}"
2Ø PRINT "ENTER YOUR AGE "; : INPUT X
```

```
30 PRINT "{ESC-SHIFT-CLEAR}" : PRINT :
   PRINT : PRINT
40 PRINT "YOUR AGE IS "; X
```

Now RUN the program. You will see that the presentation is a little more interesting. Also, notice we did not put an END command at the end of the program. In ATARI BASIC it is not necessary to enter an END command, but it is usually a good idea to do so. As we get into more advanced topics, we will see that our program can jump around, and the place we want it to END will be in the middle. We will need an END statement so that it will not crash into an area we don't want it to go. So, while an END command really has not been necessary up to now, it is nevertheless a good habit to develop.

Let's soup up our program a little more with the INPUT statement.

```
NEW <RETURN>
10 PRINT "{ESC-SHIFT-CLEAR}"
20 DIM NA$(20) : REM WILL ACCEPT UP
   TO 20 CHARACTERS
30 PRINT "WHAT'S YOUR NAME -> "; : INPUT NA$
40 PRINT
50 PRINT "WHAT'S YOUR AGE -> "; : INPUT AGE
60 PRINT
70 DIM RT$ (1) : PRINT "PRESS <RETURN>
   TO CONTINUE "; : INPUT RT$
80 ? "{ESC-SHIFT-CLEAR}" : ? : ? : ? : ? : ? : REM
   USING "?" AS SUBSTITUTES FOR PRINT
90 PRINT NA$; " IS "; AGE ; " YEARS OLD. " : REM
   BE CAREFUL WHERE YOU PUT YOUR QUOTE
   MARKS AND SEMICOLONS IN THIS LINE
100 END
```

Now we're getting somewhere. You can enter information as numeric or string variables and the output is formatted so you know what's going on. As your programs become larger and more complicated, it is very important to connect your string variables and numeric variables in such a way that it is easy to see what the numbers on the screen mean. Let's face it, a computer wouldn't be very helpful if it filled the screen with numbers, and you did not know what they meant! Line 7Ø is the format for a pause in your program. RT$ doesn't hold any information, but since INPUT statements expect something from the keyboard and a variable, RT$ (for RETURN) is as good as any.

READing In DATA

A second way to enter data into a program is with READ and DATA statements. However, instead of entering the data through the keyboard, DATA in one part of the program is READ in from another part. Each READ statement looks at elements in DATA statements sequentially. The READ command is associated with a variable which looks at the next DATA statement and places the numeric value or string in the variable. Let's look at the following example:

```
NEW <RETURN>
10 PRINT "{ESC-SHIFT-CLEAR}"
15 DIM NA$(12), OC$(15), ST$(14), CT$(10),
   SA$(10)
```

```
20 READ NA$ : REM READS NAME
30 READ OC$ : REM READS OCCUPATION
40 READ SN : REM READS STREET NUMBER
50 READ ST$ : REM READS STREET NAME
60 READ CT$ : REM READS CITY
70 READ SA$ : REM READS STATE
80 READ ZIP : REM READS ZIP CODE
90 PRINT : PRINT : PRINT
100 REM BEGIN PRINTING OUT WHAT 'READ'
    READ IN. (BE CAREFUL TO PUT IN EVERYTHING
    EXACTLY AS IT IS LISTED.)
110 PRINT NA$
120 PRINT OC$
130 PRINT SN; " " ; ST$
140 PRINT CT$ ; ", " ; SA$ ;" "; ZIP
150 END
1000 DATA DAVID GORDON, SOFTWARE TYCOON,
     8943, FULLBRIGHT AVE
1010 DATA CHATSWORTH, CALIFORNIA, 91311
```

NOTE: Spaces were left between the DATA *elements for clarity. They will be read as spaces by the* READ *statements. By either omitting spaces after the commas in the* DATA *elements or by making the* DIM*ensions of the strings longer, the output will be correct.*

In the DATA statements there is a comma separating the various elements, unless the DATA statement is at the end of a line. If you have one of the elements out of place or omit a comma, strange things can happen. For example, if the READ statement is expecting a numeric variable (such as the street address) and runs into a string (such as the street name) you will get an error message. Think of the DATA statements as a stack of strings and numbers. Each time a READ statement is encountered in the program the first element of the DATA is removed from the stack. The next READ statement looks at the element on top of the stack, moving from left to right. Go ahead and SAVE this program and let's put an error in it. (SAVE it first, though, so you will have a correct listing of how READ and DATA statements work.)

Note that you did not have to put the string elements in quote marks. In fact, if you do put a DATA statement in quotes, the string will be defined to include the quotations. For example enter the following program:

```
NEW
10 PRINT"{ESC-SHIFT-CLEAR}"
20 DIM QUOTE$(21)
30 READ QUOTE$
40 DATA "To be or not to be."
50 PRINT QUOTE$
```

When you RUN the program you will get

```
"To be or not to be."
```

Not only did the quotation marks show up in our output, but the string was able to include both upper and lower case in its definition and therefore in its output. This is one method of getting quotation marks to be part of a string. (What would happen if you simply entered QUOTE$= "To be or not to be."?)

Looping With FOR/NEXT

The FOR/NEXT loop is one of the most useful operations in BASIC programming. It allows the user to instruct the computer to go through a determined number of steps, at variable increments if desired, and execute them until the total number of steps is completed. Let's look at a simple example to get started.

```
NEW <RETURN>
10 PRINT "{ESC-SHIFT-CLEAR}"
20 DIM NA$(30) :NA$ = "<YOUR NAME>"
30 FOR I = 1 TO 10 : REM BEGINNING OF LOOP
40 PRINT NA$
50 NEXT I : REM LOOP TERMINAL
60 END
```

Now RUN the program and you will see your name printed 10 times along the left side of the screen. That's nice, but so what? OK, not too impressive, but we will see how useful this can be in a bit. But first let's look at another simple illustration to show what's happening to "I" as the loop is being executed.

```
NEW <RETURN>
10 PRINT "{ESC-SHIFT-CLEAR}"
20 FOR I = 1 TO 10
30 PRINT I
40 NEXT I
```

As we can see when the program is RUN, the value of "I" changes each time the program proceeds through the loop. Think of a loop as a child on a merry-go-round. Each time the merry-go-round completes a revolution, the child gets a gold ring, beginning with one and ending, in our example, with 10.

TRIVIA

As you begin looking at more and more programs, you will see that the variable I is used in FOR/NEXT loops a lot. Actually, you can use any variable you want, but the I keeps cropping up. Like yourself, I was most curious as to why programmers kept using the letter I, and after several moments of exhaustive research I found out. The I was the "integer" variable in FORTRAN (an early computer language), and it was used in "DO loops" since it was faster. The I also can be interpreted to stand for "increment." I told you it was trivia.

Having seen how loops function, let's do something practical with a loop. We'll fix up our CHECKBOOK program we've been playing with.

In our souped up CHECKBOOK program, we are going to use variables in many ways. First, our FOR/NEXT loop will use a variable. We'll stick with tradition and use I. Second, we will use a variable to indicate the number of loops to be executed. We will use NUMBER as the variable name. Third, we will use variables for the balance, the amount of the check, and the new balance. This program is going to be a little longer; so be sure to SAVE it to disk every five lines or so. For cassette, SAVE it about every 1Ø lines.

```
NEW <RETURN>
1Ø PRINT "{ESC-SHIFT-CLEAR}"
2Ø DIM CB$(9) : CB$ = "[ATARI KEY] CHECKBOOK
   [ATARI KEY]"
3Ø PRINT : PRINT : PRINT CB$ : PRINT
4Ø PRINT "HOW MANY CHECKS";: INPUT NUMBER
5Ø PRINT "WHAT IS YOUR CURRENT BALANCE" ; :
   INPUT BA
6Ø REM BEGIN LOOP
7Ø FOR I = 1 TO NUMBER
8Ø PRINT "YOUR BALANCE IS NOW $";BA
9Ø PRINT " AMOUNT OF CHECK #";I; "-> ";
1ØØ INPUT CK : REM VARIABLE FOR CHECK
```

```
110 BA = BA - CK : REM KEEPS A RUNNING BALANCE
120 NEXT I : REM TOP OF LOOP
130 PRINT "{ESC-SHIFT-CLEAR}" : REM CLEAR
    SCREEN WHEN ALL CHECKS ARE ENTERED
140 PRINT : PRINT : PRINT
150 PRINT "YOU NOW HAVE $"; BA ;
    " IN YOUR ACCOUNT"
160 PRINT : PRINT " THANK YOU AND
    COME AGAIN "
170 END
```

Our checkbook program is coming along, making it easier to use, and that is the purpose of computers. Now, let's look at something else with loops.

Nested Loops

With certain applications, it is going to be necessary to have one or more FOR/NEXT loops working inside one another. Let's look at a simple application. Suppose you had two teams with 10 members on each team. You want to make a team roster indicating the team number (#1 or #2) and member number (#1 through #10). Using a nested loop, we can do this in the following program:

```
NEW <RETURN>
10 PRINT "{ESC-SHIFT-CLEAR}"
20 FOR T = 1 TO 2 : REM T FOR TEAM #
30 FOR M = 1 TO 10 : REM M FOR MEMBER #
40 PRINT "TEAM #" ; T , "PLAYER #"; M
50 NEXT M
60 NEXT T
70 END
```

In using nested loops, it is important to keep the loops straight. The innermost loop (the "M loop" in our example) must not have any other FOR or NEXT statement inside of it. Think of nested loops as a series of fish eating one another, the largest fish's mouth encompassing the next smallest and so forth on down to the smallest fish.

Look at the following structure of nested loops:

```
FOR A = 1 TO N
  FOR B = 1 TO N
    FOR C = 1 TO N
      FOR D = 1 TO N
      NEXT D
    NEXT C
  NEXT B
NEXT A
```

Note how each loop begins (a FOR statement is executed) and is terminated (encounters a NEXT statement) in a "nested" sequence. If you have ever stacked a set of different sized cooking bowls, each one fits inside the other; that is because the outer edge of one is larger than the next one. Likewise, in nested loops, the "edge" of each loop is "larger" than the one inside it and "smaller" than the one it is inside.

Stepping Forward and Backward

Loops can go one step at a time, as we have been using, or they can step at different increments. For example, the following program "steps" by 1Ø.

```
NEW <RETURN>
1Ø PRINT "{ESC-SHIFT-CLEAR}"
2Ø FOR I = 1Ø TO 1ØØ STEP 1Ø
3Ø PRINT I
4Ø NEXT I
```

This allows you to increment your count by whatever you want. You can even use variables or anything else that has a numeric value. For example:

```
NEW <RETURN>
1Ø PRINT "{ESC-SHIFT-CLEAR}"
2Ø K = 5 : N = 25
3Ø FOR I = K TO N STEP K
4Ø PRINT I
5Ø NEXT I
```

Go ahead and RUN the program. The variable works just like numbers. (But you knew that, didn't you?)

It is also possible to go backwards. Try this program:

```
NEW <RETURN>
1Ø FOR I = 4 TO 1 STEP -1
2Ø PRINT "FINISHING POSITION IN RACE =";I
3Ø NEXT I
```

As we get into more and more sophisticated (and useful) programs, we will begin to see how all of these different features of ATARI BASIC are very useful. Often, you may not see the practicality of a command initially, but when you need it later on, you will wonder how you could program without it!

IN CASE YOU WONDERED

You may have noticed that the lines inside the loops were indented. If you tried that on your ATARI you probably found that as soon as you LISTed your program, all the indentations were gone. Unfortunately, that will happen, and without special utilities, there's nothing you can do about it. However, don't let it worry you. It is a programming convention for clarity to indent or "tab" loops to make it easier to understand what the program is doing, but they do not affect your program at all.

Counters

Often you will want to count the number of times a loop is executed and keep a record of it in your program for later use. For example, if you run a program that loops with a STEP of 3, you may not know exactly how many times the loop will execute. To find out, programmers use "counters," variables that are incremented, usually by +1, each time a loop is executed. The following program illustrates the use of a counter:

```
NEW <RETURN>
10 PRINT "{ESC-SHIFT-CLEAR}"
20 FOR I = 3 TO 99 STEP 3
30 PRINT I
40 N = N + 1 : REM THIS IS THE COUNTER
50 NEXT I
60 PRINT : PRINT "YOUR LOOP EXECUTED ";
   N ; " TIMES."
```

The first time the loop was entered, the value of "N" was Ø, but when the program got to line 4Ø, the value of 1 was added to N to make it 1 (i.e. Ø + 1 = 1). The second time through the loop, the value of N began at 1, then 1 was added, and at the top of the loop, line 5Ø, the value of N was 2. This went on until the program exited the loop. Then, after all the looping was finished, PRESTO! Your N told you how many times the loop was executed. Of course, counters are not restricted to counting loops, and they can be incremented by any value, including other variables you may need. For example, change line 4Ø to read

```
40 N = N + (I * 2)
```

RUN your program again and your "counter total" will be a good deal higher.

SUMMARY

This chapter has begun to show you the power of your computer, and we have really began programming. One of the most important concepts we have covered is that of the "variable." The significant feature of variables is that they "vary" (change depending on what your program does). This is true not only with numeric variables, but also with string variables. The various input commands show how we enter values or strings into variables depending on what we want the computer to compute for us. Finally, we have learned how to loop. This allows us, with a minimal amount of effort, to tell the computer to go through a process several times with a single set of instructions. With loops, we can set the parameters of an operation at any increment we want, and then sit back and let our ATARI go to work for us.

However, we have only just begun programming! In the next chapter we will begin getting into more commands and operations that allow us to delve deeper into the ATARI's capabilities and make our programming jobs easier. The more commands we know, the less work it is to write a program.

CHAPTER 4

Branching Out

Introduction

In this chapter we will begin exploring new programming constructs that will geometrically increase your programming ability. We will be examining some more sophisticated techniques, but by taking each a step at a time, you will begin using them with ease. Later, when you are developing your own programs, be bold and try out new commands. One problem new programmers have is a tendency to stick with the simple commands they have learned to get a job done. After all, why use "complicated" commands to do what simpler ones can do? Well, the answer to that has to do with simplicity. If one "complicated" command can do the work of 1Ø "simple" commands, which one is actually simpler? As you get into more and more sophisticated programming applications, your programs can become longer and subject to more bugs. The more commands you have to sift through, the more difficult it is to find the bugs; therefore, while it is perfectly OK to write a long program using a lot of simple commands while you're learning, begin thinking about short-cuts through the use of the more advanced commands.

Related to this issue of maximizing your knowledge of different commands is that of letting the computer perform the computing. This may sound strange at first, but often novices will figure everything out for the computer and use it as a glorified calculator. In the last chapter, you may remember, we set up a counter to count the times a loop was executed when we used a STEP 3 loop. We could have figured out how many loops were executed instead of letting the computer do it with the counter, but that would have defeated the purpose of programming! So, as you learn new commands, see how they can be used to perform the calculations you had to work out yourself.

Branching

So far all of our programs have gone straight from the top to the bottom with the exception of loops. However, if our ATARI is to do some real decision making, we must have some way of giving it options. When a program leaves a straight path, we refer to it either as "looping" or "branching." We already know the purpose of a loop, but what is a branch? Well, using the IF/THEN and GOTO commands, we will see. Consider the following program: *NOTE: By now you should know enough to clear memory with a NEW command, so I won't keep on insulting your intelligence by putting one at the beginning of each program.*

```
10 PRINT "{ESC-SHIFT-CLEAR}"
20 PRINT "CHOOSE ONE OF THE FOLLOWING BY
   NUMBER: "
30 PRINT
40 PRINT "1. BANANAS"
50 PRINT "2. ORANGES"
```

```
60 PRINT "3. PEACHES"
70 PRINT "4. WATERMELONS"
80 PRINT
90 PRINT "WHICH "; : INPUT X
100 PRINT "{ESC-SHIFT-CLEAR}"
110 IF X = 1 THEN GOTO 200
120 IF X = 2 THEN GOTO 300
130 IF X = 3 THEN GOTO 400
140 IF X = 4 THEN GOTO 500
150 GOTO 10 : REM THIS IS A 'TRAP' TO MAKE SURE
    THE USER CHOOSES 1, 2, 3, OR 4
200 PRINT "BANANAS" : END
300 PRINT "ORANGES" : END
400 PRINT "PEACHES" : END
500 PRINT "WATERMELONS" : END
```

As you can see, your computer "branched" to the appropriate place, did what it was told and ENDed. Not very inspiring, I admit, but it is a clear example. Now, let's try something a little more practical for your kids to play with in their math homework.

```
10 PRINT "{ESC-SHIFT-CLEAR}" : DIM AN$(1)
20 PRINT "{ATARI KEY}ADDITION GAME{ATARI KEY}"
30 PRINT : PRINT
40 PRINT "ENTER FIRST NUMBER -->" ; : INPUT A
50 PRINT
60 PRINT "ENTER SECOND NUMBER-->" ; : INPUT B
70 PRINT
80 PRINT "WHAT IS "; A ; "+" ; B ; : INPUT C
90 IF C = A + B THEN GOTO 200
100 PRINT : PRINT "THAT'S NOT QUITE IT.
    TRY AGAIN." : PRINT
110 GOTO 80
200 PRINT " THAT'S RIGHT! VERY GOOD "
210 PRINT
220 PRINT "WOULD YOU LIKE TO DO MORE? (Y/N): ";
230 INPUT AN$
240 IF AN$ = "Y" THEN PRINT "{ESC-SHIFT-CLEAR}":
    GOTO 30
250 PRINT "{ESC-SHIFT-CLEAR}" : PRINT :
    PRINT : PRINT
260 PRINT "HOPE TO SEE YOU AGAIN SOON": END
```

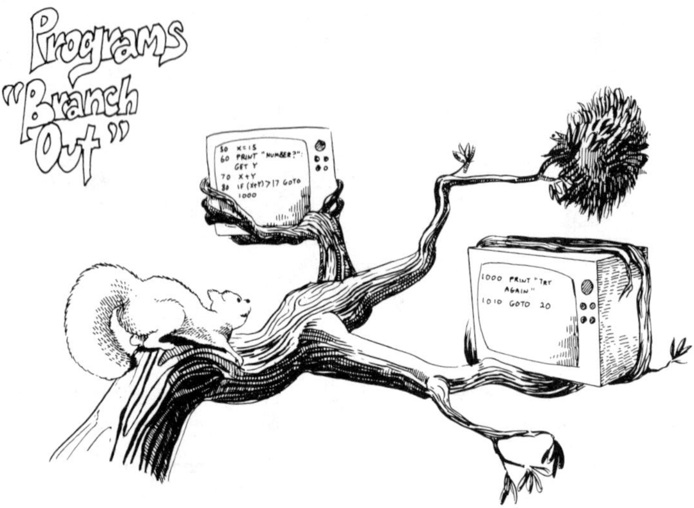

As you can see, the more commands we learn, the more fun we can have. Just for fun, change the program so that it will handle multiplication, division, and subtraction.

WHAT'S IN A NAME?

Kids (of all ages) like to have their names displayed. See if you can change the above program so that it asks the child's name; then when the program responds with either a correction or affirmation command, it mentions the child's name. (e.g., THAT'S RIGHT! VERY GOOD, SAM.) Use NAME$ as the name variable, AND be sure to DIMension it to at least 1Ø!

Let's look carefully at our program to learn something about IF/THEN statements. First, note in line 24Ø, the branch is to clear the screen (PRINT"{ESC-SHIFT-CLEAR}") if AN$ ="Y". If any other response is encountered it ends the program. You may ask why the program did not branch to line 3Ø regardless of the response since the GOTO 3Ø command is after a colon, making it a new line. Good point. The reason for that is after an IF statement, when the response or condition is null, the program immediately drops to the next LINE NUMBER. That is, any statements after a colon in a line beginning with an IF statement will be executed only if the condition of the IF statement is met. The "Y" is in quotation marks because AN$ expects a string variable. If the Y were by itself, the program would expect a value to be entered for a numeric variable. Therefore in the setting of the conditional, we must remember what kind of variable we are using. On the other hand, if we used a numeric variable, such as AN, we could have entered a line such as

```
IF AN = 1 THEN ....
```

Relationals

So far we have only used "=" to determine whether or not our program should branch. However, there are other states, referred to as "relationals," that we can also look at. The following is a complete list of the relationals we can employ:

SYMBOL	MEANING
=	Equal to
<	Less than
>	Greater than
<>	Not equal to
>=	Greater than or equal to
<=	Less than or equal to

Now let's play with some of these, and then we'll examine them for their full power. Here are some quickie programs:

```
 1Ø PRINT "{ESC-SHIFT-CLEAR}"
 2Ø PRINT "NUMBER 1-->"; : INPUT A
 3Ø PRINT "NUMBER 2-->"; : INPUT B
 4Ø IF A > B THEN GOTO 1ØØ
 5Ø IF A < B THEN GOTO 2ØØ
 6Ø IF A = B THEN GOTO 3ØØ
1ØØ PRINT "NUMBER 1 IS GREATER THAN
    NUMBER 2" : END
2ØØ PRINT "NUMBER 1 IS LESS THAN
    NUMBER 2" : END
3ØØ PRINT "NUMBER 1 IS EQUAL TO NUMBER 2"

1Ø DIM AN$ (1)
2Ø PRINT "{ESC-SHIFT-CLEAR}"
```

```
30 PRINT "DO YOU WANT TO CONTINUE? (Y/N)"; :
   INPUT AN$
40 IF AN$ <> "Y" THEN END
50 GOTO 10
```

```
 10 PRINT "{ESC-SHIFT-CLEAR}"
 20 PRINT "HOW OLD ARE YOU? "; : INPUT AGE
 30 IF AGE >= 21 THEN GOTO 100
 40 PRINT"{ESC-SHIFT-CLEAR}" : PRINT : PRINT
    "SORRY, YOU'VE GOT TO BE 21 OR OLDER TO
    COME IN HERE!" : END
100 PRINT"{ESC-SHIFT-CLEAR}" : PRINT : PRINT
    "WHAT WOULD YOU LIKE TO DRINK?"
```

OK, you have the idea of how relationals can be used with IF/THEN commands; note that they work with string as well as numeric variables. However, there is another way to use relationals. Try the following from the Immediate mode:

```
A = 10 : B = 20 : PRINT A = B
```

Your computer responded with a Ø, right? This is a logical operation. If a condition is false, your ATARI responds with a Ø, but if it is true, it responds with a 1. Now try the following little program.

```
10 PRINT "{ESC-SHIFT-CLEAR}"
20 A = 10
30 B = 20
40 C = A > B
50 PRINT C
```

When you RUN the program, you again get a Ø. This is because the variable C was defined as A being greater than B. Since A was less than B the variable C was Ø or "false." Now, let's take it a step further:

```
10 PRINT "{ESC-SHIFT-CLEAR}"
20 A = 10
30 B = 20
40 C = A > B
50 IF C = 0 THEN PRINT "A IS LESS THAN B" : END
60 IF C = 1 THEN PRINT "A IS GREATER THAN B"
```

Later, we will see further applications of these logical operations of the ATARI. For now, though, it is important to understand that a true condition is represented by a "1" and a false condition by a "Ø."

AND/OR/NOT

Sometimes we need to set up more than a single relational. Suppose, for example, that you are organizing your finances into 3 categories of expenses: (1) Under $1Ø; (2) between $1Ø and $1ØØ; and (3) over $1ØØ. With our relationals it would be simple to compare input under $1Ø and over $1ØØ. But what if we wanted to do something in between. In this case we might have some difficulty without added commands. The AND, OR and NOT statements allow us to set ranges with our relationals.

AND	If all conditions are met then true
OR	If one condition is met then true
NOT	If condition is not met then true.

For example:

```
10 PRINT "{ESC-SHIFT-CLEAR}" : DIM AN$(1)
20 PRINT "ENTER AMOUNT -->$"; : INPUT A
30 IF A < 10 THEN 100
40 IF A > 10 AND A <= 100 THEN 200
50 IF A > 100 THEN 300
100 PRINT " PETTY CASH " : GOTO 400
200 PRINT " GENERAL EXPENSES " :GOTO 400
300 PRINT " BIG BUCKS "
400 PRINT " DO YOU WISH TO CONTINUE"; :
    INPUT AN$
410 IF AN$ < > "Y" AND AN$ < > "N" THEN
    PRINT"ANSWER 'Y' OR'N' PLEASE ": GOTO 400
420 IF AN$ = "Y" THEN 20
430 PRINT"{ESC-SHIFT-CLEAR}" :
    PRINT "GOODBYE"
```

In line 4Ø we set the conditional branch to be BOTH greater than 1Ø and equal to or less than 1ØØ. The variable A had to meet both conditions to branch. Similarly, in line 41Ø, using the AND statement again, we made sure that the response had to be either Y or N.

If you are very perceptive, you may have asked yourself about some fishy format in the program. There are conditional IF/THEN lines that simply say THEN 1ØØ and stuff like that. What's going on? Shouldn't there be a GOTO statement there? Again, we have slipped in another feature of ATARI BASIC. When using IF/THEN statements, it is possible to drop the GOTO on a branch and simply put in the line number. However, note that we have used GOTO statements elsewhere in the program where no conditional is used within the same line or within a single set of colons. Until you become more familiar with programming you might want to keep your GOTO statements after IF/THEN statements, but they are not required.

Now let's use the OR and NOT statements in a program:

```
10 PRINT "{ESC-SHIFT-CLEAR}"
20 READ A
30 READ B
40 READ C
50 DATA 10,20,30
60 IF A + B = C OR A < B OR A - B = C THEN 100
70 END
100 PRINT"{ESC-SHIFT-CLEAR}" : PRINT "ONE OF
    'EM MUST BE TRUE"
```

Looking at line 6Ø we can see that A – B does not equal C; however, A + B does equal C and A is less than B. Using the OR statement, only one statement has to be true to branch. Let's try the following program:

```
10 PRINT "{ESC-SHIFT-CLEAR}"
20 READ A : READ B : READ C
30 DATA 10,20,30
40 Z = A - B = C
50 IF NOT Z THEN 100
60 END
100 PRINT " THAT'S RIGHT! A - B = C IS NOT
    RIGHT! — DID I SAY THAT RIGHT?"
```

As can be seen from the example, it is possible to use the "negation" of a formula to calculate a branch condition. In most cases, you will use < > (not equal) or the positive case, but at other times it will be simpler to employ NOT.

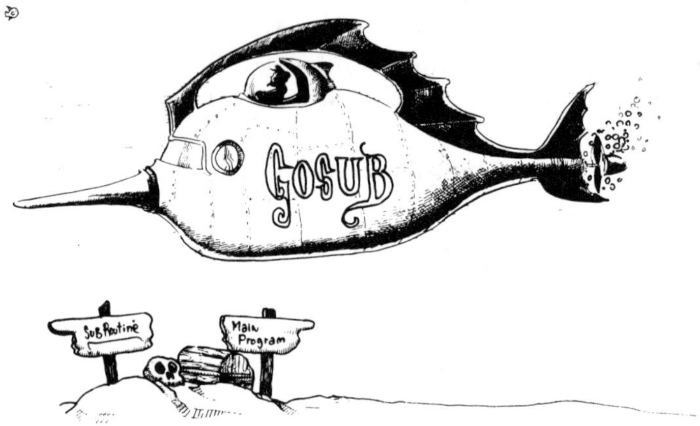

Subroutines

Often in programming there is some operation you will want your computer to perform at several different places in the program. Now, you can repeat the instructions again and again or use GOTOs all over the place to return to your original spot after branching to the operation. On the other hand, you can set up "subroutines" and jump to them using GOSUB and get back to your starting point using the RETURN command. Up to a point the GOSUB command works pretty much like the GOTO command since it sends your program bouncing off to a line out of sequence. Also, the RETURN command is something like GOTO since it also sends your program to an out-of-sequence line. However, the GOSUB/RETURN pair is unique in what it does. Let's take a look at a simple example to see how it works:

```
10 PRINT "{ESC-SHIFT-CLEAR}" : DIM A$(20)
20 A$ = "HELLO" : GOSUB 100
30 A$ = "HOW ARE YOU TODAY?" : GOSUB 100
40 A$ = "I'M FINE" : GOSUB 100
50 END
100 PRINT A$
110 RETURN
```

Our example shows that a GOSUB statement works exactly like a command on the line itself except that it is executed elsewhere in the program. The RETURN statement brings it back to the next statement after the GOSUB statement. Using the GOSUB/RETURN pair it is much easier to weave in and out of a program than using GOTO since the RETURN automatically takes you back to the jump-off point.

To better illustrate the usefulness of GOSUB, let's change our subroutine beginning at line 100 to something more elaborate. Also, in line 10 add TAB$(38) to the DIM statement. Try the following: *NOTE: We will be getting ahead of ourselves a bit with this example, but the following is meant to illustrate something very useful in* GOSUBs.

```
100 L = 19 - LEN (A$)/2
110 FOR I = 1 TO L : TAB$ (I) = " " : NEXT I
120 PRINT TAB$; A$
130 RETURN
```

Now when you RUN the program, all of your strings are centered. As you can see, a single routine handled all of the centering, and instead of having to rewrite the routine every time you wanted a string centered, all you had to do was use a GOSUB to line 100.

NEATNESS COUNTS

We really have not discussed the structure of programs too much up to this point. In part, this is because we have not really had the need to do so. However, as our instruction set grows, so too does the possibility for errors, and by now if you haven't made an error, you haven't been keying in these programs! One way to minimize errors, especially using GOSUBs, is to organize them into coherent blocks. Basically, a block is a subroutine within a range of lines. For example, you might block your subroutines by 1ØØ's or 1ØØØ's, depending on how long the subroutines are. Thus, you might have subroutines beginning at lines 5ØØ, 6ØØ and 7ØØ. It doesn't matter if the subroutine is 1 line or 1Ø lines; as long as it is confined to the block, it is easier to debug, easier for others and you to understand what is happening in the program, and in general a good programming practice. Also, we should DIM our strings at the beginning of a program instead of hither and yon as we have been doing. Up to now, it was clearer to DIM a string, in some cases, right before we used it so you were reminded what the DIM was for. We won't be doing that any more, for it will cause problems in many programs we will be writing.

Computed GOTO and GOSUB

Now we're going to get a little fancier, but in the long run, it will result in clearer and simpler programming. As we have seen, we can GOTO or GOSUB on a "conditional" (e.g., IF A = 1 THEN GOTO 2ØØ). An easier way to make a conditional jump is to use "computed" branches using the ON statement. For example:

```
10 DIM AN$(1)
20 PRINT "{ESC-SHIFT-CLEAR}" : PRINT "ENTER A
   NUMBER FROM 1 TO 5 " ; : INPUT A
30 IF A < 1 OR A > 5 THEN 20 : REM TRAP
```

```
40 ON A GOSUB 100,200,300,400,500 :
   REM COMPUTED GOSUB
50 PRINT "DO YOU WISH TO CONTINUE? (Y/N)" ; :
   INPUT AN$
60 IF AN$ <> "Y" THEN END
70 GOTO 20
100 PRINT "ONE" : PRINT : RETURN
200 PRINT "TWO" : PRINT : RETURN
300 PRINT "THREE" : PRINT : RETURN
400 PRINT "FOUR" : PRINT : RETURN
500 PRINT "FIVE" : PRINT : RETURN
```

The format for a computed GOSUB/GOTO is to enter a variable following the ON command. The program will then jump the number of "commas" to the appropriate line number. If a "1" is entered, it takes the first line number, a "2," the second, and so forth. It's a lot easier than entering:

```
70 IF A = 1 THEN GOSUB 100
80 IF A = 2 THEN GOSUB 200
   etc.
```

However, it is necessary to use relatively small numbers in the "ON" variable since there is a limited number of subroutines. If your program is computing larger numbers, convert the larger numbers into smaller ones by changing the variables. For example:

```
10 DIM AN$(1)
20 PRINT "{ESC-SHIFT-CLEAR}" : PRINT "ENTER
   ANY NUMBER--> "; : INPUT A
30 IF A < 100 THEN B = 1
40 IF A >= 100 AND A < 200 THEN B = 2
50 IF A >= 200 THEN B = 3
60 ON B GOSUB 100, 200, 300 : REM COMPUTED
   GOSUB ON 'B' VARIABLE
70 PRINT "DO YOU WISH TO CONTINUE?(Y/N)"; :
   INPUT AN$
80 IF AN$ <> "Y" THEN END
90 GOTO 20
100 PRINT "LESS THAN 100" : RETURN
200 PRINT "MORE THAN 100 BUT LESS
     THAN 200 " : RETURN
300 PRINT "MORE THAN 200" : RETURN
```

RUN the program and enter any number you want. Since the program is branching on the variable B, and not on A (the INPUT variable), you will not get an error since the greatest value of B can only be 3.

Now let's get back to relationals and see how they can be used with computed GOSUB. Remember, in using relationals, the only numbers we get are Ø's and 1's for false and true respectively. However, we can use these Ø's and 1's just like regular numbers. Try the following:

```
10 PRINT "{ESC-SHIFT-CLEAR}"
20 X = 1 : Y = 2 : Z = 3
30 A = X < Z
40 B = Y > Z
50 C = Z > X
60 PRINT "A + A =" ; A + A
70 PRINT : PRINT "A + B =" ; A + B
80 PRINT : PRINT "A + B + C =" ; A + B + C
90 END
```

Now before you RUN the program, see if you can determine what will be printed by lines 6Ø, 7Ø and 8Ø. Once you have made a determination, RUN the program and see what happens. Go ahead and do it. How'd you do? Let's go over it step by step.

1. Since X is less than Z, A will be "true" with a value of one (1). Therefore A + A (1 + 1) will equal 2.

2. Since Y is not less than Z, (Y = 2 and Z = 3, remember) B will be "false" with a value of Ø. Therefore, A + B (1 + Ø) will total 1.

3. Since Z is greater than X, C will be "true" with a value of 1. Therefore A + B + C (1 + Ø + 1) will equal 2.

If you got it right, congratulations! If not, go over it again. Remember, very simple things are happening, so don't look for a complicated explanation!

Now that we see how we can get numbers by manipulating relationals, let's use them in computed GOSUBs. The following program shows how:

```
10 DIM AN$(1)
20 PRINT "{ESC-SHIFT-CLEAR}" : PRINT "HOW BIG
   WAS THE HOME CROWD?"; : INPUT HC
30 R = 1 + (HC >= 500) + (HC >= 1000)
40 ON R GOSUB 100,200,300
50 PRINT : PRINT "DO YOU WISH TO CONTINUE?
   (Y/N) "; : INPUT AN$
60 IF AN$ <> "Y" THEN END
70 GOTO 20
100 PRINT "{ESC-SHIFT-CLEAR}" : PRINT "THE
   HOME CROWD WAS NOT VERY BIG - LESS
   THAN 500" : RETURN
200 PRINT "{ESC-SHIFT-CLEAR}" : PRINT "THE
   HOME CROWD WAS A PRETTY GOOD
   SIZE - BETWEEN 500 AND 1000." : RETURN
300 PRINT "{ESC-SHIFT-CLEAR}" : PRINT "THE
   HOME CROWD WAS VERY BIG - 1000 OR
   OVER! " : RETURN
```

This program is hinged on line 30's formula or algorithm. Let's see how it works:

1. There are 3 conditions:
   a. HC is less than 500
   b. HC is 500 or more but less than 1000
   c. HC is 1000 or greater.

2. If the first condition exists both HC >= 500 and HC >= 1000 would be false. Thus 1 + 0 + 0 = 1. Therefore R = 1.

3. If HC is >= 500 but less than 1000 then HC >= 500 would be true but HC >= 1000 would be false. Thus we would have 1 + 1 + 0 = 2.

4. Finally if HC is both >= 500 and >=1000 then our formula would result in 1 + 1 + 1 = 3.

REST AREA

At this point let's take a little rest and reflect. In programming, there is no such thing as THE RIGHT WAY and THE WRONG WAY. Certain programs are more efficient, faster or take less code and memory than others, but the computer makes no moral judgments. If a program does what you want it to do, no matter how slowly it does it or how long it took you to write it, it is "right." In the above example we used an algorithm with relationals to do something we could have done with more code. Don't expect to use such formulas right off the bat unless you have a strong background in math. If you're not used to using algorithms, don't expect to understand their full potential right away. The one we used is relatively simple, and you will find far more elaborate ones as you begin looking at more programs. The main point is to keep plugging ahead. With practice, you will learn all kinds of little shortcuts and formulas, but if you get stuck along the way, just keep on going. Remember, as long as you can get your program running the way you want it to, you're doing the "right" thing.

Strings and Relationals

Before we leave our discussion of computed GOTOs and GOSUBs with relationals, let's take a look at how relationals handle strings. Try the following:

```
DIM A$(1), B$(1) : A$ = "A" : B$ = "B" :
PRINT B$ > A$
(Return)
(Result=) 1
```

Surprised? In addition to comparing numeric variables, relationals can compare alphabetic string variables with "A" being the lowest and "Z" the highest. (Actually, any string variables can be compared, but we will just look at the alphabetic ones here.) So, if we ask if B$ is greater than A$, we get a "1" (true) since B$ was a B and A$ was an A. Now you might be wondering what on earth you could possibly want to do with this knowledge. Well, in sorting strings (like putting names in alphabetical order) such an operation is crucial. Let's make a simple string sorter for sorting two strings.

```
10 DIM A$(20), B$(20) : PRINT "{ESC-SHIFT-CLEAR}"
20 PRINT "WORD #1 --> " ; : INPUT A$
30 PRINT "WORD #2 --> " ; : INPUT B$
40 PRINT : PRINT : PRINT
50 IF A$ < B$ THEN PRINT A$ : PRINT B$
60 IF A$ > B$ THEN PRINT B$ : PRINT A$
```

Just what you needed! A program that will put two words in alphabetical order!

Arrays

The best way to envision arrays is as a kind of variable. As we have seen, we can name variables A, X1 and so forth. An array uses a single name with a number to differentiate different variables. Consider the following two lists, one using regular variables and the other using an array:

Variable	**Array**
A = 1	A(1) = 1
B = 2	A(2) = 2
C = 3	A(3) = 3
D = 4	A(4) = 4

Again, you may well ask, "So what? Why not just use regular numeric variables instead of arrays?" Well, for one thing, it can be a lot easier to keep track of what you're doing in a program using arrays, and for another, it can save a lot of time. Consider the following program for INPUTing a list of 10 employees' numbers from a list of names using an array.

```
10 PRINT "{ESC-SHIFT-CLEAR}" : DIM PAY (10)
20 FOR I = 1 TO 10
30 PRINT "EMPLOYEE #"; I ; : INPUT P
40 PAY(I) = P
50 NEXT I
```

```
10Ø PRINT "{ESC-SHIFT-CLEAR}" : FOR I = 1 TO 1Ø
11Ø PRINT "EMPLOYEE #"; I; " GETS $"; PAY(I)
12Ø NEXT I
```

Now write a program that does the same thing using non-array variables. It would take a lot more code to do so, but go ahead and try it. Use the variables PAY1 through PAY1Ø for the names just to see what it would take.

If you re-wrote the program, you saw how much time using arrays saved, but before going on let's take a closer look at how the program worked with the FOR/NEXT loop and array variable:

1. The FOR/NEXT loop generated the numbers sequentially so that the array would be the following:

   ```
   FOR I = 1 TO 1Ø
   PAY(1) <--First time through loop
   PAY(2) <--Second time through loop
   PAY(3) <--Third time through loop
   PAY(4) etc.
   PAY(5)
   PAY(6)
   PAY(7)
   PAY(8)
   PAY(9)
   PAY(1Ø)
   NEXT I
   ```

2. Each value INPUT by the user was stored in a sequentially numbered array variable.

3. Output, using the PRINT statement, was generated by the FOR/NEXT loop sequentially supplying numbers to be entered into array variables.

Now, to get used to the idea that an array variable is a variable, enter the following:

```
A(1Ø) = 432 : PRINT A(1Ø) <RETURN>
XYZ(9) = 2.432 : PRINT XYZ(9) <RETURN>
J(5) = 321 : PRINT J(5) <RETURN>
```

OK, maybe it didn't take all that to convince you that an array is a variable with a number in parentheses after it, but it's easy to forget and think of arrays as something more exotic than they are.

The DIMension of an ARRAY

As with strings, it is necessary to DIMension arrays. It is done in the same way as with strings. The following is an example of the format for DIMensioning an array.

```
10 PRINT "{ESC-SHIFT-CLEAR}"
20 DIM AB(150) : REM DIMENSION OF
   ARRAY VARIABLE 'AB'
30 FOR I = 1 TO 150
40 AB(I) = I
50 NEXT I
60 FOR I = 1 TO 150
70 PRINT AB(I),
80 NEXT I
```

RUN the program as it is written. It should work fine. Now delete line 20 by simply entering 20. (Remember how we learned to delete single line numbers by entering that number?) Now RUN the program, and you will get ERROR- 9 AT LINE 40. That's because there was no DIM statement in line 20. So, whenever you create arrays be sure to DIM them.

DO IT YOURSELF DIM

It is perfectly all right to DIM an array with a variable. That is, you can write your program so that you enter the DIMension as you go along. For instance, if the first line is something like,

```
10 PRINT "HOW BIG IS THE ARRAY?"; : INPUT N
```

The variable N can be used to DIM your array (e.g., DIM X (N)). The FOR/NEXT loops that generate the array elements can be topped with an N (e.g., FOR I = 1 TO N). This option gives you more flexibility in writing programs with arrays.

Multi-dimensional Arrays

So far, all we have examined are single dimension arrays. However, it is possible to have arrays with two or more dimensions. Let's begin with two-dimensional arrays, and examine how to use arrays with more than a single dimension.

The best way to think of a two-dimensional array is as a matrix. For example, if our array ranged from 1 to 3 on two dimensions the entire set would include: A(1,1) A(1,2) A(1,3) A(2,1) A(2,2) A(2,3) A(3,1) A(3,2) and A(3,3). By laying it out on a matrix, we can think of the first number of the subscript as a row and the second as a column. This makes it much clearer:

	Column #1	**Column #2**	**Column #3**
Row #1	A(1,1)	A(1,2)	A(1,3)
Row #2	A(2,1)	A(2,2)	A(2,3)
Row #3	A(3,1)	A(3,2)	A(3,3)

Again, it is important to remember that each element in the array is simply a type of variable. Now let's use a two-dimension array in a program.

```
10 DIM V(3,3) : REM 2 DIMENSIONAL ARRAY "V"
20 DIM STOCK$(20), MONTH$(10)
30 PRINT "{ESC-SHIFT-CLEAR}"
40 PRINT "{ATARI-KEY} COMPUTER STOCK
   {ATARI-KEY}" : PRINT
50 FOR I = 1 TO 3
60 READ STOCK$
70 FOR K = 1 TO 3
80 READ MONTH$
90 PRINT "VALUE OF "; STOCK$; " FOR"; MONTH$ :
   INPUT W
100 V(I,K) = W
110 NEXT K : NEXT I
120 RESTORE : REM RESET THE 'READ' POINTER
    BACK TO THE FIRST DATA STATEMENT
130 PRINT "{ESC-SHIFT-CLEAR}"
200 *** REM OUTPUT THE VALUES ***
210 PRINT "{ATARI-KEY} MONTHLY VALUES OF
    COMPUTER STOCK {ATARI-KEY}"
```

```
220 PRINT
230 FOR I = 1 TO 3
240 READ STOCK$
250 FOR K = 1 TO 3
260 READ MONTH$
270 PRINT STOCK$; " FOR"; MONTH$; "= $"; V(I,K)
280 NEXT K : NEXT I
290 END
1000 *** REM DATA STATEMENTS ***
1010 DATA Jumbo Computers, January, February,
     March
1020 DATA Super Computers, January, February,
     March
1030 DATA Marvel Computers, January, February,
     March
```

When you RUN this program, you will be asked to enter the values for the various stocks for the first quarter of the year (January, February, and March). Then, the program, using the two-dimensional array, will print out your list for you.

We put a new BASIC statement into this program, RESTORE. What this does is start reading the DATA statements from the beginning. In this way, we can "re-use" the same data statements we did the first time, instead of having to key in a whole new set of DATA statements for the output.

To make sure you understand how everything works, let's go over the program step by step:

STEP 1: We DIMensioned our array with 3 and 3. This gives us a total of 9 values we can enter. Then we DIMensioned our strings, STOCK$ and MONTH$ so that they will be long enough to READ their values from the DATA statements beginning in line 1010.

STEP 2: We set up a "nested loop" with I and K both with a top value of 3. The first time through the I loop, STOCK$ was "Jumbo Computers" and then the K loop generated MONTH$ values of "January, February , March" on the three times through the K loop. Thus, the first time through both loops with K and I equal to "1", our array was V(1,1). The second time through the K loop, the array element was V(1,2). That is V(I,K), equaled 1 for I and 2 for K. In this way we generated values for array elements V(1,1) through V(3,3).

STEP 3: After all of the values for the array were entered with INPUT statements and transferred to the array, V(I,K) = W, the screen was cleared and the READ pointer was reset to the beginning with RESTORE.

STEP 4: The I and K loops were set up again beginning at line 23Ø and we re-read the DATA statements into our strings. This time, instead of entering data, we output the information stored in our array, generated by the I and K loops.

It is also possible to have several more dimensions in an array variable. As you add more and more dimensions, you have to be careful not to confuse the different aspects of a single array. Sometimes, when a multi-dimensional array becomes difficult to manage (or use), it is better to break it down into several one- or two-dimensional arrays.

SUMMARY

We covered a good deal in this chapter, and if you understood everything, excellent! If you did not, don't worry, for with practice, it will all become very clear. Whatever your understanding of the material, though, experiment with all the statements. Be BOLD and daring with your computer's commands, and as long as you have a disk or cassette on which you can practice your skills, the worst that can happen is that you will erase a few programs!

We learned that your ATARI computer can compute! Using the IF/THEN commands and relationals we can give the computer the power of "decision making." Using subroutines it is possible to branch at decision points to anywhere we want in our program. Computed GOTOs and GOSUBs allow the execution to move appropriately with a minimal amount of programming.

Finally, we examined array variables. Arrays allow us to enter values into sequentially arranged variables (or elements). Using FOR/NEXT loops it is possible to quickly program multiple variables up to the limits of our DIMensions. Not only do arrays assist us in keeping variables orderly, they save a good deal of work as well.

In the next chapter, we will begin working with commands which help arrange everything for us. As our programs become more and more sophisticated, we will need to keep better track of what we're doing. By organizing our programs into small, manageable chunks, we can create clear, useful programs.

CHAPTER 5

Organizing the Parts

Introduction

Unless we organize as we accumulate more and more information, work, or just about anything else, things get confusing. Good organization allows us to do more and to handle more complex and larger problems. These principles hold with programming as well. As we learn more commands, we can do more things, but the more we do, the more likely we are to get tangled up and lost.

One of the areas which is likely to be the first to suffer from overflow is that of formatting output. Variables get mixed up, arrays are misnumbered and the screen is a mess. In order to handle this kind of problem, we will deal extensively with text and string formatting. Not only will we be able to put things where we want them, but we will do it with style!

The second major area of disorganization is I/O (INPUT/OUTPUT). Some of the problem has to do with formatting, but even more elementary is the problem of organizing the input and output so that data is properly analyzed. Data has to be connected to the proper variables and be subject to the correct computations. Thus, in addition to examining string formatting, we will also look at organizing data manipulation.

Formatting Text

In Chapter 1 we said that the ATARI keyboard works in many ways like a typewriter. One feature of a typewriter is its ability to set tabs so that the user can automatically place text a given number of spaces from the left margin. With your ATARI, you can TAB in much the same way.

We have been using the ESC-SHIFT-CLEAR sequence to clear our screen. In the same way, we use our TAB key. Enter the following:

```
PRINT "{ESC-TAB} HERE" <RETURN>
     HERE
```

When you entered ESC-TAB within the quote marks, you got a little left-facing arrow. Your computer read that to mean, "Go to the first tab stop and output the next character at that point." Now let's add another tab stop :

```
PRINT "{ESC-TAB} {ESC-TAB} HERE" <RETURN>
     HERE
```

This time you got two arrows, and your message, HERE was printed at the second tab stop, 14 spaces from the left side. Depending on where we want our output to be placed on the screen, we can enter our tabs in different places. In addition, we can change our tabs for special output. Suppose we have six columns of numbers and we want our output to line up the six columns evenly. First, we will clear our tabs by pressing the TAB key, and at each tab stop entering {CTRL-TAB}. Second, we will set our new tabs at five spaces apart. To do this, we start on the left hand side and press the SPACE bar five times, enter {SHIFT-TAB} and press the SPACE bar five more times until we have set six tabs. To make sure we have our tabs set the way we want, we simply press the TAB key to see if the cursor stops where we intended. Now enter the following program:

```
10 PRINT {ESC-SHIFT-CLEAR}
20 FOR I = 1 TO 6
30 PRINT "{ESC-TAB} #"; I ;
40 NEXT I
50 PRINT ""
60 FOR J = 1 TO 6 : PRINT "{ESC-TAB} " ; : NEXT J
```

When you RUN the program, you will see all of your columns lined up and underlined. (To get the underline character, press SHIFT "–".) You should also note that in line 5Ø, we put in a PRINT "". This was so that the next TAB would not be the left hand side of the screen. (The far left tab is a TAB you *cannot* clear!)

Now let's have some fun with our commands. Here's a little program which will give you an idea of how to place text within your program.

```
10 DIM MS$(30), A$(1)
20 PRINT "{ESC-SHIFT-CLEAR}" : FOR I = 1
   TO 4 : PRINT : NEXT I : PRINT "ENTER
   MESSAGE--> "; : INPUT MS$
30 PRINT : PRINT "HORIZONTAL PLACEMENT
   (1-37) -> "; : INPUT H
40 PRINT : PRINT "VERTICAL PLACEMENT
   (1-24) -> "; : INPUT V
50 PRINT "{ESC-SHIFT-CLEAR}"
60 FOR VER = 1 TO V : PRINT : NEXT VER :
   FOR HOR = 1 TO H : PRINT " "; : NEXT HOR :
   PRINT MS$
70 PRINT : PRINT "HIT RETURN TO CONTINUE
   OR 'Q' TO QUIT ";
80 INPUT A$
90 IF A$ < > "Q" THEN 20
100 END
```

As you can see, spaces and PRINT statements can be used to format the output of text horizontally and vertically. The variables (H and V in our example) serve to give us different screen locations. Using the above program, what do you think would happen if you entered "THIS IS A LONG STRING", a HORIZONTAL placement of 35 and a VERTICAL placement of 24? Since the maximum horizontal position is 38 and the maximum vertical placement is 25, the string (MS$) will go over the boundaries. Go ahead and try it to see what happens. In fact, it would be a good idea to test the limits of TAB and vertical placement with this program to get a clear understanding of their parameters.

Position It!

Now that we have examined how to move the cursor around with tabs and loops, let's do some easy formatting! (Why didn't we do it the easy way, first?) The POSITION command allows you to enter text or graphic characters on an X,Y axis with X being the horizontal position and Y the vertical. The format for the POSITION statements is:

```
POSITION X,Y : PRINT "HERE"
```

Try the following little program to see how easy it is to use compared to our previous efforts:

```
10 PRINT "{ESC-SHIFT-CLEAR}" : DIM AN$(1)
20 PRINT "HORIZONTAL (0-39)" ; : INPUT H
30 PRINT "VERTICAL (0-23)" ; : INPUT V
40 POSITION H,V : PRINT "X"; : FOR PAUSE = 1
   TO 100 : NEXT PAUSE
50 POSITION 10, 22 : PRINT "HIT RETURN TO
   CONTINUE"; : INPUT AN$
60 PRINT "{ESC-SHIFT-CLEAR}" : GOTO 20
```

See how easy that is! Now let's see if you can write a program which will stick your name right in the middle of the string. I'm not going to tell you how to do it, but if you can figure it out, then you can position just about anything you want. *HINT:* Use a string variable for your name and the LEN function.

Paddle and Joystick Formatting

NOTE: If you do not have paddles and/or joysticks, skip this section.

Paddle formatting of text or graphics can add a lot to your computer's usefulness. To get started, plug your paddles into "slot 1" on the front or side of your computer. (ATARI 4ØØ/8ØØ's have four paddle/joystick jacks on the lower front of the computer, and ATARI 12ØØXL's have only two, located on the left side - labelled "CONTROLLERS" on all machines.) One of the paddles will be PADDLE(Ø) and the other will be PADDLE(1). To find out which is which, enter the following little program:

```
10 PRINT "{ESC-SHIFT-CLEAR}"
20 P0 = PADDLE(0)
30 POSITION 10,10 : PRINT P0; " ";
40 GOTO 20
```

When you run this program, you will see some numbers in the middle of the screen. Turn the knobs on your paddles. One of the paddles will cause the numbers to change. That paddle is PADDLE(Ø). Label that paddle PØ and the other one P1. The values generated from the paddles can be used in programs just like variables. In fact, in this little test program, we used the variable PØ to be the value of PADDLE(Ø). You can format output with your paddles if you want. For example, you might make PADDLE(Ø) = H and PADDLE(1) = V, and then using POSITION H,V place text on the screen with your paddles. However, the values of the paddles range from 1 to 228, and you would have to be careful not to have your text positioned in a location beyond 39 horizontally or 23 vertically! Just for fun, try the following little PADDLE ADD program to see that paddle values are treated the same as any others.

```
10 PRINT "{ESC-SHIFT-CLEAR}"
20 P0 = PADDLE(0) : P1 = PADDLE(1)
30 POSITION 10,10 : PRINT P0;"  ";
40 POSITION 10,11 : PRINT P1;"  ";
50 POSITION 9,12 : PRINT "+___ ";
60 POSITION 10,13 : PRINT P0 + P1
70 GOTO 20
```

Interesting, huh? Now I think you could format that a little better, don't you? Let's see if you can line up the numbers a little better than that. Again, you're on your own! *HINT: Use* IF/THEN *and* "<".

FIRE! Another programmable feature of your paddles is the "fire button." When the button is pressed it's value is "Ø", and when it is not being pressed, it is "1". PADDLE(Ø) fire button is PTRIG(Ø) and PADDLE(1)'s is PTRIG(1). (I bet the PTRIG stands for PADDLE TRIGGER.) All we have to do to use the fire buttons is to make something happen when their value changes. The following program shows how this is done.

```
10 PRINT "{ESC-SHIFT-CLEAR}"
20 FIREØ = PTRIG(Ø) : FIRE1 = PTRIG(1)
30 IF FIREØ = Ø THEN GOSUB 1ØØ
40 IF FIRE1 = Ø THEN GOSUB 2ØØ
50 GOTO 2Ø
100 REM *** A LITTLE ANIMATION ***
110 PRINT "{ESC-SHIFT-CLEAR}"
120 FOR I = Ø TO 37
130 POSITION I,1Ø : PRINT "->"
140 FOR P = 1 TO 3 : NEXT P
150 POSITION I,1Ø : PRINT " "
160 NEXT I
170 POSITION 38,1Ø : PRINT "->"
180 POSITION 34,11 : PRINT "THUNK!"
190 RETURN
200 REM *** A LITTLE MORE ANIMATION ***
210 PRINT "{ESC-SHIFT-CLEAR}"
220 FOR I = 37 TO Ø STEP -1
230 POSITION I,1Ø : PRINT "<-"
240 FOR P = 1 TO 3 : NEXT P
250 POSITION I,1Ø : PRINT " "
260 NEXT I
270 POSITION Ø,1Ø : PRINT "<-"
280 POSITION Ø,11 : PRINT "BONK!"
290 RETURN
```

Later, when we get to graphics, we will play some more with animation, the paddles and graphics, but now let's look at the joysticks. They work on the same principle as paddles except they have only nine values based on the position of the paddle. The following diagram shows the joystick's value relative to its stick's position:

JOYSTICK POSITION VALUES

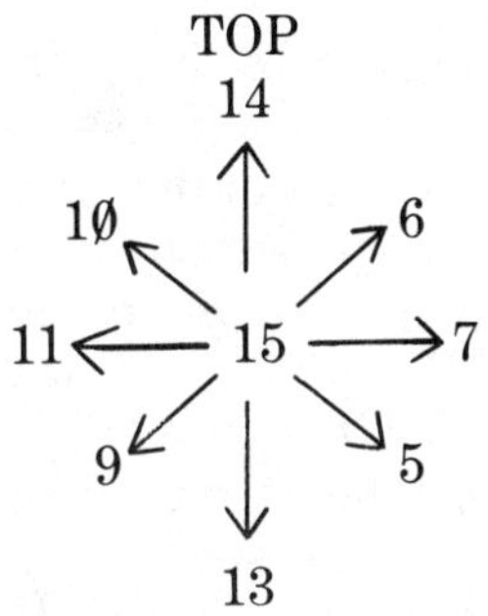

Those values give us a lot less to work with. The following program will help you see the values as you move the stick:

```
10 PRINT "{ESC-SHIFT-CLEAR}"
20 JOYØ = STICK(Ø)
30 POSITION 2Ø, 1Ø : PRINT JOYØ; " ";
40 GOTO 2Ø
```

The fire button is STRIG(Ø) or STRIG(1) with a default value of "1" and a pressed value of "Ø". Let's use it to shoot some horizontal lines across the screen and at the same time redefine the stick values:

```
1Ø PRINT "{ESC-SHIFT-CLEAR}"
2Ø VPOS = STICK(Ø) : FIREØ = STRIG(Ø)
3Ø IF VPOS = 14 THEN V = 5
4Ø IF VPOS = 15 THEN V = 1Ø
5Ø IF VPOS = 13 THEN V = 15
6Ø IF FIREØ=Ø THEN PRINT "(ESC-SHIFT-CLEAR)" :
   FOR I= Ø TO 39:POSITION I,V: PRINT "–" : NEXT I
7Ø GOTO 2Ø
```

By moving the stick up and down and pressing the fire button, it is possible to put a line of dashes across the screen in different vertical positions. Soon you'll be able to use the sticks to blast aliens back to Mars! For practice, see if you can shoot vertical lines from different horizontal positions. When you've done that, see if you can shoot both vertical and horizontal lines!

Unraveling Strings

Our discussion of strings up to this point has involved whole strings. That is, whatever we define a string to be, no matter how long or short, can be considered a whole string. For example, if we define R$ as WALK, then we can consider WALK to be the whole of R$. Likewise, if we defined R$ as A VERY LONG AND WORDY MESSAGE then, A VERY LONG AND WORDY MESSAGE would be the whole string of R$. There will be occasions, however, when we want to use only part of a string or tie several strings together. (When we get into data base programs, we will find this to be very important.) Also, there are applications where we will need to know the length of strings, find the numeric values of strings, and even change strings into numeric variables and back again.

TRUST ME!

I hate to admit it, but when I first learned about all of the commands we are about to discuss, I thought, "Boy, what a waste of time!" It was enough to get the simple material straight, but why in the world would anyone want to chop up strings and put them back together again? If you want only a certain segment of a string, why not simply define it in terms of that segment? And if you want a longer string, then just define it to be longer! Those were my thoughts on the matter of string formatting. However, I have now come to the point where I find it very difficult to even conceive of programming without these powerful commands. So, trust me! String formatting commands are terrific little devices to have, and if you do not see their applicability right away, you will as you begin writing more programs.

String Formatting

We will divide our discussion of string formatting into four parts: 1) Calculating the length of a string; 2) Locating parts of strings; 3) Changing strings to numeric variables and back again; and 4) Tying strings together (concatenation).

Calculating the LENgth of Strings

Sometimes it is necessary to calculate the length of a string for formatting output. Happily, your ATARI is very good at telling you the length of a particular string. By the command, PRINT LEN (A$) you will be given the number of characters, including spaces, your string has. Try the following little program to see how this works:

```
10 DIM A$(38) : DIM AN$(1) : PRINT
   "{ESC-SHIFT-CLEAR}"
20 PRINT "NAME OF STRING-> "; : INPUT A$
30 PRINT A$; " HAS "; LEN(A$); " CHARACTERS"
40 PRINT : PRINT " MORE (Y/N) ";
50 INPUT AN$
60 IF AN$ = "Y" THEN 20
```

Now to see a more practical application, we will look at a modified version of the centering routine we used in the last chapter.

```
10 DIM S$ (38), A$(1)
20 PRINT "{ESC-SHIFT-CLEAR}" : PRINT "ENTER
   A STRING LESS THAN 39 CHARS" : INPUT S$
30 PRINT "{ESC-SHIFT-CLEAR}"
40 L = 19 - LEN(S$)/2 : FOR C = 1 TO L-1 : PRINT
   "(SPACE)"; : NEXT C : PRINT S$
50 FOR I = 1 TO 20: PRINT : NEXT I : PRINT "HIT
   RETURN TO CONTINUE OR 'Q' TO QUIT ";
60 INPUT A$
70 IF A$ < > "Q" THEN 20
80 END
```

Now that we can see how to compute the LENgth of a string and then use that LENgth to compute our tabbing, let's see how we can control the input with the LEN command. Suppose you want to write a program which will print out mailing labels, but your labels will hold only 3Ø characters. You want to make sure all of your entries are 3Ø or fewer characters long, including spaces. To do this we will write a program which checks the LENgth of a string before it is accepted.

```
10 DIM NA$(40), AN$(1)
20 PRINT "{ESC-SHIFT-CLEAR}"
30 PRINT "ENTER A NAME LESS THAN 30 " : PRINT
   "CHARACTERS INCLUDING SPACES" :
   PRINT "-> "; : INPUT NA$
40 IF LEN (NA$) > 29 THEN GOTO 100 : REM TRAP
50 PRINT : PRINT NA$
60 PRINT : PRINT "ANOTHER NAME?(Y/N) ";
70 INPUT AN$
80 IF AN$ < > "Y" THEN END
90 GOTO 20
100 PRINT "{ESC-SHIFT-CLEAR}" : PRINT "PLEASE
   USE 30 CHARACTERS OR LESS "
110 PRINT : GOTO 20
```

Now break the rule!!! Go ahead and enter a string of more than 3Ø characters to see what happens. (If your computer gets snotty with you, you can always re-program it. It helps to remind it of that fact periodically.) If the program was entered properly, it is impossible to enter a string of more than 3Ø characters. *NOTE: We intentionally* DIM*ed* NA$ *to be greater than 3Ø so that the* LEN *of* NA$ *could be greater. If you* DIM *a string to a given length, it will accept any size string but terminate it after the* DIM *size has been exceeded.*

From the above examples, you can begin to see how the LEN command can be useful in several ways. There are many other ways that such commands can be employed to reduce programming time, clarify output, and compute information. The key to understanding its usefulness is to experiment with it and see how other programmers use the same command.

Substrings

Suppose you want to use a single string variable to describe three different conditions, such as "POOR FAIR GOOD", but you want to use only part of that string to describe an outcome. Using substrings, it is possible to PRINT only that part of the string you want. For example, the following program lets you use a single string to describe three different conditions:

```
 1Ø DIM X$(14), F$(1), AN$(1)
 2Ø PRINT "{ESC-SHIFT-CLEAR}" : X$ ="POOR
    FAIR GOOD"
 3Ø PRINT "HOW DO YOU FEEL TODAY? (<P>OOR,
    <F>AIR OR <G>OOD)";
 4Ø INPUT F$ : IF F$ = "" THEN 4Ø
 5Ø IF F$ = "P" THEN PRINT X$(1,4)
 6Ø IF F$ = "F" THEN PRINT X$(6,4)
 7Ø IF F$ = "G" THEN PRINT X$(1Ø)
 8Ø PRINT : PRINT : PRINT "ANOTHER GO?(Y/N) ";
 9Ø INPUT AN$ : IF AN$ = "" THEN 9Ø
1ØØ IF AN$ = "Y" THEN 2Ø
```

Let's face it, it would have been easier to simply branch to a PRINT 'GOOD' 'FAIR' or 'POOR' and no less efficient. But, no matter, it was for purposes of illustration and not optimizing program organization.

Lines 5Ø through 7Ø have a similar format except that line 7Ø has only a single number after X$. Let's see what's going on. When you enter a string variable and two numbers in parentheses following it, the string is printed from the position of the first number to the position of the last number. The position "place" is determined by counting the string's characters from left to right beginning with "1." If there is only a single number in parentheses following the string variable, the characters from that position to the end of the string are printed. Since GOOD made up the last four characters of X$, beginning in position 1Ø, all we had to do to get it to PRINT "GOOD" was to enter X$(1Ø) instead of X$(1Ø,14). To give you some immediate experience with these commands, try the following:

```
DIM W$(11) :W$ = "WHAT A MESS" : PRINT W$(6)
<RETURN>
```
(Result = A MESS)

```
DIM G$(9) : G$ = "BURLESQUE" : PRINT G$(4,6)
<RETURN>
```
(Result = LES)

```
DIM X$(16) : X$ = "A PLACE IN SPACE" :
PRINT X$(5,7) : PRINT X$(14)<RETURN>
```
(Result = See if you can guess!)

Another trick with partial strings is to assign parts of one string to another string. For example,

```
10 DIM BIG$(30), LITTLE$(4), AWY$(5), LG$(4)
20 PRINT "{ESC-SHIFT-CLEAR}" :BIG$ =
   "LONG LONG AGO AND FAR FAR AWAY"
30 LITTLE$ = BIG$(11,13)
40 AWY$ = BIG$(27,30)
50 LG$ = BIG$(1,4)
60 PRINT : PRINT : PRINT AWY$;" ";LG$;" ";LITTLE$
70 REM BEFORE YOU RUN IT, SEE IF YOU CAN
   GUESS THE MESSAGE.
```

For an interesting effect, try the following little program:

```
 10 DIM NA$(30), AN$(1)
 20 PRINT "{ESC-SHIFT-CLEAR}"
 30 PRINT "YOUR NAME"; : INPUT NA$
 40 FOR I = LEN (NA$) TO 1 STEP -1 :
    PRINT NA$(I,I); : NEXT I
100 REM *** SLOWER WITH DELAY LOOP ***
110 PRINT : PRINT : PRINT "NOW IN SLOW
    MOTION" : PRINT
120 PRINT "{ATARI KEY} PRESS RETURN TO
    CONTINUE {ATARI KEY}"; : INPUT AN$
130 FOR I = LEN (NA$) TO 1 STEP -1 : PRINT
    NA$(I,I); : FOR J = 1 TO 100 : NEXT J : NEXT I
140 PRINT : PRINT "AGAIN (Y/N)" ; : INPUT AN$
150 IF AN$ = "Y" THEN 20
```

Now you have probably been wondering ever since you got your computer how to make it print your name backwards. Well, now you know! (If your name is BOB you probably didn't notice it was printed backwards - try ROBERT.) Actually, the above exercise did a couple of things besides goofing off. First, it is a demonstration of how loops and substrings can be used together for formatting output. Second, we showed how output could be slowed down for either an interesting effect or simply to give the user time to see what's happening.

Changing Strings to Numbers and Back Again

Now we're going to learn about changing strings to numbers and numbers to strings. If you're like me, when I first found out about these commands, I thought they were pretty useless. After all, if you want a string use a string variable, and if you want a number use a numeric variable. Simple enough, but again, once you understand their value, you'll wonder how you ever did without them. To get started, let's RUN the following program:

```
10 DIM NA$(11),X(5)
20 PRINT "{ESC-SHIFT-CLEAR}"
30 FOR I = 1 TO 5 : READ NA$
40 X(I) = VAL (NA$(LEN(NA$),LEN(NA$)))
50 NEXT I : RESTORE
60 FOR I = 1 TO 5 : READ NA$
70 PRINT "OVERTIME PAY FOR ";
    NA$(1,LEN(NA$)-1); "= $"; X(I) * (1.5 * 7) : NEXT I
80 DATA SMITH 7, JONES 8, MCKNAP 6,
   JOHNSON 2, KELLY 3
```

Using DATA that were originally in a string format, we were able to change a portion of that string array to a numeric array. By making such a conversion, we were able to use our mathematical operations on line 70 to figure out the overtime pay for someone receiving time and a half at seven dollars ($7) an hour. We now have a list of who got what and the total overtime paid!

It always helps to do a few immediate exercises with a new command to get the right feel, so try these:

```
DIM A$(3) :A$ = "123" : PRINT VAL(A$) + 11
<RETURN>
DIM Q$(4) :Q$ = "99.5" : PRINT VAL(Q$) * 7
<RETURN>
DIM SALE$(5) : SALE$ = "44.95" : PRINT "ON
SALE AT HALF PRICE ->$"; VAL(SALE$) / 2
<RETURN>
DIM DO$(7), DN$(6) : DO$ = "$103.88" :
DN$ = "$18.34" : PRINT
VAL (DO$(2)) + VAL (DN$(2)) <RETURN>
```

NOTE: Since you may want to SAVE *the above examples on tape or disk, all you have to do is to add a line number and* SAVE *them as little programs.*

From Numbers to Strings

All right, now let's go the other way. We saw why we might want to change strings to numbers, but we may also want to change numbers to strings. To make the conversion we use the STR$ command. For example, look at the following program:

```
10 DIM A$(20) : PRINT "{ESC-SHIFT-CLEAR}"
20 PRINT "ENTER A NUMBER WITH 5 DIGITS ":
   PRINT " AFTER THE DECIMAL POINT " ; : INPUT A
30 A$ = STR$(A)
40 PRINT : PRINT A$(1,4)
```

As you can see, you have truncated the number to four characters including the decimal point. Now, let's do some in the Immediate mode to get the idea firmly into your mind, and a little later we will do something very practical with these commands.

```
DIM A$(4) : A = 5.00 : A$ = STR$(A) : PRINT A$
<RETURN>
```

(Result = 5 – What happened?!)

```
DIM V$(4) : V = 2345 : V$ = STR$(V) : PRINT V$
<RETURN>
DIM BUCKS$(5) :BUCKS = 22.36 : BUCKS$ =
STR$(BUCKS) : PRINT BUCKS$ (1,2) <RETURN>
```

Remember these commands, and when you are dealing with decimal points you will often find them handy. However, even the string cannot preserve the Ø's directly from a numeric variable. Later we will see how to fix that.

Tying Strings Together: Concatenation

We have seen how we can take a portion of a string and PRINT it to the screen. Now, we will tie strings together. This is called CONCATENATION and is accomplished by using the "+" sign with strings. For example:

```
1Ø DIM NF$(2Ø), NL$(2Ø) : PRINT "{ESC-SHIFT-
   CLEAR}"
2Ø PRINT "YOUR FIRST NAME -> "; : INPUT NF$
3Ø PRINT "YOUR LAST NAME -> "; : INPUT NL$
4Ø NF$ (LEN (NF$)+1) = NL$
5Ø PRINT NF$
```

A little messy, huh? However, you can see how to tie NF$ and NL$ together into a single larger string. Now, change line 4Ø to read

```
4Ø PRINT NF$; " " ; NL$
```

and delete line 5Ø. This time when you RUN the program, your name will turn out fine. This change did *not* concatenate string variables, but instead PRINTed the strings along with a "space" between the first and last names. Thus, even though we can concatenate strings, it is not always a good idea to do so. However, there are definite purposes for concatenation. Let's take a look at a very important one.

One of the problems with the way BASIC formats numbers is that it drops Ø's off the end. For example, try the following:

```
PRINT 19.8Ø
PRINT 5.ØØ
```

In dealing with dollars and cents, this can be a real pain in the neck, and it doesn't look very good. So, using concatenation and our VAL and STR$ commands, let's see if we can fix that.

```
1Ø DIM T$(1Ø), Z1$(1), Z2$(3), R$(1), NT$(15)
2Ø PRINT "{ESC-SHIFT-CLEAR}" : PRINT "BE SURE
   TO INCLUDE ALL CENTS!" : PRINT : PRINT
3Ø PRINT "HOW MUCH SPENT "; : INPUT S
4Ø T = T + S
5Ø T$ = STR$(T)
6Ø NT$ = "ØØØ" : NT$(LEN(NT$)+1)= T$ :
   REM CONCATENATE 3 "Ø's" ONTO T$
7Ø Z1$ ="Ø" : Z2$ = ".ØØ"
8Ø IF NT$ (LEN (NT$) – 1, LEN (NT$)–1) = "." THEN
   NT$(LEN (NT$) + 1) = Z1$ : GOTO 1ØØ
9Ø IF NT$ (LEN (NT$) –2, LEN (NT$) –2) < > "."
   THEN NT$ (LEN (NT$) +1) = Z2$
1ØØ PRINT : PRINT : PRINT "YOU NOW HAVE
```

```
        SPENT $"; NT$
110 PRINT "PRESS RETURN TO CONTINUE OR
        'Q' TO QUIT";
120 INPUT R$
130 IF R$ = "Q" THEN END
140 GOTO 20
```

This may look pretty complicated, but let's break it down to see what has been done.

1. We entered numeric variables in line 3Ø and computed their sum in line 4Ø.

2. The sum represented by T was then converted to a string variable T$ in line 5Ø.

3. In line 6Ø we padded T$ with three Ø's to give it a minimum length we will need in lines 8Ø and 9Ø.

4. Line 8Ø computes the second from the last character in NT$. If that character is a decimal point (.), then we know it must be a figure that dropped off the last cent column. (e.g., 5.4, 19.5, etc.) So we tack on a "Ø" by concatenating NT$ with Z1$ and jump to line 1ØØ.

5. Line 9Ø computes the third from the last character, and if it is not a decimal point (.) then we know it must have dropped all the cents completely — an even dollar number. So we tack on the decimal point and two Ø's (.ØØ), Z2$.

6. Finally, in line 1ØØ we print out our results but first drop the padding we added in line 6Ø using NT$(4), the substring beginning with the fourth character in the string.

All of this may seem a bit complicated just to get our Ø's back, but actually, the entire process was done in 6 lines (5Ø through 1ØØ). SAVE or CSAVE the program, and when you need those Ø's in your output, just include those lines! (Be careful, though, this will not work with subtraction when you get below $1!)

Setting Up Data Entry

Now that we have a firm grip on numerous commands, it is time we begin thinking seriously about organizing our programs. The first thing we must do is arrange our data entry in a manner that we ourselves and others can understand. This involves blocking elements of our program and deciding what variables and arrays we will be using. Also, when we enter data, we want to make sure that we are entering the correct type of data; so we have to set "traps" so that any input that is over a certain length or amount can be checked against our parameters. Let's look at a way to make our strings a certain length (no shorter or longer a length than we want). We've already discussed how to keep strings to a maximum length, so let's see how to keep them to a minimum as well. This latter process is referred to as "padding."

```
1Ø DIM CM$(2Ø), R$(1), PAD$(1Ø) : PAD$ =
   "XXXXXXXXXX" : N = 1Ø
2Ø PRINT "{ESC-SHIFT-CLEAR}" : FOR I = 1 TO 8 :
   PRINT : NEXT I : PRINT "YOUR COMPANY-->"; :
   INPUT CM$
3Ø IF LEN(CM$) <= 1Ø THEN 7Ø
4Ø IF LEN(CM$) > 1Ø THEN PRINT "1Ø OR FEWER
   CHARACTERS PLEASE" : REM TRAP FOR TOO
   LONG A NAME
5Ø PRINT : PRINT "{ATARI KEY} HIT RETURN TO
   CONTINUE {ATARI KEY}"; : INPUT R$
6Ø GOTO 2Ø
7Ø IF LEN(CM$) < 1Ø THEN CM$ (LEN(CM$+1 ))=
   PAD$(N) : N = N - 1 : GOTO 7Ø
8Ø PRINT "{ESC-SHIFT-CLEAR}" : FOR I = 1 TO 8 :
   PRINT : NEXT I : PRINT "THE COMPUTER HAS
   DECIDED THAT "
9Ø PRINT CM$; " SHOULD GIVE YOU A RAISE!"
```

Now if YOUR COMPANY <CM$> is less than 1Ø characters, you will see some X's stuck on the end. These were put there to show you how padding works. Now change the X's to spaces in the definition of PAD$ in line 1Ø and see what happens. (i.e., PAD$ = "   ".) Go ahead. The second time you ran the program, if your company's name was less than 1Ø characters, there were a lot of blank spaces after the company name. To remove the spaces, we would enter:

```
75 IF CM$(LEN(CM$), LEN(CM$)) = " " THEN
   CM$ = CM$(1, LEN(CM$)-1) : GOTO 75
```

It may not make much sense to add spaces and then remove them, but with certain applications, you will want to tie several strings together and then divide them up based on a certain length for various parts of the string. After dividing the big string into smaller ones, you will want to get rid of the padding. This is especially true when you begin writing data base programs. For the time being, though, just note how padding works.

Setting Up Data Manipulation

Once you have organized your input, the next major step is performing computations with your data. There are essentially two kinds of data manipulation you will deal with:

1. NUMERIC - Manipulating numeric data with mathematical operations.

2. STRING - Manipulating strings with concatenation and substring commands.

Most of the string manipulations are for setting up input or output, so we will concentrate on manipulating numeric data. We will use a simple example that keeps track of three manipulations: (1) additions; (2) subtractions; and (3) running balance. This will be our checkbook program we started earlier.

```
10 DIM CB$(22), AN$(1) :
   PRINT "{ESC-SHIFT-CLEAR}"
20 REM ### BEGIN INPUT & HEADER BLOCK ###
30 CB$ = "{ATARI-KEY} =COMPUTER
   CHECKBOOK={ATARI-KEY}": L=19-LEN(CB$)/2:
   FOR C = 1 TO L-1 : PRINT " ";: NEXT C : PRINT
   CB$ : REM =HEADER=
40 FOR I = 1 TO 4 : PRINT : NEXT I : PRINT "ENTER
   YOUR CURRENT BALANCE-> $"; : INPUT BA
50 PRINT : PRINT "1. ENTER DEPOSITS": PRINT :
   PRINT "2. DEDUCT CHECKS"
```

```
55 PRINT : PRINT "3. EXIT"
60 FOR I = 1 TO 7 : PRINT : NEXT : PRINT
   "{ATARI KEY} CHOOSE BY NUMBER {ATARI-KEY}"; :
   INPUT A
70 ON A GOTO 100,200,400
80 GOTO 60: REM TRAP
90 REM END OF INPUT BLOCK
100 REM ### DATA MANIPULATION
    ROUTINE NO. 1 ###
110 PRINT"{ESC-SHIFT-CLEAR}" : FOR I = 1
    TO 6 : PRINT : NEXT I : PRINT "ENTER AMOUNT
    OF DEPOSIT $"; : INPUT DP
120 BA = BA + DP: REM RUNNING BALANCE
130 PRINT : PRINT : PRINT "YOU NOW HAVE $";
    BA ;" IN YOUR ACCOUNT"
140 PRINT : PRINT "{ATARI-KEY}MORE DEPOSITS?
    (Y/N) {ATARI-KEY}"; : INPUT AN$
150 IF AN$ = "Y" THEN 110
160 PRINT : PRINT "WOULD YOU LIKE TO
    DEDUCT CHECKS? (Y/N) ";: INPUT AN$
170 IF AN$ = "N" THEN 400
180 IF AN$ = "Y" THEN 200
190 PRINT"{ESC-SHIFT-CLEAR}" : GOTO 160 :
    REM TRAP & END OF DATA MANIPULATION
    ROUTINE NO.1
200 REM ### DATA MANIPULATION
    ROUTINE NO. 2 ###
210 PRINT"{ESC-SHIFT-CLEAR}" : FOR I = 1
    TO 6 : PRINT : NEXT I : PRINT "ENTER
    AMOUNT OF CHECK $"; : INPUT CK
220 BA = BA - CK: REM RUNNING BALANCE
230 PRINT : PRINT "YOU NOW HAVE $";BA;" IN
    YOUR ACCOUNT"
240 PRINT : PRINT "MORE CHECKS (Y/N) - 'Q'
    TO QUIT ";: INPUT AN$
250 IF AN$ = "Y" THEN 210
260 IF AN$ = "Q" THEN 400
270 PRINT : PRINT "ANY DEPOSITS (Y/N) ";:
    INPUT AN$
280 IF AN$ = "Y" THEN 100
290 GOTO 240: REM TRAP & END OF DATA
    MANIPULATION BLOCK NO. 2
400 REM ### TERMINATION BLOCK ###
```

```
410 PRINT"{ESC-SHIFT-CLEAR}" : FOR I = 1
    TO 380: PRINT "$";: NEXT I
420 PRINT "YOU NOW HAVE A BALANCE OF $"; BA
```

This program is designed to provide a simple illustration of how to block data manipulation. However, there are some problems with it in the output. We are not getting the Ø's on the end of our balance! This is an output problem we will discuss in the following section, but before we continue, make sure you understand how we blocked the data manipulation. We used only three variables:

BA = BALANCE
CK = CHECK
DP = DEPOSIT

When we subtracted a check, we simply subtracted CK from BA, and when we entered a deposit, we added DP to BA. In this way we were able to keep a running balance and at the very end BA was the total of all deposits and checks. By keeping it simple and in blocks we were able to jump around and still keep everything straight.

Organizing Output

Let's go back to our program and repair it so that our balance will have the Ø's where they belong. This is essentially a problem of output, because all of the computations have been done, and they correctly tell us our balance, but it doesn't look right with the missing Ø's. However, we don't want to have to enter the lines for converting our balance into a string variable every time the running balance is printed. Therefore, we will put the subroutine for our conversion in a block. Looking at our COMPUTER CHECKBOOK program, it just so happens that there is a block available in the 3ØØ's - our luck is with us! We'll use that block to format our output.

```
300 REM ### FORMAT OUTPUT ###
310 BA$ = STR$(BA)
320 NBA$ = "000" : NBA$(LEN(NBA$)+1) = BA$ :
    REM CONCATENATE THREE "0's" ONTO BA$
330 Z1$ ="0" : Z2$ = ".00"
```

```
340 IF NBA$ (LEN (NBA$) — 1, LEN (NBA$)-1) = "."
      THEN NBA$(LEN (NBA$) + 1) = Z1$
      : GOTO 360
350 IF NBA$ (LEN (NBA$) -2, LEN (NBA$) -2) <> "."
      THEN NBA$ (LEN (NBA$) +1) = Z2$
360 RETURN
370 REM END OF OUTPUT BLOCK
```

Now, all we have do is to change a few lines in our program so that when there is an output of our balance, it will jump to the subroutine between lines 300 and 350 and then RETURN to output BA$. The following lines in our COMPUTER CHECKBOOK program should be changed and/or added:

```
5 DIM BA$(20), NBA$(23), Z1$(1), Z2$(3)
125 GOSUB 300
130 PRINT : PRINT : PRINT "YOU NOW HAVE $";
      NBA$(4); "IN YOUR ACCOUNT"
225 GOSUB 300
230 PRINT : PRINT "YOU NOW HAVE $"; NBA$(4);
      " IN YOUR ACCOUNT"
415 GOSUB 300
420 PRINT "YOU NOW HAVE A BALANCE OF $";
NBA$(4)
```

Now if you put everything together properly, you should have a handy little program for working with your checkbook. Just to make sure you got everything, here's the complete program with all the subroutines and changes we made:

```
5 DIM BA$(20), NBA$(23), Z1$(1), Z2$(3)
10 DIM CB$(22), AN$(1) : PRINT
    "{ESC-SHIFT-CLEAR}"
20 REM ### BEGIN INPUT & HEADER BLOCK ###
30 CB$ = "{ATARI-KEY} =COMPUTER
    CHECKBOOK= {ATARI-KEY}":
    L = 19 - LEN (CB$) / 2: FOR C = 1 TO
    L-1 : PRINT " ";: NEXT C : PRINT
    CB$ : REM =HEADER=
40 FOR I = 1 TO 4 : PRINT : NEXT I : PRINT
    "ENTER YOUR CURRENT BALANCE-> $";
    : INPUT BA
50 PRINT : PRINT "1. ENTER DEPOSITS": PRINT :
```

```
   PRINT "2. DEDUCT CHECKS"
55 PRINT : PRINT "3. EXIT"
60 FOR I = 1 TO 7 : PRINT : NEXT : PRINT
   "{ATARI KEY} CHOOSE BY NUMBER {ATARI-KEY}"; :
   INPUT A
70 ON A GOTO 100,200,400
80 GOTO 60: REM TRAP
90 REM END OF INPUT BLOCK
100 REM ### DATA MANIPULATION ROUTINE
    NO. 1 ###
110 PRINT"{ESC-SHIFT-CLEAR}" : FOR I = 1 TO 6 :
    PRINT : NEXT I : PRINT "ENTER AMOUNT OF
    DEPOSIT $"; : INPUT DP
120 BA = BA + DP: REM RUNNING BALANCE
125 GOSUB 300
130 PRINT : PRINT : PRINT "YOU NOW HAVE $";
    NBA$(4) ;" IN YOUR ACCOUNT"
140 PRINT : PRINT "{ATARI-KEY}MORE DEPOSITS?
    (Y/N) {ATARI-KEY}"; : INPUT AN$
150 IF AN$ = "Y" THEN 110
160 PRINT : PRINT "WOULD YOU LIKE TO DEDUCT
    CHECKS? (Y/N) ";: INPUT AN$
170 IF AN$ = "N" THEN 400
180 IF AN$ = "Y" THEN 200
190 PRINT"{ESC-SHIFT-CLEAR}" : GOTO 160 :
    REM TRAP & END OF DATA MANIPULATION
    ROUTINE NO.1
200 REM ### DATA MANIPULATION ROUTINE
    NO. 2 ###
210 PRINT"{ESC-SHIFT-CLEAR}" : FOR I = 1 TO 6 :
    PRINT : NEXT I : PRINT "ENTER AMOUNT OF
    CHECK $"; : INPUT CK
220 BA = BA - CK: REM RUNNING BALANCE
225 GOSUB 300
230 PRINT : PRINT "YOU NOW HAVE $";
    NBA$(4) ;" IN YOUR ACCOUNT"
240 PRINT : PRINT "MORE CHECKS (Y/N) - 'Q'
    TO QUIT ";: INPUT AN$
250 IF AN$ = "Y" THEN 210
260 IF AN$ = "Q" THEN 400
270 PRINT : PRINT "ANY DEPOSITS (Y/N) ";:
    INPUT AN$
280 IF AN$ = "Y" THEN 100
```

```
290 GOTO 240: REM TRAP & END OF DATA
    MANIPULATION BLOCK NO. 2
300 REM ### FORMAT OUTPUT ###
310 BA$ = STR$(BA)
320 NBA$ = "000" : NBA$(LEN(NBA$)+1) = BA$ :
    REM CONCATENATE 3 "0's" ONTO BA$
330 Z1$ ="0" : Z2$ = ".00"
340 IF NBA$ (LEN (NBA$) - 1, LEN (NBA$)-1) = "."
    THEN NBA$(LEN (NBA$) + 1) = Z1$
    : GOTO 360
350 IF NBA$ (LEN (NBA$) -2, LEN (NBA$) -2) <> "."
    THEN NBA$ (LEN (NBA$) +1) = Z2$
360 RETURN
370 REM END OF OUTPUT BLOCK
400 REM ### TERMINATION BLOCK ###
410 PRINT"{ESC-SHIFT-CLEAR}" : FOR I = 1 TO 380:
    PRINT "$";: NEXT I
415 GOSUB 300
420 PRINT "YOU NOW HAVE A BALANCE OF $";
    NBA$(4)
```

Scroll Control!

One of the big problems in output occurs when you have long lists that will scroll right off the screen. For example, the output of the following program will kick the output right out the top of the screen:

```
10 PRINT "{ESC-SHIFT-CLEAR}"
20 FOR I = 1 TO 100 : PRINT I : NEXT I
```

Instead of numbers, suppose you have a list of names you have sorted or some other output you wanted to see before they zipped off the top of the screen. Depending on the desired output, screen format and so forth, there are several different ways to control the scroll. Consider the following:

```
10 DIM A$ (1) : PRINT "{ESC-SHIFT-CLEAR}"
20 FOR I = 1 TO 100
30 IF I = 20 THEN GOSUB 100
40 IF I = 40 THEN GOSUB 100
50 IF I = 60 THEN GOSUB 100
```

```
60 IF I = 80 THEN GOSUB 100
70 PRINT I : NEXT I
80 END
100 PRINT : PRINT : PRINT "{ATARI-KEY} HIT
    RETURN TO CONTINUE{ATARI-KEY}"; : INPUT A$
110 PRINT "{ESC-SHIFT-CLEAR}" : RETURN
```

REMEMBER!! You and not the computer are in CONTROL! You can have your output any way you want it. To use more of the screen, you can have output tabbed to another column. For example,

```
10 PRINT "{ESC-SHIFT-CLEAR}"
20 FOR I = 1 TO 20
30 PRINT I; "{ESC-TAB} {ESC-TAB}"; I + 20
40 NEXT I
```

(See if you can add a third column from 41 to 60.) When you RUN the above program, you may want your numbers in the first column to be right justified. To do that add the following four lines:

```
25 IF I < 10 THEN GOTO 100
50 END
100 PRINT " "; I; "{ESC-TAB} {ESC-TAB}"; I + 20
110 GOTO 40
```

Alternatively, you could do the same thing with only one line:

```
25 IF I < 10 THEN PRINT " "; I; "{ESC-TAB}{ESC-TAB}";
   I + 20 : NEXT I
```

The first method is a little clearer since we broke it down into several parts, but the second is more efficient, quicker and takes less work.

Well, you get the idea. Format your ouput in a manner that best uses the screen and suits your needs and get that scroll under control!

SUMMARY

The formatting of programs makes the difference between a useful and not-so-useful application of your computer. The more organized and clear your program is, the better the chances are for simple yet effective programming. Formatting is more than an exercise in making your input/output fancy or interesting. It is a matter of communication between your ATARI and you! After all, if you can't make heads or tails of what your computer has computed, the best calculations in the world are of absolutely no use.

In the same way it is important to have your computer tell you what you want, it is also important to write your programs so that you and others can understand what is happening. By using blocks, it is easier to organize and later understand exactly what each part of your program does. Obviously, it is possible to write programs sequentially so that each command and subroutine is in an ascending order of line numbers, but to do so means that you will have to repeat simple and/or complex operations that could be better handled as subroutines. Also, it will be considerably more difficult to locate bugs and make the appropriate changes. In other words, by using a structured approach to programming, you make it simpler, not more difficult.

Finally, you should begin to see why there are commands for substrings and the importance of the TAB key. These are handy tools for organizing the various parts in a manner that gives you complete control over your computer's output. What may at first seem like a petty, even silly command in ATARI BASIC, upon a useful application, can be appreciated as an excellent tool. Therefore, as we delve deeper into your computer, look at the variety of commands as mechanisms of more efficient and ultimately simpler control and not a complex "gobbleygook" of "computerese" for geniuses. After all, if you've come this far, you should realize that what you know now looked like the work of "computer whizzes" when you first began.

CHAPTER 6

Some Advanced Topics (But Not Too Difficult Once You Get To Know Them)

Introduction

The topics of this chapter are more code like and contain the kinds of commands that look frightening. At least that's how I interpreted them when I first saw them. Many of the functions can be done with commands we already know, but many cannot. Still others, as we will see, can be accomplished better using these new commands. Like so much else you have seen in this book, what at first may appear to be impossible is really quite simple once you get the idea. More importantly, by playing with the commands, you can quickly learn their use.

The first thing we will learn about is the ASCII code. ASCII (pronounced ASS-KEY) stands for the AMERICAN STANDARD CODE for INFORMATION INTERCHANGE. Essentially, this is a set of numbers which have been standardized to mean certain characters. The ASCII code on your ATARI is based on a slightly different ASCII, called ATASCII so that the several graphic characters and special keys on the ATARI can be accessed. In ATARI BASIC the CHR$ (character string) command ties into ATASCII and can be used to directly output ATASCII. As we will see, the CHR$ command is very useful for outputting special characters.

The next commands have to do with directly accessing locations in your computer's memory. The first, POKE, puts values into memory and the second, PEEK, looks into memory addresses and returns the values there. We will examine several different uses of these two commands. These commands are essential for producing certain types of graphics and sound.

The ATASCII Code and CHR$ Functions

In a couple of places we have used an ESC sequence to produce various results, such as ESC-SHIFT-CLEAR to clear the screen, or ESC-TAB to make the output jump to a given tab stop. In our program, we get a little bent arrow between quote marks to indicate the screen will be cleared or various other symbols depending on the statement we are using. Using the CHR$ function, we can directly access any combination of keyboard characters or functions. For example, if we want a single inverse letter, in lower case, instead of having to press the ATARI KEY before and after the desired character and then the CAP/LOWR key, we enter the CHR$ value of the letter. In APPENDIX C of your Basic Reference Manual there is a complete listing of ATASCII which you will want to examine. Whenever we want to access a character we just enter the CHR$ and the decimal value of the character we want. For example, enter the following:

```
PRINT CHR$(65) <RETURN>
```

You got an A. That's simple enough and not too interesting. On the other hand, try the following little program, and I'll bet you couldn't do it without using the CHR$ function:

```
10 PRINT CHR$(125) : REM USES ATASCII
   FOR {ESC-SHIFT-CLEAR}
20 DIM QU$(1), BUZ$(1), AN$(1) : QU$ = CHR$(34)
   : BUZ$ = CHR$(253) : REM USES ATASCII
   : VALUE FOR QUOTE MARKS AND BUZZER
30 FOR I = 1 TO 20 : PRINT : NEXT I : PRINT
   "HIT RETURN TO CONTINUE OR ";
40 PRINT QU$ ; "Q" ; QU$ ; " TO QUIT ";
50 PRINT BUZ$; : INPUT AN$
60 IF AN$ = CHR$(81) THEN END
70 PRINT "To be continued . . . "
```

RUN the program and look carefully. Note the quotes around the Q. If we tried to PRINT a quote mark, the computer would think it got a command to begin printing a string. However, by defining QU$ as CHR$(34) we were able to slip in the quote marks and not confuse the output! (Just for fun, see if you can do that without using the CHR$ command.) Also, did you notice how we began the program? Instead of using the ESC-SHIFT-CLEAR key, we used CHR$(125). We did not have to put in the quote (") marks around CHR$(125) as we did with ESC-SHIFT-CLEAR. Likewise, we defined BUZ$ as CHR$(253) to produce a buzzer sound to remind the user to press either RETURN or Q. To see what different characters you have available, RUN the following program:

```
10 PRINT CHR$(125)
20 FOR I = 1 TO 255
30 IF I = 125 THEN PRINT " "; " ";: NEXT I
40 PRINT CHR$(I); " "; : NEXT I
```

Voila! There you have all of your symbols. Well, actually we got all but the last two. We heard CHR$(253) with the buzzer, but since CHR$(254) backs over itself, it is invisible. However, if we have an ESC sequence *before* those characters we can see them. CHR$(27) is the CHR$ code for ESC, so let's see if we can use it to get our characters on the screen. Insert the following lines to do so:

```
30 IF I = 125 OR I = 253 OR I = 254 OR I = 255
   THEN PRINT CHR$(27); CHR$(I);" "; : NEXT I
35 IF I > 255 THEN END
```

Now we can see all of our characters, including the CLEAR and BUZZER symbols, but we don't hear the buzzer! Originally, we substituted a " " for CLEAR since we didn't want everything to disappear when CHR$(125) was printed out. (Remove lines 30 and 35 to see what happens!)

The following is a little programs with which you can practice. See if you can guess what they will produce before running them:

```
10 DIM LB$(7), RB$(1), AT$(5)
20 LB$ = CHR$ (219) : RB$ = CHR$(221)
   : AT$ = "ATARI"
30 LB$(LEN(LB$) + 1) = AT$
40 LB$(LEN(LB$) + 1) = RB$
50 PRINT CHR$(125) : L = 19 – LEN(LB$)/2 – 1
60 FOR I = 1 TO L : PRINT CHR$(31);
   : NEXT I : PRINT LB$
```

DO IT THE EASY WAY

The following little program provides you with the perfect opportunity to write the bulk of your program with your editor. Key in lines 10 and 20 normally. After line 20, simply "walk" the cursor back to line 20 and enter 30, change the 10 to 15 and press RETURN. Do that for the rest of the lines, only adding the appropriate line number and FOR/NEXT value. This shortcut can be applied to *lessen* programming errors since once a line is correctly entered, it will be automatically correct if it is simply duplicated. Gives you more time for mountain climbing.

```
10 PRINT CHR$(125) : PRINT : PRINT : PRINT
20 FOR I = 1 TO 10 : PRINT CHR$(160); :
   NEXT I : PRINT : PRINT
30 FOR I = 1 TO 15 : PRINT CHR$(160); :
   NEXT I : PRINT : PRINT
40 FOR I = 1 TO 20 : PRINT CHR$(160); : NEXT I
   : PRINT : PRINT
50 FOR I = 1 TO 12 : PRINT CHR$(160); : NEXT I
   : PRINT : PRINT
```

The above program shows how to create bars for a graph using CHR$ commands. The same thing could have been done with the ATARI KEY and the space bar, but using the

CHR$ function, it is clearer and less cumbersome. In the next chapter, covering graphics, we will use the CHR$ command a good deal in creating pictures, charts and graphs.

The following program is a handy little device for printing out all of the CHR$ values to screen. Save it to tape or disk to use as a handy reference guide to look up CHR$ values and symbols.

CHR$ MAP

```
10 PRINT CHR$(125) : N = 0 : COUNTER = 0
   : DIM AN$(1)
20 FOR I = 1 TO 255
30 COUNTER = COUNTER + 1 : IF COUNTER = 76
   THEN GOSUB 300
40 N = N + 1 : IF N = 4 THEN GOSUB 200
50 IF I = 3 OR I = 4 OR I = 5 OR I =28 OR I = 29
   OR I = 30 OR I = 31 THEN 100
55 IF I = 125 OR I = 127 OR I = 158 OR I = 159
   OR I = 253 OR I = 254 OR I = 255 THEN 100
60 PRINT I; " = "; CHR$(I); CHR$(127);
70 NEXT I
80 END
100 PRINT I; " = "; CHR$(27); CHR$(I);
    CHR$(127); : NEXT I
110 GOTO 70
200 N = 0 : PRINT : RETURN
300 PRINT : PRINT "{ATARI KEY} PRESS RETURN
    TO CONTINUE {ATARI KEY}"
310 COUNTER = 0 : INPUT AN$ : PRINT
    CHR$(125) : RETURN
```

The program CHR$ MAP can be used as a handy eference for you to look up the CHR$ values of different symbols. You may have noticed that the program branches to a subroutine at line 100 if I has various values. This was to minimize the effect the special and CTRL characters had on screen formatting. All line 100 did was to add an ESC sequence, CHR$(27), so that the function would not be executed. Even so, there were still a few strange format outputs which would take more programming to repair. Also, note how we worked with the tabs. Instead of using {CTRL-TAB}, we used CHR$(127) in lines 6Ø and 1ØØ to get the tabs we wanted. However, in line 3ØØ, we did not attempt to put our prompt message in with CHR$ codes, but instead simply used the ATARI KEY to toggle the inverse mode. (Let's face it boys and girls, we could have done it with CHR$ but that would have been a lot of work! Using CHR$s would have been interesting, but it would have been a really *dumb* application.)

POKES and PEEKS : Looking inside your ATARI's Memory.

At first you won't have too many uses for POKEs and PEEKs, but as you begin exploring the full range of your computer's capacity, they will be used more and more. Basically, a POKE command places a value into a given memory location and a PEEK command returns the value stored in that location. For example, try the following:

```
POKE 2Ø48, 255 : PRINT PEEK (2Ø48) <RETURN>
```

You should have gotten "255" since the POKE command entered that value into location 2Ø48 and PRINT PEEK (2Ø48) printed out the value of that address. That's relatively simple, but more is going on than storage of numbers.

The key importance of POKE and PEEK involves what occurs in a given memory location when a given value is entered. In some locations nothing other than the storage of the number will occur, as in our example above. However, with other memory locations, very precise events occur. What we will do in the remainder of this section is to examine some of the more useful locations for POKEing and PEEKing in your ATARI. We will not be getting into the more complex elements of POKEs and PEEKs, however.

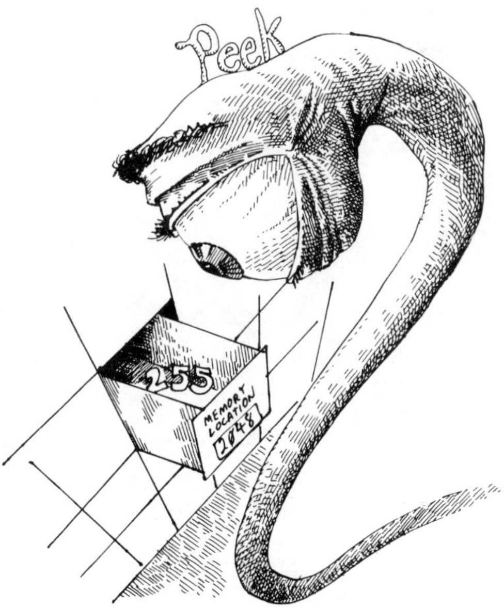

A TALE OF TWO NUMBER SYSTEMS

When using POKEs and PEEKs, we use decimal numbers for accessing locations. However, much of what is written about special locations in your TECHNICAL REFERENCE NOTES available for your ATARI is written in HEXADECIMAL, generally referred to as HEX. Since we've used decimal notations for counting all our lives, it seems to be a "natural" way of doing things. However, decimal is simply a "base 1Ø" method of counting and we could use a base of anything we wanted. For reasons I won't get into here, "base 16", called HEXADECIMAL is an easier way to think about using a computer's memory, and that's why so much of the notation we see is in HEX. HEX is counted in the same way as decimal except it is done in groups of 16, and it uses alphanumeric characters instead of just numeric ones. You can usually tell if numbers are HEX since they are typically preceded by a dollar-sign (e.g., $45 is not the same as decimal 45), and often there are alphabetic characters mixed in with numbers. (e.g., FC58, AAB, 12C). The following is a list of decimal and hexadecimal numbers.

Decimal	**Hexadecimal**
Ø	$Ø
1	$1
2	$2
3	$3
4	$4
5	$5
6	$6
7	$7
8	$8
9	$9
1Ø	$A
11	$B
12	$C
13	$D
14	$E
15	$F
16	$1Ø

As you can see, instead of starting with double digit numbers at 1Ø, hexadecimal begins double digits at decimal 16 with a $1Ø. In the "Major Memory Locations of Interest" in your ATARI TECHNICAL REFERENCE NOTES, the hexadecimal numbers are given. (Your ATARI BASIC REFERENCE MANUAL has some locations of interest in both hexadecimal and decimal.)

A ROTTEN TRICK!!

When you start POKEing and PEEKing into different locations of your ATARI, you will not always get what you expect. In the decimal addresses from 1536 through 1791, you will be pretty safe, since this is the User Basic area. However, other locations are the "homes" of special routines which will react directly to anything POKEd into them. For example, if you POKE 694,255 all of your keys will give you strange results, and you have to press SYSTEM/RESET to get it back to normal. Now if you slipped that into one of your programs and gave it to a friend, it would goof up his machine, and that would be a Rotten Trick! Of course, you wouldn't ever do anything like that. Would you?

Now let's take a look at some places to POKE. We will begin with your text screen.

POKEing the Text Screen

Another use of POKEs is to enter a character to a location on your next screen. Each character has a different value between Ø and 255. Your screen can be envisioned as a set of addresses on a 4Ø by 24 grid beginning at a decimal location we call "SCREEN" and ending at SCREEN + 4Ø * 24. That gives you exactly 96Ø locations on your screen where you can place text. The addresses are contiguous, and by using FOR/NEXT loops, it is a simple matter to enter sequential lines of text. Or, using POKEs, you can put text anywhere on the screen you want.

First, though, it is necessary to find where your computer is storing screen display. Depending on what program is in your computer and what it is doing at a given point, the location of SCREEN will vary. That's why we are defining it as a variable! (On some computers, the screen display addresses are constant.) To get started, we have to examine a special address that tells us where the beginning screen memory is currently located. The "pointers," at locations 88 and 89, tell us where the screen starts. Therefore, it is necessary to PEEK those locations. However, the locations actually have a reversed hexadecimal code which has to be converted to a useful decimal code. The formula

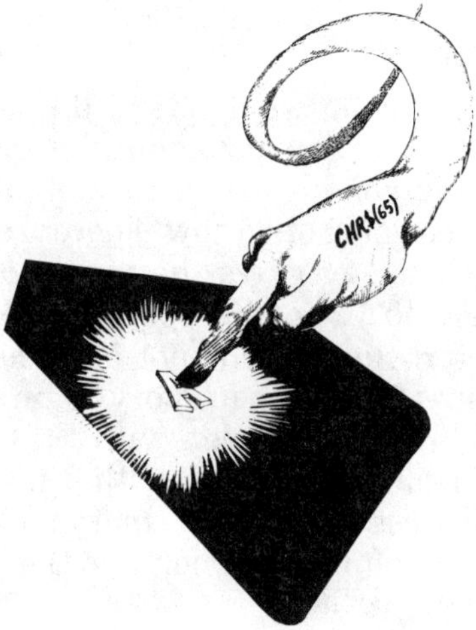


```
PEEK(88) + 256 * PEEK(89)
```

will give us that starting address; therefore, we will define our variable SCREEN to be

```
SCREEN = PEEK(88) + 256 * PEEK(89)
```

To get an idea of what happens when we POKE characters directly into memory, try the following program: (Give it to your true love.)

```
1Ø PRINT CHR$(125)
2Ø SCREEN = PEEK(88) + 256 * PEEK(89)
3Ø FILL = 4Ø * 24
4Ø FOR I = Ø TO FILL - 1
5Ø POKE SCREEN + I, 64
6Ø NEXT I
```

If you have been paying attention, you should have absolutely no idea of what made that happen! Where did those hearts come from? The ATASCII code for hearts is Ø, but we POKEd the screen with 64. Also, why in the world did the horizontal screen go all the way to 4Ø instead of 38 like we have seen up to now? (Now hold on, don't go back to the ALIEN FROG BLASTER game and give up programming just yet.) All that's happened is that you have been given more POWER over what your computer does. Let's take it one step at a time.

1. First, in line 3Ø we defined FILL as 4Ø * 24. That means we are now using all 4Ø horizontal columns of your screen instead of the defaulted 38 that we have been using up to now. There are still 24 vertical rows, so the 24 stays the same as always. Thus, there are 4Ø * 24 or 96Ø spots on the screen to put a character. Since each spot is an address and the addresses for screen memory begin with SCREEN, we filled up the screen with FILL -1. (We used FILL -1 since we began with Ø instead of 1.) The first address of screen memory [SCREEN + Ø] is the upper left hand corner, and the last is the lower right hand corner.

2. Second, the values for POKEd characters are different from CHR$ values. Thus, a "64" is a heart when POKEd into screen memory. The nice thing about POKEing in a character is that it does not function but is only displayed. (Remember when we made our CHR$ list and things went crazy when a control character was inserted without an ESC sequence?) The following program will give you a list of all the characters that can be POKEd in your screen memory.

```
10 PRINT CHR$(125)
20 SCREEN = PEEK(88) + 256 * PEEK(89)
30 FOR V = 1 TO 10 : PRINT : NEXT V
40 FOR I= 0 TO 255
50 POKE SCREEN + I, I
60 NEXT I
70 PRINT : PRINT : PRINT : PRINT : PRINT
```

Now you see that all the characters can be POKEd in without affecting your tabbing or anything else. Also, note that we tabbed vertically with line 3Ø to vertical position 1Ø, but our first character was printed in vertical position 1 on the screen (top row). That is, while the cursor was at Row 1Ø, the output began in Row 1. This is because we were filling an address and not PRINTing a character to the screen. This gives you total control over where your characters will be placed.

We also used an "offset" in our program. In programming, offsets are important for keeping track of things. In line 5Ø, we used the offset from SCREEN to be +I. This means that whatever the address of SCREEN is, we add the value of I to it. This allowed us to sequentially place all of our characters in memory locations instead of the same one over and over. (To see what happens without an offset, remove the +I from line 5Ø. All of the characters will be printed in the upper left hand corner.) In several programs, we will be doing that to let the computer do all the computations for us. (REMEMBER: A good program lets the computer do the hard work!)

In order to easily see what characters are produced with different values we POKE into screen locations, the following program allows you to INPUT a value and then displays the character on the screen for you. Of particular interest in this program are lines 5Ø and 6Ø. Line 5Ø prints out a message and ends it with a blank instead of a semicolon. However, when the program is RUN the character output is right next to the end of the string we entered in line 5Ø. The reason for that is we POKEd the output in a screen address right next to the end of our string. We could have placed a semicolon, comma or blank at the end of line 5Ø and the output would have been in the same place. Try it and see.

```
10 DIM AN$(1)
20 PRINT CHR$(125) :PRINT: PRINT : PRINT
   "ENTER A NUMBER FROM 0 TO 255-> ";
   : INPUT X
30 IF X > 255 THEN 20
40 FOR I = 1 TO 11 : PRINT : NEXT I
50 PRINT "THE CHARACTER FOR "; X ; " IS->"
60 SCREEN = PEEK(88) + 256 * PEEK(89)
70 VMOVE = 40 : HMOVE = 28
```

```
80 POKE SCREEN + 15 * VMOVE + HMOVE, X
90 PRINT : PRINT : "HIT RETURN TO CONTINUE
   OR 'Q' TO QUIT"
100 INPUT AN$
110 IF AN$ < > "Q" THEN 20
120 END
```

HOW TO FIND PLACES TO POKE

We've seen how to POKE some interesting locations in memory for information we need. With all the memory in an ATARI, how do we know what to POKE? Well, this is a little advanced for beginners, but you won't be a beginner all your life; so here are some tips. First of all, in APPENDIX I of your BASIC REFERENCE MANUAL which comes with your computer, is a list of memory locations. The decimal locations tell you where to PEEK for the information you need. This is only a partial list, but now you know how to use it. To get all the technical information, along with a lot more insight into how your ATARI works, get a copy of the ATARI TECHNICAL REFERENCE NOTES. This is a big, complicated set of notes, but with a little study you can use it. The trick is to know what to look for. For example, to find the beginning address for screen memory, I had to look up "Screen Memory Address" on page 222 in the OPERATING SYSTEM USER'S MANUAL (which is part of the TECHNICAL REFERENCE NOTES). There was a brief description of SAVMSC along with the notation (ØØ58,2). Now, since the notations are given in HEX, I knew that the ØØ58 was 88 in decimal, and the "2" indicated that 2 bytes were used; so, the pointers were located at decimal locations 88 and 89. To convert from hexadecimal to decimal, I simply used a handy little program which lists out hexadecimal values from Ø to 255, reproduced below. (Also, there's a nice decimal to hex conversion program in Appendix H of your BASIC REFERENCE MANUAL.) I admit that this is a little hairy for beginners, but once you get the hang of it, you can really start to delve into your computer's "mind."

DECIMAL - HEX CONVERSION PROGRAM

```
10 DIM AN$(1) : PRINT CHR$(125)
20 DIM HD$(26): HD$= "{ATARI-KEY} HEX - DECIMAL
   CONVERSION (ATARI-KEY)"
30 L = 20 - LEN (HD$)/2 : POSITION L, 0 : PRINT HD$
40 FOR N = 0 TO 255
50 PRINT "$"; : REM THE $ IS USED TO REPRESENT
   HEX NUMBERS
60 H = INT (N)/16 : H = INT(H) : GOSUB 200
70 H = N - INT(H) : 16 : H = INT(H) * GOSUB 200
80 PRINT "="; N ; CHR$(127)
90 C = C + 1 : IF C =4 THEN PRINT : C = 0
100 C2 = C2 + 1 : IF C2 = 76 THEN C2 = 0 : PRINT : PRINT
    "{ATARI-KEY} HIT RETURN TO CONTINUE {ATARI-KEY}";
    : INPUT AN$ : PRINT CHR$(125)
110 NEXT N
120 END
200 REM *** CONVERSION ROUTINE ***
210 PRINT CHR$(48+ H + 7 * (H > 9));
220 RETURN
```

CHART IT!

In addition to having labels stuck all over my computer, I have a number of charts. The nice thing about a chart is that it has everything from a single category together in one place. You should make or buy or somehow get your hands on charts which will summarize POKEs, PEEKs and other handy locations and addresses. Also, in several computer magazines, you can find charts. Make copies of the charts and using rubber cement, paste them to cardboard and keep them handy. In the chapter on printers, we'll see how to print out our HEX - DECIMAL CONVERSION program.

Resetting the Text Window

As we saw with the POSITION command, we can use two extra columns to the left of our text window. For example:

```
POSITION Ø,5 : PRINT "X";
```

will print an X at the far left-hand side of our screen in row 5. Using a special POKE, we can change that. Decimal address 82 sets the left margin of our screen. For example, load a program into memory and enter:

```
POKE 82, Ø
```

Now LIST your program. It lists along the far left side instead of where it normally does. Enter the following:

```
FOR I = 1 TO 4Ø : PRINT "1"; : NEXT I
```

As you can see, you now have a 4Ø column screen instead of a 38 column screen. To get it back to a 38 column screen, enter:

```
POKE 82,2
```

Now let's change the right margin of the screen. This time we will POKE address 83 instead of 82. Enter:

```
1Ø POKE 83,1Ø
2Ø FOR I = 1 TO 38 : PRINT "1"; : NEXT I
RUN
```

This time, you were only able to print out nine 1's before the next line started. Now, LIST the program. You still have a right margin of 1Ø; so even your LIST comes out funny. (By the way, how come you only get nine columns when you POKEd the right margin to 1Ø? See if you can figure it out, and remember that column Ø is at the far left side and your left column begins at 2 in the default condition.) To quickly get everything back to normal, press SYSTEM RESET.

Having done that, let's change *both* the left and right margins and see what happens:

```
10 PRINT CHR$(125)
20 POKE 82, 20 : POKE 83, 30 : PRINT
30 FOR I = 1 TO 11 * 23 : PRINT CHR$(128);
   : NEXT I
40 PRINT "ENTER #"; : INPUT A : REM This just holds
   things so you can look at the screen.
```

RUN and LIST the program. This will give you a clear idea of what happens when the text window is reset. Nothing is harmed, and it gives you greater flexibility in formatting your screen output. Finally, for an interesting effect add line 5∅:

```
50 POSITION 2,0 : POKE 82,2 : POKE 83,19 : LIST
```

This does a double window change!

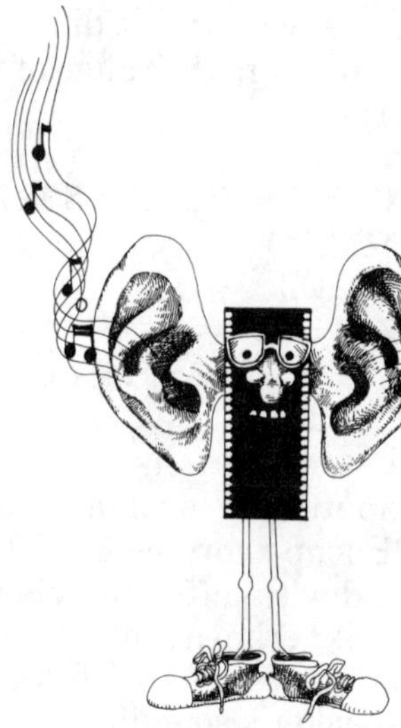

Sources of Sound

Now that we have seen that besides simply POKEing numbers in empty memory locations, we can also POKE in values at special locations to get some immediate results, we are ready to take a look at the ATARI's fantastic sound capabilities. There are two sources of sound which can be generated. On the one hand, we can click the speaker. This involves POKEing memory location 53279 with a ∅ and building loops to give it different effects. On the other hand you can generate sound through your TV's speaker. For this, we use the Atari BASIC word SOUND. This will give us a good deal of power in generating sound. *NOTE: If you are using a monitor without a speaker, the* SOUND *command will not work. It will be necessary to install an external speaker or hook up your computer to a TV.* We will keep everything simple and provide programs and instruction on how to get started.

Tweaking the Speaker

We have buzzed the speaker with CHR$(253), but now we will POKE memory location 53279 with Ø to click it. If this is done with different delays, we can get different effects. The following program runs through the range of tones produced by the internal speaker:

```
10 PRINT CHR$(125) : BUZZ = 53279
20 FOR J = 1 TO 20
30 FOR I = 1 TO 200
40 POKE BUZZ, 0
50 FOR PAUSE = 1 TO 20 STEP J : NEXT PAUSE
60 NEXT I : NEXT J
```

The buzz starts like a sputtering airplane and then increases in speed as the PAUSE loop shortens until it reaches a high pitch. By playing around with different delay loops, you can create different effects. Experiment until you find a sound you like. Remember, all it takes is a PAUSE loop of a different length to change the speaker's sound!

Sound Off!

Turn up the sound of your TV set and let's really make some racket! The format of the SOUND statement in BASIC is as follows:

```
SOUND voice, pitch, distortion, loudness
```

When each of these parameters is set to a value, different sounds, including musical notes, can be generated from your TV's speaker. The sound will continue until it is turned off with SOUND Ø,Ø,Ø,Ø. To control the duration of a sound, delay loops are used. To get started, let's make a little sound and then see what we've done:

```
10 PRINT CHR$(125)
20 SOUND 3, 127, 8, 15
30 FOR DURATION = 1 TO 400 : NEXT DURATION
40 SOUND 0, 0, 0, 0
```

What was that sound? A rocket as heard from the inside of a spaceship, of course! Well, it can be anything you want, and you can change it. Just for fun, using your editor, change the values in line 2Ø to see what you get. Be careful, though. The first number has to be between Ø and 3; the second between Ø and 255; the third, even numbers between Ø and 14; and the fourth, between Ø and 15.

Now let's see what we have been doing. We will examine the four values plus the DURATION loop and then make a program which examines the various sounds.

1. VOICE (Ø-3) Think of the voices as separate speakers, and you can have all four speakers (Ø-3) going simultaneously, or turn on some and not others. Individual SOUND commands must be used for each voice or speaker.

2. PITCH (Ø-255) The pitch value produces the frequencies which make specific notes or sounds. With 256 tones available, there is a full range of notes you can produce.

3. DISTORTION (even numbers, Ø-14) This is the variable for "sound effects." A value of 1Ø produces a pure tone, while other even numbers give varying amounts of distortion. Odd numbers result in clicks.

4. VOLUME (Ø-15) This parameter simply turns up the volume to a given level. If you want a constant sound but you want to make it sound as though it is getting closer or further away, vary the volume in your SOUND command.

5. DURATION This is *not* part of the SOUND command, but it is a loop which will make the sounds last a varying amount of time until the values of the SOUND statement are changed or until they are turned off with SOUND (Ø-3),Ø,Ø,Ø.

Now let's whip up a program which will allow us to explore the different sounds we can make. Make notes of the sounds you like so that you can incorporate them in your programs later on.

```
10 DIM AN$(1)
20 PRINT CHR$(125) :PRINT "VOICE Ø-3";
   : INPUT VOICE
30 PRINT "PITCH Ø-255"; : INPUT PITCH
40 PRINT "DISTORTION Ø-14"; : INPUT DISTORTION
50 PRINT "VOLUME Ø-15"; : INPUT VOLUME
60 PRINT "DURATION "; : INPUT DURATION : PRINT
   CHR$(125)
70 SOUND VOICE,PITCH, DISTORTION, VOLUME
80 FOR D = 1 TO DURATION : NEXT D
90 FOR N = Ø TO 3 : SOUND N,Ø,Ø,Ø : NEXT N
100 PRINT : PRINT "THAT SOUND WAS MADE BY:"
110 PRINT "VOICE = "; VOICE
120 PRINT "PITCH = "; PITCH
```

```
130 PRINT "DISTORTION ="; DISTORTION
140 PRINT "VOLUME = "; VOLUME
150 PRINT : PRINT "{ATARI KEY} PRESS RETURN
    TO CONTINUE{ATARI KEY}" : PRINT "{ATARI KEY}
    OR 'Q' TO QUIT {ATARI KEY}"; : INPUT AN$
160 IF AN$ <> "Q" THEN GOTO 20
```

To experiment with multiple voices simultaneously, enter INPUT statements for more variables and on separate lines between lines 70 and 80, enter additional SOUND statements. As you may have noted, line 90 is already set up to turn off the sound on all voices.

SUMMARY

This chapter has ventured into the ATARI's memory, and while you are not expected to understand all of the nuances of our discussion, I hope that you have a general idea of how ATASCII values work and a little about addresses and locations. Most important is that you have tried the commands introduced and attempted to use them in your programs. The more you use different commands, the more you begin to understand what is happening.

The CHR$ function introduced ATASCII values. Some of the uses of CHR$ allow us to access characters not available in our programming. We can loop through different values or enter text characters with numeric variables using CHR$.

The POKE command enters a value to a decimal address and the PEEK command retrieves a value from an address. Special locations in your ATARI's memory have special functions, such as the ATASCII screen values. More advanced uses of POKE and PEEK can provide ways of virtually writing machine-level subroutines. Making different sounds on the ATARI was accomplished using POKEs to tweak the computer's built in speaker with a series of delays to produce a variety of sounds. To really get sound, we saw that the SOUND command in BASIC could easily produce a wide range of noise and music on four different voices simultaneously. These sounds can be integrated with text and graphics to produce anything from sound prompts to output to games.

CHAPTER 7

Using Graphics

Introduction

One of the nicest features of the ATARI is its graphics capabilities. There are three kinds of graphics: (1) Keyboard Graphics, (2) Screen Graphics and (3) Player/Missile Graphics. Keyboard graphics are something like text except that we use a lot more color and figures instead of letters and numbers. The way the graphics are used, however, we can access both graphics and text simultaneously. This feature is especially useful for labeling our graphics, such as charts or figures we may wish to create. As a matter of fact, if you have pressed the CTRL key and one of the other keys simultaneously, you may have already accessed some of your computer's graphics capabilities.

Screen graphics have the most varied number of possibilities. Different screen sizes, color combinations, resolutions, text expansion, and drawing words in BASIC are available to the user. You can really turn your computer into an artist's palette with graphics on the ATARI!

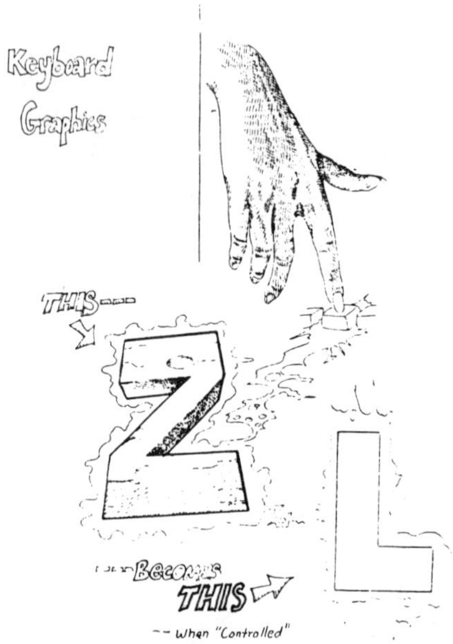

Player/Missile graphics are wholly different from keyboard and screen graphics, and they are a good deal more difficult to use. However, player/missile graphics give you an incredible amount of flexibility and power in creating figures in fine detail, especially animated ones for game applications. Once you become adept at using player/missile graphics, there are limitless possibilities for the creation of colorful animated characters.

Keyboard Graphics

Keyboard graphics are very simple to use, since you can enter figures directly from the keyboard. To create a single figure simply PRINT that figure in the same way you would a letter or number. For example, if you enter

```
PRINT "{CTRL-,}" : REM CONTROL - COMMA
```

you will get a heart figure. However, to create more interesting graphics, you will want to enter commands from the Program mode. This can be done by writing a series of PRINT statements, entering the drawing as you go along. For example, let's make a graphic rocket ship. We'll keep it simple and program a one stage rocket. (It would be a good idea to SAVE or CSAVE this program to disk or tape, as well as the others in this section. SAVE them under different file names since, even though some will have the identical results, they are programmed differently.)

```
10 PRINT CHR$(125)
20 PRINT " {CTRL-H} {CTRL-J}"
30 PRINT " {CTRL-V} {CTRL-B}"
40 PRINT " {CTRL-V} {CTRL-B}"
50 PRINT " {CTRL-V} {CTRL-B}"
60 PRINT " {CTRL-V} {CTRL-B}"
70 PRINT " {CTRL-H} {CTRL-V} {CTRL-B} {CTRL-J}"
80 PRINT " {CTRL-M} {CTRL-M}"
```

When you are finished writing the program you should be able to see a "Rocket" on your screen – even before you RUN the program. When you do RUN it, the screen will clear and a "Rocket" will appear in the upper left hand corner of your TV. In the same way, you can draw anything else you want with the different shapes and characters on your keyboard.

Let's take another look at our "Rocket" and see if we can improve the program. First, note that lines 3Ø through 6Ø are identical. Instead of having to re-write those lines, let's use our GOSUB commands, treating the repeated lines as subroutines. Using your editor, change line 3Ø to line 1ØØ, adding a colon and RETURN after line 1ØØ. Now change lines 3Ø to read:

```
30 FOR I = 1 TO 4 : GOSUB 100 : NEXT I
```

Add line 9Ø END. The program should now look as follows:

```
10 PRINT CHR$(125)
20 PRINT " {CTRL-H} {CTRL-J}"
```

```
30 FOR I = 1 TO 4 : GOSUB 100 : NEXT I
70 PRINT "{CTRL-H} {CTRL-V} {CTRL-B} {CTRL-J}"
80 PRINT "{CTRL-M} {CTRL-M}"
90 END
100 PRINT "{CTRL-V} {CTRL-B}" : RETURN
```

Now that didn't save a lot of programming time, but if you begin to think of keyboard graphics as you would any other program, you will want to look for shortcuts both to save memory space and to minimize programming redundancy.

EDIT IT!!

If you did not use your editor to change the above lines, you are working too hard! All that is required when you edit a line is to enter the changes and hit RETURN. To change a line to a different line number, simply enter the new line number over the old line number. For example, to change line 30 in our original "Rocket" to line 100, simply use the cursor key to walk up to line 30, place the cursor over the 3, enter 100 and press RETURN. When you LIST the program, line 30 will still be there in its original form, but there will now be a line 100 identical to line 30.

We will be leaving keyboard graphics now, but not for good since we may want to use them later on. The main thing to understand in this section is that figures and symbols can be output very much like text. You are simply sending information to your computer's screen. In the next section keep this in mind as we explore other screens in your ATARI computer.

Screen Graphics

There are nine GRAPHICS screens on your ATARI. We have been working on the GRAPHICS 0 screen thus far, and now we will look at the others. Since screens 1 through 8 have different characteristics, we will examine the screen in groups of common features. Our discussion of the screens will be in the following groups:

GRAPHIC SCREENS	GROUP
1,2	A
3,5,7	B
4,6	C
8	D

GROUP A: Big Text Screens

This first group of screens, GRAPHICS 1 and GRAPHICS 2, prints big text on your screen. To set either graphics screen, enter

```
GRAPHICS 1 (GR. 1)
```

or

```
GRAPHICS 2 (GR. 2)
```

As soon as you set a graphics screen, everything on it is cleared; so if you write big text on GRAPHICS 1 and then enter GRAPHICS 2, your text from GRAPHICS 1 will disappear. Therefore, while these two screens are similar, they cannot be used together without more advanced programming techniques beyond the scope of this book. *NOTE: We have been using fully spelled out commands. With* GRAPHICS *we will make an exception and use* GR. *instead of* GRAPHICS *since, when you* LIST *your program after entering* GR., GRAPHICS *will appear fully spelled out. It's magic!*

Both GRAPHICS 1 and 2 leave four lines of text at the bottom of the screen. When you enter GR. 1, for example, the screen will go black except for a little blue window at the bottom. GR. Ø will return everything to the full text screen where we do all of our programming. In our programs, we will be putting in a little "utility" to get back to GRAPHICS Ø after we have seen the effects on the GRAPHICS screen. This utility is:

```
5ØØ INPUT AN$ : GR. Ø : LIST
```

It is not to be considered anything other than a routine which will quickly get back the program listing. When you are finished with a graphics program, it should be removed.

To print out big text in GR. 1 or 2, you have to use PRINT #6 (or ? #6) for output. Upper and lower case change the color of the printed text; so if you see lower case in your program, don't expect to get it in your screen output. To get started, enter the following program:

```
10 DIM AN$(1)
20 GR. 1
30 PRINT #6; "This Is In BIG" : PRINT #6; "letters"
40 PRINT #6 : REM WORKS JUST LIKE "PRINT"
   ON GR. 0
50 PRINT #6; "This is graphics 1"
60 PRINT #6 : PRINT #6
70 PRINT #6; "PRESS RETURN";
200 INPUT AN$ : GR. 0 : LIST
```

When you RUN the program, you will be presented with letters in double width with the upper case in one color and the lower case in another. (Remember what you entered as lower case will be upper case on the output.)

Now, to see GR. 2, simply change line 20 to:

```
20 GR. 2
```

and the 1 in line 50 to 2. This time you will get the same message, but the text will be double width *and* double length.

If you want to use the full graphics screen, you add 16 to the GR. mode. For example, if you want full screen for GR. 1, you would enter GR. 1 + 16 (or GR. 17). However, with full screen graphics, you have to hold onto the screen with a loop or it will think it is supposed to go back to GR. 0. For example, change the above program by adding the following:

```
20 GR. 1 + 16
80 FOR PAUSE = 1 TO 1000 : NEXT PAUSE
```

Now when you RUN the program, there is no little text window at the bottom of the screen, and after the PAUSE loop, all you get on your screen is a question mark waiting for you to press RETURN. Experiment with these two screens.

Color

We interrupt our discussion of different screen to bring you COLOR! This may seem like a rude place to insert color, but I wanted you to see some different graphics screens first.

Setcolor

To get started enter the following from GR. Ø:

```
SETCOLOR 2,3,8
```

Your screen turned a yellow-orange. OK, but why? First, let's see what the different numbers mean.

SET COLOR [register numbers Ø-4], [color Ø-15], [luminance Ø-14 <even numbers>]

1) **Register number** These five registers vary in their effect depending on which mode you are in. In general, though, they direct color changes to different "switches" in memory.

2) **Color** There are 16 codes for colors. The following table shows how to obtain different colors by entering different codes.

COLOR	**CODE**
Aqua	1Ø
Blue	7
Blue-Green	9
Blue-Purple	6
Gold	1
Green	12
Green-Blue	11
Grey	Ø
Light-Blue	8
Orange	2 & 15
Orange-Green	14
Pink	4
Red	3
Violet	5
Yellow-Green	13

These colors work with the various modes to set background and border color. Later we will discuss the COLOR command, which is *different* from SETCOLOR.

3) **Luminance** This sets the color to different levels of brightness, using even numbers from Ø to 14. The Ølevel produces an almost black level and 14 an almost white level.

Now that we have an idea of the different colors, set your screen to GR. Ø, and let's take a tour of the different background and border colors available to you. In this, GR. Ø, the number 2 register sets background color, and the number 4 register the border:

```
10 PRINT CHR$(125) : DIM AN$(1)
20 FOR BORDER = Ø TO 15
30 FOR BACKGROUND = Ø TO 15
40 SETCOLOR 4, BORDER, 8
50 SETCOLOR 2, BACKGROUND, 8
60 PRINT : PRINT : PRINT "BORDER ="; BORDER
70 PRINT : PRINT "BACKGROUND ="; BACKGROUND
80 PRINT: PRINT : PRINT "PRESS RETURN";: INPUT
   AN$ : PRINT CHR$(125)
90 NEXT BACKGROUND : NEXT BORDER
```

Now let's examine luminance. To do this we will simply change the above program as follows:

```
20 FOR LUMINANCE = Ø TO 14 STEP 2
50 SETCOLOR 2, BACKGROUND, LUMINANCE
60 PRINT : PRINT : PRINT "LUMINANCE =";
   LUMINANCE
90 NEXT BACKGROUND : NEXT LUMINANCE
```

(Delete line 4Ø)

The above two programs ought to give you a good idea of how to change colors and luminance to all kinds of combinations. If you're really sharp, I'll bet you noticed that by changing luminance, you can also change colors. So how many different combinations of colors can you get by changing luminance with colors? *HINT: Count the number of times you had to press* RETURN *in the second program.*

Now that we have seen how SETCOLOR can change background and border colors along with luminance in GR. Ø, let's see what it can do with GR. 1 and GR. 2. We will use GR. 1 in our examples of coloring and lighting text since it and GR. 2 have the same effects. The first thing we learned about GR. 1 and GR. 2 is that the color of the TEXT changes with upper and lower case and with inverse and normal text. To see the different colors we can get with different SETCOLOR combinations and text styles, enter the following program: Notice that we placed GR. 1 *inside* our loop.

```
10 DIM AN$(1)
20 FOR HUE = 0 TO 15
30 GR. 1
40 SETCOLOR 0, HUE, 8
50 PRINT #6; "THIS IS UPPER CASE"
60 PRINT #6; "this is lower case"
70 PRINT #6; "{ATARI KEY} THIS IS UC INVERSE
   {ATARI KEY}"
80 PRINT #6; "{ATARI KEY} this is lc inverse
   {ATARI KEY}"
90 PRINT #6; : PRINT #6; "HUE ="; HUE
100 PRINT #6 : PRINT #6 : PRINT #6; "(press return)"
110 INPUT AN$
120 NEXT HUE
200 GRAPHICS 0 : LIST
```

In order to change background and border colors in GR. 1 and GR. 2, it is necessary to use register number 4. The default color of black may not be what you need, so let's see what we can do. Add the following line to the above program:

```
35 SETCOLOR 4, 5, 8
```

Now you have a violet border and background. You can also change the luminance to get just the right combination of background and text color. Try changing the luminance values in line 35 to 4 and in line 35 to 1Ø. (Remember the last value in SETCOLOR is for luminance.) Just for fun, see if you can set a blue background the same color *and* luminance as the text window. You can then print big text on what appears to be GR. Ø. (Amaze your dog.)

At this point let's summarize our understanding of color and graphics modes in a little chart. The next graphics we discuss will take a leap into another type of graphics.

SETCOLOR REGISTER	MODE	EFFECTS
Ø	Ø	NUL
1	Ø	Character luminance
2	Ø	Background color
3	Ø	NUL
4	Ø	Border color
Ø-3	1,2	Character color
4	1,2	Background and Border

Now we are all set to forge onward!

Screen Graphics (continued)

GROUP B : Plotting and Drawing

The most useful way to conceive of graphic screens 3,5 and 7 is in terms of different gradations of points placed on the screen. In GR.3, the points plotted are large and blockish looking, in GR. 5 they are smaller blocks, and in GR. 7, the plots are little blocks, almost points. Depending on your application, one mode or another will be best.

To get started, let's take a look at three new commands: COLOR, PLOT and DRAWTO. The COLOR command, tells the computer what foreground or "plotted" color to draw to the screen in. PLOT, in the following form:

```
PLOT [horizontal], [vertical]
```

tells the computer where to plot a block. For example, the following program plots a block in GR. 3 in the upper left hand corner and lower right hand corner of the graphics screen. (Remember, line 2ØØ is just our utility to get back to our "programming screen.")

```
10 GR. 3
20 COLOR 1
30 PLOT 0,0
40 PLOT 39,19
200 DIM AN$ (1) : INPUT AN$ : GR. 0 : LIST
```

Now let's look at DRAWTO. It "draws" a line from PLOT h,v to DRAWTO h,v. For example, in the program we just examined, change line 40 to read:

```
40 DRAWTO 39,19
```

This time when you RUN the program, you have a diagonal line (looking like a staircase) from the upper left to lower right corners of your graphics screen.

Screen Sizes

When we change from GR. 3 to GR. 5 or 7, the same commands work, but the results are different. Change the program so that line 10 reads:

```
10 GR. 5
```

and then after running it, change it to

```
10 GR. 7
```

In both cases everything worked fine, except the line produced by DRAWTO was shorter and finer. With GR. 5, the line went a little beyond the middle of the screen, but it still looked more like a staircase than a line. However, with GR. 7, the staircase turned into a dotted line, and it didn't even reach the middle of the screen. Since the printed blocks are smaller for GR. 5 and 7 than for GR. 3, it is possible to have a larger number of plot positions on the screen. If we add 16 to our GR., we get rid of the text window at the bottom and have even more vertical room for our drawings. The following chart shows the different sizes of the graphics windows:

GRAPHICS MODE	MIXED	FULL
3	4Ø by 2Ø	4Ø by 24
5	8Ø by 4Ø	8Ø by 48
7	16Ø by 8Ø	16Ø by 96

When you are making your plots, it is important to remember that the first vertical or horizontal plot position is Ø and not 1; so think of your highest plot positions as 1 less than the numbers on the above chart. For example, the highest PLOT vertically on GR. 3 in the mixed graphics and text mode is 19 and not 2Ø. (REMEMBER, though, that Ø through 19 are 2Ø positions to plot.

Now that we can COLOR, PLOT and DRAWTO, what kind of useful things can we do with these screens? One use is to make graphs. Using the lower resolution graphics we can make bar graphs, and with the higher resolution we can make line graphs. Let's start off with a horizontal bar graph using GR. 5. Also, while we're at it, let's use the different COLORs available. In GROUP B graphics, we have four colors — one background and three foreground. For a quick look at these colors, let's run through them in a little program:

```
10 DIM AN$(1)
20 GR. 3
30 FOR C = 0 TO 3
40 COLOR C
50 PLOT 0,0
60 DRAWTO 39,19
70 PRINT "COLOR = ";C
80 PRINT "PRESS RETURN "; : INPUT AN$ : PRINT
   CHR$(125) : NEXT C
200 INPUT AN$ : GR. 0 : LIST
```

As you saw, COLOR Ø is the same color as the background. (Actually, you did not see anything except a black screen!) Therefore, we really have only three colors with which to work on the graphics screen. OK, now to our graph. *NOTE: Put in Lines 1Ø and 3ØØ-31Ø first!*

```
10 PRINT CHR$(125) : DIM TI$(30), AN$(1)
20 PRINT "TITLE OF GRAPH"; : INPUT TI$
```

```
30 PRINT "HOW MANY PLOTS (1-10)"; : INPUT NP
40 IF NP > 10 THEN PRINT CHR$(253);
   "NO MORE THAN 10!" : GOTO 30
50 DIM P(NP)
60 FOR I - 1 TO NP
70 PRINT "VALUE FOR PLOT (0-79) "; I : INPUT VP
80 IF VP > 79 THEN PRINT CHR$(253);
   "NO MORE THAN 79!" : GOTO 70
90 P(I) = INT (VP) : NEXT I
100 REM *** DRAW THE GRAPH ***
110 REM
120 REM ** FIRST DRAW THE SIDES IN COLOR 1 **
130 REM
140 GR. 5 : COLOR 1
150 PLOT 0,0 : DRAWTO 0,39 : DRAWTO 79,39
160 REM
170 REM ** NEXT DRAW THE BARS IN COLOR 2 **
180 REM
190 COLOR 2
200 FOR I = 1 TO NP
210 PLOT 0, I * 3 : DRAWTO P(I), I * 3
220 NEXT I
230 REM
240 REM ** STICK IN THE TITLE **
250 REM
260 L = 19 - LEN (TI$)/2 : FOR I = 1 TO L
    : PRINT " "; : NEXT I : PRINT TI$
270 REM *** THAT'S ALL ***
300 REM **** UTILITY - REMOVE AFTER GRAPH
    IS COMPLETED ****
310 INPUT AN$ : GRAPHICS 0 : LIST
```

RUN the program and see how nicely you can present data graphically. The program is severely limited in that it does only a maximum of 10 plots and values from 0 to 79. It is simple to change the number of plots above 10. You need only change the trap value in line 40 to a higher number, and change the offset in line 150 to I * 2 or simply I. Changing the values to greater than 79 is a little trickier, but we will see how to do that in a bit. First, though, let's take a look at a different kind of graph, a line graph using GR. 7. We will also see how to use all three colors on a graph and how to set up more informative labels in the "text window" at the bottom of the screen. This graph is pretty fancy, as a matter of fact, so there are several REM statements to tell you what's happening. (REMEMBER to put in the "utility" at the end of the program after you enter line 10.)

```
10 DIM AN$(1), MN$(12), TI$(30) : MN$ =
   "JFMAMJJASOND" : PRINT CHR$(125)
20 PRINT "NAME OF THIS CHART" ; : INPUT TI$
30 PRINT "FIRST YEAR, LAST YEAR"; : INPUT
   YEAR1, YEAR2
40 PRINT "NUMBER OF MONTHS: (1-12)" ; : INPUT M
50 PRINT "NUMBER OF YEARS: (1-3)" ; : INPUT Y
60 DIM PM (M,Y) : REM ** USE A TWO-DIMENSIONAL
ARRAY TO HANDLE ALL PLOTTING **
70 FOR YR = 1 TO Y
80 FOR MO = 1 TO M
90 PRINT "PLOT VALUE YR "; YR; " MONTH ";
   MO : PRINT "MAXIMUM VALUE=79"; : INPUT PLOT
100 IF PLOT > 79 THEN PRINT CHR$(253) : GOTO 90
110 PM (MO,YR) = INT (PLOT) : REM ** PUT THE
    INTEGER VALUE IN THE ARRAY 'PM' **
120 NEXT MO : NEXT YR
200 REM
210 REM *** MAKE A LINE GRAPH ***
220 REM
230 REM ** FIRST MAKE THE SIDES **
240 REM
250 GR. 7 : COLOR 2
260 PLOT 0,0 : DRAWTO 0,79 : DRAWTO 159,79
270 REM
280 REM ** DRAW THE LINES **
290 REM
300 FOR YR = 1 TO Y
310 PLOT 0, 39 : REM ** START IN CENTER OF
    VERTICAL AXIS **
320 FOR MO = 1 TO M
330 COLOR YR : REM ** DIFFERENT COLOR
    FOR EACH YEARLY LINE **
340 DRAWTO 12 * MO, 79 - PM(MO,YR) : REM **
    SUBTRACT PLOT VALUE FROM 79 **
350 NEXT MO : NEXT YR
360 REM
370 REM ** USE SUBSTRINGS OF MN$ TO
    LABEL MONTHS **
```

```
380 REM
390 FOR I = 1 TO M : PRINT " "; MN$(I,I); " ";
    : NEXT I
400 PRINT : PRINT TI$; " FOR "; YEAR1;
    " TO "; YEAR2
500 REM
510 REM *** UTILITY - REMOVE WHEN FINISHED ***
520 INPUT AN$ : GR. 0 : LIST
```

Now that should give you a near professional looking graph! (And you thought you couldn't program!) Line 340 is important, for it reverses your values so that the higher values will appear higher on your screen. Remember, since the top of your vertical axis is 0, your higher plot values would be lower on the screen if we simply used DRAWTO to the values we entered. For example, if one value was 20 and another was 40, the vertical position of 40 would be lower than vertical position 20. By subtracting the plot value from 79 (the highest vertical value we can plot on GR. 7) we make the lines appear higher for higher values. Thus, 40 becomes 39 and 20 becomes 59.

Now let's see if we can solve the problem of the maximum value of a plot. To do this, we will use GR. 3 since it has the fewest number of plotting positions, and if we can do it with GR. 3, the same principles can be applied to the other graphics modes. While we're at it, let's do something about changing the SETCOLOR. For GR. 3, 5, and 7, we use register 4 for changing both background and border colors.

```
10 PRINT CHR$(125) : DIM AN$(1), PV(2)
20 PRINT "MAX VALUE->"; : INPUT MV
30 RATIO = 19.9/MV : REM THIS SETS UP THE RATIO
   FOR ANY LINE AS A RATIO OF 20 - .1
40 FOR I = 1 TO 2
50 PRINT "PLOT VALUE->"; I; : INPUT PV
60 IF PV > MV THEN PRINT CHR$(253) : GOTO 50
70 PV(I) = INT (PV * RATIO)
80 NEXT I
100 REM *** MAKE THE CHART ON GR. 3 ***
110 GR. 3 : SETCOLOR 4,3,6 : COLOR 1
120 REM * FIRST MAKE THE SCALE MARKS *
130 FOR SM = 0 TO 20 STEP 4
140 PLOT 0, SM : DRAWTO 39, SM : NEXT SM
```

```
150 REM * NEXT CHANGE THE COLOR AND
    DRAW THE GRAPH *
160 COLOR 2
170 FOR I = 1 TO 2
180 PLOT 10 * I, 19 : DRAWTO 10 * I, 19 - PV(I)
200 REM *** LABEL YOUR CHART WITH THE
    TEXT WINDOW ***
210 L = 6 : FOR TAB = 1 TO L : PRINT
    "{ESC-CTRL-RIGHT ARROW}"; : NEXT TAB : PRINT
    "PLOT"; I
220 NEXT I : REM ** THIS IS FROM THE LOOP
    THAT STARTED ON LINE 170 **
230 PRINT : PRINT "MARKS = "; MV/5;
    " MAX VALUE = "; MV
240 REM * KILL THE CURSOR AND GO INTO
    ENDLESS LOOP *
250 POKE 755,0 : GOTO 250
260 REM * PRESS 'BREAK' AND THEN 'CONT'
    TO GO ON *
300 REM *** UTILITY WHILE WORKING WITH
    GRAPH ***
310 INPUT AN$ : GR. 0 : LIST
```

As you can see, changing the maximum possible value of what can be plotted simply requires the algorithm we used in line 3Ø. By dividing the maximum plotting position minus .1 by the maximum value to be entered as a plot value, all values can be proportionally adjusted so that your chart will reflect relative differences in your plot values. This little trick allows you to graphically plot any values you want! We also cleaned up the display by POKEing 755 with a Ø in line 25Ø to remove the cursor. Using the BREAK key and then the CONT command, we can get to our utility on line 3ØØ. (Not too elegant, I admit, but it gives a clean display of your chart.)

GROUP C: Graphics that Conserve Memory

GRAPHICS 4 and 6 are essentially like those in GROUP B, but they only have one foreground color. GR. 4 has the same resolution as GR. 5 while GR. 6 has the same resolution as GR. 7, and both use about half the memory. If you are writing longer programs or programs that use more memory or you are using the ATARI 400 with the minimum memory configuration, GROUP C graphics may be needed. (Don't worry if you have only 16K of memory, though, there's still plenty of room!) To test this graphics group, replace GR. 5 with GR. 4 and GR. 7 with GR. 6 in the programs from the GROUP B programs above. Make sure to have all COLORS = 1.

Let's take a look at a new command here. This command can be used in the other graphics modes we have discussed, but GROUP C graphics should have something new! The command is XIO, and is used for filling in boxes. The format for XIO is:

```
XIO 18, #6, Ø,Ø, "S:"
```

Now that's a strange format, but it's the only one used, so it shouldn't be too difficult to remember. We also have to learn a new POKE. It is 765 and is POKEd with the COLOR number we want to fill our box with. Since GROUP C graphics only have 1 foreground color, this should be simple. We will POKE 765,1. Also, we have to use POSITION. With this application, though, we do not POSITION text output, but we POSITION the cursor only. (We cannot see it on the graphics screen, but it's there.) We POSITION the cursor to the lower vertical and leftmost horizontal placement. The following program illustrates how to do this:

```
1Ø PRINT CHR$(125)
2Ø GR. 6 : COLOR 1
3Ø PLOT Ø,Ø : DRAWTO 159,79 : DRAWTO Ø,79
   : DRAWTO Ø,Ø
4Ø POSITION Ø,79
5Ø POKE 765,1 : REM ** POKE IN COLOR 1 **
6Ø XIO 18, #6,Ø,Ø, "S:"
2ØØ DIM AN$(1) : INPUT AN$ : GR. Ø : LIST
```

That should have filled your screen with COLOR 1. Now change line 4Ø to:

```
4Ø POSITION Ø, 39
```

RUN the program again, and this time the screen only fills halfway. Now change line 4Ø to:

```
40 POSITION 79, 79
```

This time around, you got a diagonal fill, leaving a black triangle on the left side. Experiment with different positions and different graphics modes with the XIO command. Be sure to try it with different colors, in the appropriate modes, by POKEing 765 with 1, 2, or 3.

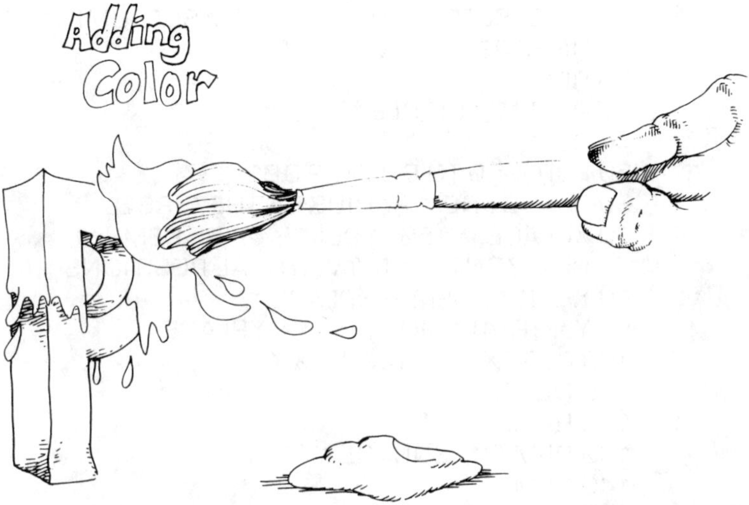

GROUP D GRAPHICS: High Resolution

The final screen graphics we will examine is GR. 8, the only mode in GROUP D. GRAPHICS 8 has a resolution of 320 by 160 (mixed) and 320 by 192 (full). That means it is possible to have much finer drawings on the screen. The only problem with GR. 8 is the limited colors. We can get only one color at a time but, using two luminances, it is possible to draw on the screen. Essentially, we have a background of one luminance and draw in a foreground color of another luminance. Given the high resolution, we could make finer line graphs, but let's do some drawing instead. (If you want to do graphs with GRAPHICS 8, just change the programs we have already done to GR. 8 along with the parameters to adjust to the higher resolution.)

Since we have been drawing only graph lines, straight ones from one point to another, let's take a look at how to draw circles. Using the SIN (sine) and COS (cosine) functions in BASIC, we can PLOT and DRAWTO curves on the high resolution screen of GR. 8. (We'll throw in a couple of straight line geometric figures in our program as well, just to make sure you can see how they are done.)

```
10 GR. 8 : SETCOLOR 1,0, 12 : REM SET LUMINANCE
   OF FOREGROUND TO 12
20 REM
30 REM **** CIRCLE ****
40 REM
50 FOR I = 0 TO 6.3 STEP 0.01
60 R = 40 : REM RADIUS OF THE CIRCLE
70 XPLACE = 150 : YPLACE = 75 : REM
   HORIZONTAL AND VERTICAL POSITIONS
80 X = R * COS(I) + XPLACE
90 Y = (R/4) * SIN (I) / 0.3 + YPLACE
100 PLOT X,Y : DRAWTO X,Y
110 NEXT I
120 REM
130 REM **** SQUARE ****
140 REM
150 PLOT 10,20 : DRAWTO 10,50 : DRAWTO 50,50
    : DRAWTO 50,20 : DRAWTO 10,20
160 REM
170 REM **** TRIANGLE ****
180 REM
190 PLOT 30,60 : DRAWTO 50,80 : DRAWTO 10, 80
    : DRAWTO 30,60
200 REM
210 REM **** PARALLELOGRAM ****
220 REM
230 PLOT 20,90 : DRAWTO 50,90 : DRAWTO 40,110
    : DRAWTO 10,110 : DRAWTO 20,90
300 REM
310 REM **** UTILITY ****
320 REM
330 DIM AN$(1) : INPUT AN$ : GRAPHICS 0 : LIST
```

With those shapes, you can make just about anything you want. If you are a better artist than I (and everyone I know certainly is!), you can do all sorts of artwork. However, it can be a lot of programming to stick in all the plots and lines you need for an artistic masterpiece. Why not use our game paddles to do the PLOTs and DRAWTOs for us? Then all we'd rave to do is to turn the paddles and push buttons to get our pictures drawn on the screen. The following program does just that. Before we key it in, let's see how it works. (If you do not have paddles, you can either skip this program or use INPUT statements to enter the values of X and Y.)

We use POKE 755,Ø to get rid of the cursor, as you will remember. Then we use POKE 656,Ø, a new one. This POKE sets the cursor to the top of the text window in the mixed graphics mode. Since we will be using the text window to display the X (horizontal) and Y (vertical) positions for PLOT and DRAWTO, we will need that information in one place all the time. Next, we define PADDLE(Ø) + 46 to be our X position and PADDLE(1) to be our Y position. We added the 46 to PADDLE(Ø) to center our position on the horizontal axis since the paddle value only goes to 228 and our screen goes to 36Ø. On the other hand, since our vertical axis is only 16Ø, we had to limit the value of PADDLE(1) to 159 so as not to put the cursor out of range. In order to PLOT and DRAWTO, we put in subroutines beginning at lines 2ØØ and 3ØØ respectively. We set up PTRIG(Ø) to jump to the PLOT subroutine and PTRIG(1) for the DRAWTO subroutine. This allows us to move the horizontal and vertical position of our cursor without dragging a line with it if we desire. We put in a single buzzer [CHR$(253)] to PLOT when the button on Paddle Ø [PTRIG(Ø)] is pressed and two buzzers when the button on Paddle 1 [PTRIG(1)] is pressed to remind us whether we are using PLOT or DRAWTO.

To use the program, hook up your paddles in "Controller Jack 1" and RUN the program. Turning the paddles to get the desired position for your first PLOT, press the button on Paddle Ø. Then change the positions and press the button on Paddle 1, and you will get a line. If you want to add to the line, simply change the horizontal and vertical values and press the Paddle 1 button again. If you want to draw another line which is not connected, change the positions and press the button on

Paddle Ø. Then, after moving the horizontal and vertical positions again, draw another line by pressing the button on Paddle 1.

```
10 GR. 8 : SETCOLOR 1,0,12
20 POKE 755,0 : POKE 656,0
30 X = PADDLE (0) + 46 : Y = PADDLE(1)
40 IF Y > 159 THEN Y = 159
50 IF PTRIG(0) = 0 THEN GOSUB 200
60 IF PTRIG(1) = 0 THEN GOSUB 300
70 PRINT "HOR=";X;" VER="; Y; " "
80 FOR PAUSE = 1 TO 10 : NEXT
   PAUSE : GOTO 20
200 REM
210 REM *** PLOT POINT ***
220 REM
230 PRINT CHR$(253) : POKE 656,0
240 PLOT X,Y
250 RETURN
300 REM
310 REM *** DRAWTO POINT ***
320 REM
330 PRINT CHR$(253) : FOR J = 1 TO 50 : NEXT
    J : PRINT CHR$(253) : POKE 656,0
340 DRAWTO X,Y
350 RETURN
```

Animation

We have spent a good deal of time working on charts in the various GRAPHICS mode since it is important to see the practical applications of such graphics. Often users simply see screen graphics as something to draw mosaic pictures on and nothing else; however, as we have seen, it is possible to make very good practical use of them as well. Now let's have a little fun with animation before going on to player/missile graphics. To do so we will return to keyboard graphics since they give us several different little shapes to move.

Animation in keyboard graphics can be used in games and for special effects. However, we will touch upon only some elementary examples to provide you with the concepts of how animation works. Basically, by placing a figure on the keyboard, covering it up, and then putting it in a new position, you can create the illusion of moving figures. It works in exactly the same way as animated cartoons. A series of frames are flashed on the screen sequentially. Even though each individual frame has a stationary figure, by rapidly flashing a series of such frames, the figures appear to move. Your computer does the same thing. For example, the following little program appears to bounce a ball in the upper left hand corner:

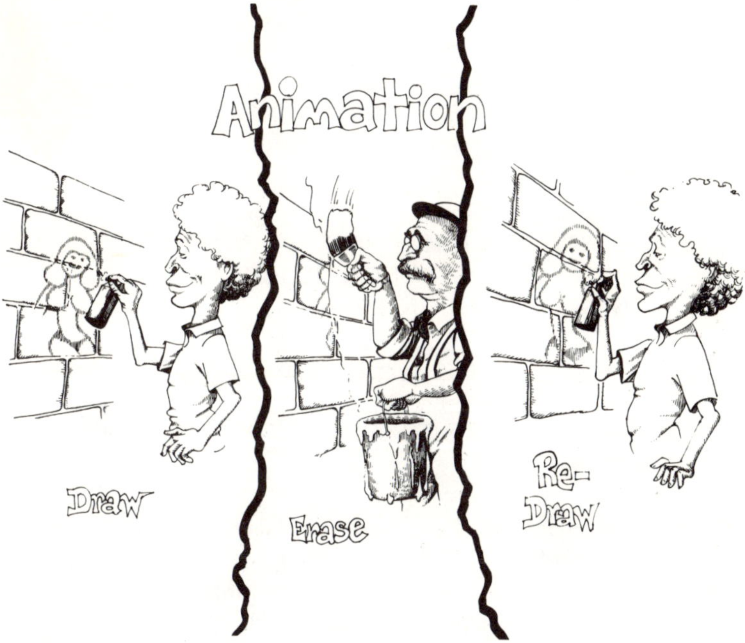


```
10 PRINT CHR$(125) : POKE 755,Ø
2Ø PRINT "(CTRL-T) " : REM SPACE BETWEEN
   CTRL-T AND SECOND QUOTATION MARK
3Ø FOR I = 1 TO 1ØØ : NEXT I
4Ø PRINT CHR$ (28); " (CTRL-T)" : REM
   SPACE BETWEEN FIRST QUOTATION MARK
   AND CTRL-T
5Ø FOR I = 1 TO 1ØØ : NEXT I
6Ø PRINT CHR$(28);: GOTO 2Ø
```

What appeared to be a moving "ball" was actually a figure being placed on the screen, erased, and then placed in a different location. Now, let's do the same thing on the vertical axis. Also, just for fun, let's add some sound and special effects.

```
10 PRINT CHR$(125) : POKE 755,0
   :REM *** REMOVE CURSOR AND BEGIN
   ANIMATION BLOCK ***
20 FOR I = 0 TO 22
30 POSITION 20,I : PRINT "(CTRL-T)" : REM A
   WHITE BALL WILL APPEAR ON YOUR SCREEN
40 FOR J = 1 TO 50 : NEXT J : REM DELAY
   LOOP TO SLOW MOVEMENT
50 POSITION 20,I : PRINT "(SPACE)" : REM PUTS
   SPACE WHERE BALL WAS
60 NEXT I
70 GOSUB 200
90 POSITION 20,I : PRINT "*" : END : REM
   *** END ANIMATION BLOCK ***
200 REM *** SOUND EFFECTS ***
210 SOUND 0,128,12,14
220 FOR DU = 1 TO 50 : NEXT DU
    : REM SET DURATION
240 SOUND 0,0,0,0 : REM TURN OFF SOUND
250 RETURN
```

By experimenting with different algorithms, you can create a wide range of effects. If you have played arcade games with movement and sound, you now have an idea of how they were created. Now, go ahead and start working on that SUPER SPACE BLASTER ALIEN EATER game.

Player/Missile Graphics

Now that we have an idea of how to go about using graphics on the different graphics screens, let's take a look at a very powerful aspect of your ATARI: player/missile graphics. First, we'll have to explain what player/missiles are and what you may want to use them for. Essentially, a player/missile is a figure in memory. Depending on what you place in special memory locations, you will get different figures or player/missiles. They can be used in animation and game development, but they also may be used to liven up virtually any presentation.

The good news about player/missiles in your ATARI is that you have a tremendous amount of control in their creation since you enter them in a translated binary code. The bad news is that they are a bit tricky to understand. However, if we organize ourselves into the basic components of programming player/missiles, the effort will be worth the trouble. To pique your interest let's start with a simple example. Key in the following, and you will get a little "Player/Missile Rocket." We'll explain what happened later on, but for now, key in the program and watch what happens.

```
10 PRINT CHR$(125)
20 X = 50 : Y = 50 : REM X (HORIZONTAL) AND Y
   (VERTICAL) COORDINATES OF PLAYER/MISSILE
30 TOR = PEEK (106) - 8 : REM FIND TOP OF
   RAM AND SUBTRACT 8
40 POKE 54279, TOR : REM STORE HIGH BYTE
   OF TOR AT THIS ADDRESS
50 PMB = 256 * TOR : REM PLAYER/MISSILE BEGIN
60 RES = 559 : POKE RES,46 : REM POKE RESolution
   46 FOR DOUBLE OR 64 FOR SINGLE
70 ENABLE = 53277 : POKE ENABLE, 3 : REM 3
   TO ENABLE AND 0 TO DISABLE
80 HOR = 53248 : POKE HOR, X : REM HORIZONTAL
   POSITION FOR PLAYER #0
90 P0 = 512 : REM PLAYER #0
100 REM
110 REM ******************************************
120 REM SET UP PLAYER DATA FOR PLAYER #0
130 REM ******************************************
140 REM
150 FOR I = PMB + P0 TO PMB + P0 + 128 : POKE I,0
    : NEXT I : REM CLEAR OUT PLAYER #0
160 C0 = 704 : POKE C0, 3 * 16 + 6 : REM
    COLOR FOR PLAYER #0
170 REM COLOR IS 16 TIMES COLOR VALUE
    PLUS LUMINANCE - COLOR 3 = RED/ORANGE
200 REM
```

```
210 REM ***********************
220 REM POKE IN PLAYER #0
230 REM ***********************
240 REM
250 FOR I = PMB + P0 + Y TO PMB + P0 + 6 + Y
    : READ D : POKE I,D : NEXT I
260 REM 6 = NUMBER OF DATA ELEMENTS -1
300 REM
310 REM ********************
320 REM MOVE PLAYER #0
330 REM ********************
340 REM
350 FOR I = X TO X + 150 : POKE HOR, I : NEXT I
400 REM
410 REM ***************
420 REM PLAYER DATA
430 REM ***************
440 REM
450 DATA 192, 224, 62, 127, 62, 224, 192
```

Now if everything is done correctly, you should see a little "space rocket" move horizontally across your screen. There's a lot more you can do with player/missiles, but let's use the above example to explain what is happening. The first concept to examine is that of binary arithmetic. If we conceive of our player/missiles as little dots on the screen which are together in blocks, we can understand both binary math and player/missiles. To begin, we will examine an 8 bit byte, numbered from 7 to ∅, each containing a ∅ or 1 — the only two numbers in the binary system.

7	6	5	4	3	2	1	∅
∅	1	∅	1	1	∅	1	∅

For your computer to do math, it must convert everything into the binary system, and the 65∅2 microprocessor in your ATARI does this in chunks called bytes 8 bits long. The above binary number ∅1∅11∅1∅ is translated into the decimal number 9∅, and whenever you key in 9∅, your computer translates it into ∅1∅11∅1∅.

It makes this conversion automatically, but in order to make player/missiles, it will be necessary for you to do it. However, it is really quite simple. In binary arithmetic, since we have only two digits, whenever we run out of unique combinations, we tack on a ∅ to the end and start over again. We do the same in decimal math. For example, when we get to 9 in decimal, we start over with a 1 and tack on a ∅ to get 1∅. Couting in binary, we have the following:

∅ = ∅
1 = 1
1∅ = 2
11 = 3
1∅∅ = 4
1∅1 = 5
11∅ = 6
111 = 7
1∅∅∅ = 8

It's just like when we reach 9, 99, or 999, we start over with 1 and add another digit. In binary, we start over with 11, 111, 1111, etc. since we only have ∅ and 1 to work with. However, because we are not used to working in a binary system, we have to have a simple way to convert binary to decimal. To make it simple for you, the following little program will automatically convert binary into decimal.

BINARY TO DECIMAL CONVERSION

```
1Ø PRINT CHR$(125)
2Ø DIM H$(9) : DIM AN$(1)
3Ø PRINT "BIN:";: INPUT H$
4Ø IF H$ = "Q" THEN END : REM PRESS 'Q' TO QUIT
5Ø IF LEN (H$) < > 8 THEN PRINT CHR$(125)
   : PRINT : GOTO 3Ø
6Ø D1 = VAL (H$(1,1)) * 128 + VAL(H$(2,2))
   * 64 + VAL (H$(3,3)) * 32
7Ø D2 = VAL (H$(4,4)) * 16 + VAL (H$(5,5)) * 8 + VAL
   (H$(6,6)) * 4 + VAL (H$(7,7)) * 2 + VAL (H$(8))
8Ø DECIMAL = D1 + D2
9Ø PRINT : PRINT "DECIMAL= ";DECIMAL
1ØØ POSITION 5,2Ø : PRINT "{ATARI-KEY} HIT
    RETURN TO CONTINUE {ATARI-KEY}";
    : INPUT AN$
11Ø PRINT CHR$(125) : PRINT : GOTO 3Ø
```

Another simple way of making conversions is to remember that each bit has a different value depending on whether there is a Ø or 1 in the bit. Let's look at these values and how they can be used for conversion:

"On Value"	128	64	32	16	8	4	2	1	
Bit Number	7	6	5	4	3	2	1	Ø	
	Ø	1	Ø	1	1	Ø	1	Ø	
	Ø +	64 +	Ø +	16 +	8 +	Ø +	2 +	Ø	= 9Ø

To get our decimal value (9Ø), just add the sum of the "on values."

Now the obvious question is "Why bother?" Well, since player/missiles are made up of little dots or pixels which are created by the various bits being ON, we can create any shapes we want by turning on the combination of bits we want. Then by converting the binary patterns to decimal, we can POKE in the bit patterns from BASIC. To begin, let's see how our "space rocket" in the above program was created. Here's what you'll need:

1. Some graph paper.
2. A pencil and clean eraser
3. A ruler

On the graph paper, draw an 8 wide by 7 long matrix. (The width has to be 8, but the length of figures can be longer or shorter.) We will use the binary conversion program to enter the numbers from the leftmost square or bit to the rightmost square in the byte.

Let's take a look at the following figure and see how the player/missile data is created.

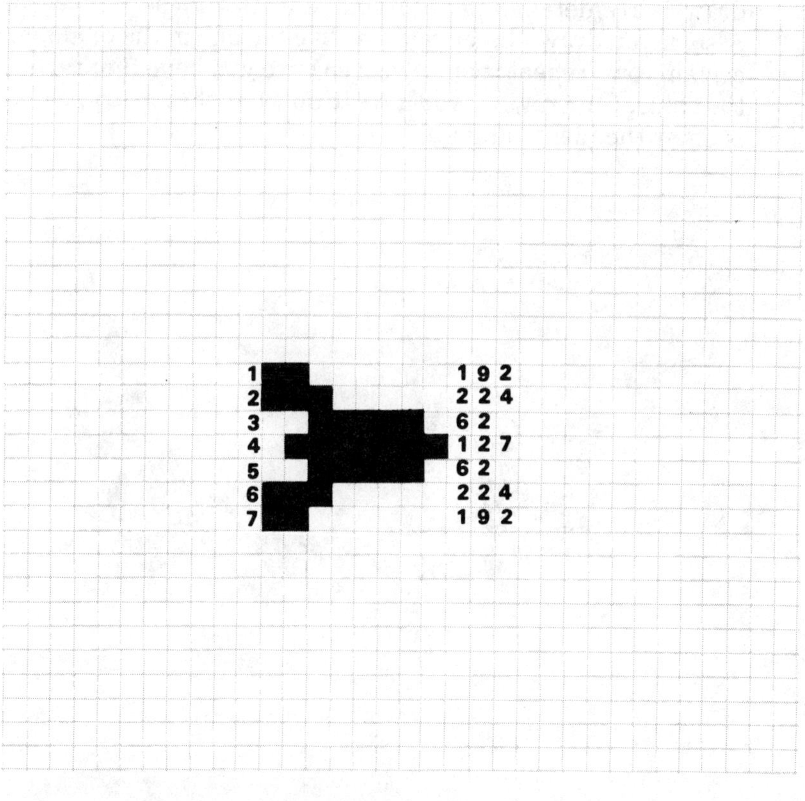

Let's look at Row #1 and see how we converted a piece of our drawing.

ROW #1

"On Value"	128	64	32	16	8	4	2	1
Bit Number	7	6	5	4	3	2	1	Ø
	1	1	Ø	Ø	Ø	Ø	Ø	Ø

128 + 64 + Ø + Ø + Ø + Ø + Ø + Ø = 192

Now, while the process is admittedly somewhat involved and exacting, it is more a matter of organization than complexity. After all, it is relatively simple to draw a player/missile on graph paper once you have your plot set up, and since you can draw fairly detailed shapes your efforts will be rewarded. Also, if you draw player/missiles like the one in the example, certain rows repeat themselves; so once you have figured out the values for a row, all you have to do when they are repeated is enter the identical data.

SAVE YOUR PLAYER/MISSILES

Once you have figured out a player/missile and have all the data laid out, it would be wise to save that player/missile to disk. By using line numbers over 4ØØ in subsequent applications, just load the data for the player/missile into memory, and then program the parameters from lower line numbers. (i.e. commands which turn on graphics, order moves, READ DATA, etc.) This will save you the trouble of having to re-do figures you have already worked out. Also, you can change part of your player/missile to make new player/missiles. So if you save your player/missile drawings, you can add or modify lines; then, rather than having to begin all over again, simply by adding new DATA you can modify existing player/missiles to create what appear to be entirely new ones. (In the next chapter we will see how player/missiles can be saved with LIST, making their inclusion into new programs even easier.)

Now that we see how to create player/missiles, the next step is to get them to do tricks for us. First of all, we have to be aware of the layout of the area through which we move. It does not matter what screen is used in moving your player/missiles. In fact, if you add a line at the beginning of our example program for GRAPHICS 2, 3, 4 — right on up to GRAPHICS 8 — the little rocket will act the same as it does on the default GRAPHICS Ø screen. (Go ahead and try it!) In our example, we used only part of the available vertical area for a player missile — seven out of a possible 256. However, we did use the entire eight horizontal pixels available to us.

Movement is through an independent screen, superimposed on any current graphics screen. Roughly, horizontal can be from Ø to 256, and for most practical purposes, the maximum Y (vertical) value is 12Ø. Horizontal movement is accomplished by changing the value of the horizontal register (53248 for Player #Ø). The movement created by rapid change of this register is smooth and animated, but vertical movement is more complicated and slower. By changing the value of Y and entering the different values into the register, it will appear to move to different locations. A little trick with vertical movement is to have a Ø value in the first and last bytes of your player/missile. In this way, it is possible, incrementing the vertical position by 1, to smoothly redraw the player/missile in consecutive vertical positions without smearing the screen with the last or first byte. The following little program shows how to move diagonally. We will use our rocket, but we have added a Ø to the first and last bytes (Ø's in the first and last DATA statements). Don't write this entire program! Take the ORIGINAL PROGRAM and using your EDITOR, just make the necessary changes!

```
10 PRINT CHR$(125)
20 REM X (HORIZONTAL) AND Y (VERTICAL)
   COORDINATES) OF PLAYER/MISSILE ARE
   DEFINED IN MOVEMENT SECTION
30 TOR = PEEK (106) - 8 : REM FIND TOP OF
   RAM AND SUBTRACT 8
40 POKE 54279, TOR : REM STORE HIGH BYTE
   OF TOR AT THIS ADDRESS
50 PMB = 256 * TOR : REM PLAYER/MISSILE BEGIN
60 RES = 559 : POKE RES,46 : REM POKE RESolution
   46 FOR DOUBLE OR 62 FOR SINGLE
70 ENABLE = 53277 : POKE ENABLE, 3 : REM 3
   TO ENABLE AND Ø TO DISABLE
80 HOR = 53248 : REM HORIZONTAL POSITION
   FOR PLAYER #Ø
90 PØ = 512 : REM PLAYER #Ø
100 REM
110 REM ******************************************
120 REM CLEAR PLAYER DATA AREA AND
    SET COLOR
130 REM ******************************************
140 REM
150 FOR I = PMB + PØ TO PMB + PØ + 128
    : POKE I, Ø : NEXT I :
    REM CLEAR OUT PLAYER #Ø
160 CØ = 7Ø4 : POKE CØ, 3 * 16 + 6 : REM
    COLOR FOR PLAYER #Ø
170 REM COLOR IS 16 TIMES COLOR VALUE
    PLUS LUMINANCE - COLOR 3 = RED/ORANGE
300 REM
```

```
310 REM ******************************************
320 REM MOVE & CREATE PLAYER #0 IN X AND
    Y DIRECTIONS
330 REM ******************************************
340 REM
350 FOR Y = 20 TO 100
360 RESTORE : X = Y : POKE HOR, X
370 FOR I = PMB + P0 + Y TO PMB + P0 + 8 + Y
    : READ D : POKE I, D : NEXT I
380 NEXT Y
400 REM
410 REM *****************
420 REM PLAYER DATA
430 REM *****************
440 REM
450 DATA 0, 192, 224, 62, 127, 62, 224, 192, 0
460 REM NOTE 0'S TACKED ON TO BEGINNING
    AND END OF DATA
```

At this point, before going on to multiple players, missiles, and other features of these special graphics, let's stop and go over the first program to see exactly what we did. It is important to use descriptive variables and lots of REM statements with these graphics since we will be using more than a single player and missile. To keep it all straight and to help in understanding, use the variables and REM statements. It takes up memory, but even on the smallest ATARI 400, you have plenty of room for these examples. Don't worry about understanding everything at this point, but with time and practice, you will see the importance of the organizing concepts we are using. We will now go over the program step by step.

Step 1 LINES 10-20. In line 10 we simply cleared the screen. Since player/missiles will crash right on through anything on the screen, it is very important to clear things up first. In line 20, we defined the initial X and Y coordinates using the variables X and Y. (Better to be clear than original!)

Step 2 LINES 30-50. The first thing we did was to locate the Top Of Ram (TOR) and subtract 8. This value is used in lines 40 and 50. First, in line 40, we store TOR in location 54279, a special address used in player/missile graphics. Then, in line 5Ø, we use the value in TOR times 256 to define our Player/Missile Begin (or PMBASE as it is also called). These same lines are used in all player/missile graphic programs.

Step 3 LINES 6Ø-9Ø. The decimal memory address which controls RESolution is at 559, so we defined RES = 559. Then we POKEd RES with 46 for double resolution. Had we wanted single resolution, we would have POKEd RES with 62. Likewise, to ENABLE our player/missiles, we defined the enable/disable address as ENABLE and POKEd it with 3 to crank up our player/missiles. A Ø to ENABLE will turn them off. Next we defined the HORizontal position register of Player #Ø to HOR. Player #Ø horizontal register is 53248. (Since each player and missile has an individual horizontal position register, we should have defined it as HPØ or some similar name, but for the first time around, I wanted to be a bit more descriptive with this register.) The following are the values for different horizontal positions registers for all four players and missiles along with variable names we will use:

HP# = Horizontal position player #.
HM# = Horizontal position missile #.
HPØ = 53248
HP1 = 53249
HP2 = 5325Ø
HP3 = 53251
HMØ = 53252
HM1 = 53253
HM2 = 53254
HM3 = 53255

As we will see, it is important to have individual registers for both players and missiles. This is because you may want to separate a missile from a player. (e.g., Blast the heathens!)

Finally, we defined Player #Ø as PØ. There are offsets for each player using double and single resolution. The offset values for double and single resolution are:

DOUBLE	SINGLE
PØ = 512	PØ = 1Ø24
P1 = 64Ø	P1 = 128Ø
P2 = 768	P2 = 1536
P3 = 896	P3 = 1792

Step 4 LINES 1ØØ-17Ø. The first thing we must do is to clear the player/missile area in memory we are going to use. This is 128 bytes we want to fill with Ø's. Each player has the same number of bytes, so using the 128 offset will clear any player we want. Next, we set the color. Each player/missile has its own color register, as follows:

CØ = 7Ø4
C1 = 7Ø5
C2 = 7Ø6
C3 = 7Ø7

Using the formula COLOR * 16 + LUMINANCE, we can create 16 hues (Ø-15) with 8 different luminances. That's 128 different colors! (The bad guys are green, remember.)

Step 5 LINES 2ØØ-26Ø. In all those REM statements, only line 25Ø is relevant. Using the values we generated or defined, we now create a player. We made a loop beginning at the Player Missile Begin + Player Missile # + Vertical position and ending at that location plus the number of bytes minus one. This gave us the correct range of addresses to store the player DATA.

Step 6 LINES 3ØØ-35Ø. This block too has only one significant line. Line 35Ø sets up a loop using the horizontal position X, which we defined with a beginning value of 5Ø, and using it we POKE the HOR (for horizontal placement) variable. This makes our play move.

Step 7 LINES 4ØØ-45Ø. Among the REM statements, we stuck our DATA in line 45Ø for the player we created on graph paper.

Now, if we keep things straight with variables defining offsets and registers rather than trying to remember a whole slew of numbers, writing more complex programs is much easier. By and large, we let the computer do the figuring rather than try and do it ourselves. For example, we could multiply our desired color values by 16 and add the luminance and put in a single number when POKEing in the player/missile colors. However, when we go back and read that program, we probably wouldn't have the slightest idea of what that number means. In fact, we could have entered POKE 7Ø4, 54 and had the same results as POKE CØ, 3 * 16 + 6, but which one is clearer? (You said, "Neither?")

Expanding Players

Each player has three possible relative sizes: normal, double, and triple. It is a simple matter to change the sizes of players, since each has a Size register. By POKEing a Ø, 1 or 3 into the register address, the player/missile will appear in single, double or triple size respectively. The values for the different registers are as follows:

SIZE REGISTERS

SØ = 53256
S1 = 53257
S2 = 53258
S3 = 53259

To test this out, enter the following line in our original program:

```
170 SØ = 53256 : POKE SØ, 1
```

That will give you a double sized player/missile. If you POKE SØ with 3, your player/missile will be triple sized. By changing the sizes of your player/missiles, you can make them appear to get closer or further away. Experiment with them!

MULTIPLE PLAYERS

In order to have multiple player/missiles, it is necessary to enter data into a different part of memory and control a second, third, and even fourth player missile. Again, rather than rewriting an entire new program, let's just fix up our first one to include another player/missile. (If there are extra player/missiles in memory, either by POKEing the player/missile locations with Ø's or turning off your computer, you can clear out the unwanted player/missiles.)

```
1Ø PRINT CHR$(125)
2Ø X=Ø : Y=5Ø : REM SET X AND Y COORDINATES
3Ø TOR = PEEK (1Ø6)-8 : REM FIND TOP OF
   RAM AND SUBTRACT 8
4Ø POKE 54279, TOR : REM STORE HIGH BYTE
   OF TOR AT THIS ADDRESS
5Ø PMB=256*TOR : REM PLAYER/MISSILE BEGIN
6Ø RES=559 : POKE RES,46 : REM POKE RESolution
   46 FOR DOUBLE OR 62 FOR SINGLE
7Ø ENABLE = 53277 : POKE ENABLE, 3 : REM 3
   TO ENABLE AND Ø TO DISABLE
8Ø HØ = 53248 : H1 = 53249 :REM HORIZONTAL
   POSITION FOR PLAYER #Ø AND PLAYER #1
9Ø PØ = 512 : P1 = 64Ø : REM OFFSETS FOR
   PLAYERS #Ø AND #1
1ØØ REM
11Ø REM ***********************************
12Ø REM CLEAR PLAYER DATA AREA AND
                   SET COLOR
13Ø REM ***********************************
14Ø REM
15Ø FOR I = PMB + PØ TO PMB + PØ + 128
    : POKE I,Ø: NEXT I: REM CLEAR OUT PLAYER #Ø
155 FOR I = PMB + P1 TO PMB + P1 + 128
    : POKE I,Ø: NEXT I: REM CLEAR OUT PLAYER #1
16Ø CØ = 7Ø4 : POKE CØ, 3 * 16 + 6 : C1 = 7Ø5
    : POKE C1, 6 * 16 + 6 : REM COLOR
    FOR PLAYERS #Ø & #1
17Ø REM COLOR IS 16 TIMES COLOR VALUE PLUS
    LUMINANCE - COLOR 3 = RED/ORANGE &
    COLOR 6 = PURPLE/BLUE
```

```
200 REM
210 REM *****************************
220 REM CREATE PLAYERS #0 & #1
230 REM *****************************
240 REM
250 FOR I = PMB + P0 + Y TO PMB + P0 + 6 + Y:
READ D : POKE I, D : NEXT I
260 FOR I = PMB + P1 + Y + 10 TO PMB + P1 + 6 + Y
    + 10 : READ D1 : POKE I, D1 : NEXT I
270 REM NOTE THAT AN 'OFFSET' OF 10 WAS
    ADDED TO THE Y VALUE FOR PLAYER #1
280 REM THIS WAS SO THAT THE PLAYERS WOULD
    BE IN DIFFERENT VERTICAL LOCATIONS
300 REM
310 REM ***************************
320 REM MOVE PLAYERS #0 & #1
330 REM ***************************
340 REM
350 FOR I = X TO 255 : POKE H0, I : POKE
    H1, 255-I : NEXT I
360 REM HAVE PLAYERS FLY IN OPPOSITE
    DIRECTIONS
400 REM
410 REM *******************
420 REM PLAYER DATA
430 REM *******************
440 REM
450 DATA 192, 224, 62, 127, 62, 224, 192
460 DATA 7, 15, 126, 252, 126, 15, 7
```

We've been referring to player/missiles, but we haven't done anything with the missiles. To understand missiles, you'll have to put on your thinking cap a little; they are not quite like players, but in most ways they are. Missiles reside in the offset from 384 to 511, right below Player #Ø. However, they are separated "horizontally" instead of "vertically," as are players. For example, the offset for Player Ø begins at 512, Player 1 at 64Ø and so forth. However, all the missiles, Ø-3, reside in the same memory. To access a missile, you have to carve up a byte into 4 parts:

MISSILE MEMORY STORAGE

"On Value"	128	64	32	16	8	4	2	1
Bit Number	7	6	5	4	3	2	1	Ø
	M3		M2		M1		MØ	

Each missile only occupies a part of each byte. Therefore, to access *Missile Ø*, instead of POKEing in the missile in a range of addresses between 384 and 511, simply POKE in *any* address in that range and 1 or 2. For *Missile 3*, you would POKE in 64 or 128, for *Missile 2*, 16 or 32 and for *Missile 1*, 4 or 8. Now let's take a look at a program using a missile. We'll use our rocket, and while we're at it, we make some sound effects for "shooting" our missile.

```
10 PRINT CHR$(125)
20 X = 50 : Y = 60
30 TOR = PEEK (106) - 8 : POKE 54279, TOR
40 PMB = 256 * TOR
50 RES = 559 : POKE RES, 46 : ENABLE = 53277
   : POKE ENABLE,3
60 HOR = 53248 : POKE HOR, X : MHOR =
   53252 : REM MHOR IS THE MISSILE'S
   HORIZONTAL REGISTER
70 P1 = 512 : MISSILE =384 : MOFFSET = 3 : REM
   MOFFSET IS TO PUT THE MISSILE IN THE
   MIDDLE OF OUR PLAYER
80 FOR I = PMB + MISSILE TO PMB + P1 + 128
   : POKE I,0 : NEXT I : REM CLEAR MISSILE AND
   PLAYER AREAS
90 C1 = 704 : POKE C1, 3 * 16 + 6
100 PSIZE = 53256 : POKE PSIZE, 1 : REM
    DOUBLE SIZE PLAYER
110 FOR I = PMB + P1 + Y TO PMB + P1 + Y + 6
    : READ D : POKE I,D : NEXT I
120 POKE PMB + MISSILE + Y + MOFFSET,2 : REM
    CREATE MISSILE 0
130 SOUND 0, 90, 8, 15
140 FOR PAUSE = 1 TO 50 : NEXT PAUSE
150 SOUND 0, 0, 0, 0
```

```
160 FOR X = 55 TO 255 : POKE MHOR,X : NEXT
    X : REM FIRE MISSILE
170 GOTO 130
200 DATA 192, 224, 62, 127, 62, 224, 192
```

Line 120 is where we create our missile. We used the offset MOFFSET in order to put the missile right on the nose of our rocket. Otherwise, it would have been up on the top fin. The register MHOR controls the horizontal movement of the missile, and the vertical control is the same as the Y value which places the player vertically.

Moving Player/Missiles with the Paddles

Another important aspect of moving player/missiles is using them with paddles. The horizontal movement is excellent, but the vertical is somewhat clunky without more advanced techniques. Basically, you define the horizontal (X) movement as one paddle and the vertical (Y) movement as another. We will use PADDLE(0) as our horizontal controller and PADDLE(1) as the vertical. (Just edit your original program to put this in!)

PLAYER PADDLE MOVEMENT

```
10 PRINT CHR$(125)
20 X = PADDLE(0) : Y = PADDLE(1)
30 TOR = PEEK (106) - 8 : POKE 54279, TOR
40 PMB = 256 * TOR
50 RES = 559 : POKE RES, 46 : ENABLE = 53277
   : POKE ENABLE,3
60 HOR = 53248 : POKE HOR, X
70 P1 = 512
80 FOR I = PMB + P1 TO PMB + P1 + 128 : POKE
   I,0 : NEXT I
90 C1 = 704 : POKE C1, 3 * 16 + 6
100 PSIZE = 53256 : POKE PSIZE, 1
110 Y = PADDLE(1) : IF Y > 80 THEN Y = 80
120 IF Y < 20 THEN Y = 20
130 FOR I = PMB + P1 TO PMB + P1 + 128 : POKE
    I,0 : NEXT I
140 FOR I = PMB + P1 + Y TO PMB + P1 + Y + 6
    : READ D : POKE I,D : NEXT I
```

```
150 X = PADDLE(0) : POKE HOR,X
160 RESTORE : IF PADDLE(1) > Y + 1 OR
     PADDLE(1) < Y - 1 THEN 110
170 GOTO 150
200 DATA 192, 224, 62, 127, 62, 224, 192
```

As you will see, the vertical movement is slow and seems to bounce rather than rise smoothly. That's because it has to be redrawn every time the Y value in PADDLE(1) changes more than plus or minus one. However, if you leave PADDLE(1) alone, you will see how easy it is to move the player horizontally.

The final characteristic of player/missile graphics we should cover is single line resolution. Here, the players look less blocky, but they take up more memory. Basically, to get single line resolution we change a few parameters of our variables. (By the way, you should now see the value of using variables instead numbers all the time, since in this next program, all we have to do is change a few variables.)

SINGLE LINE RESOLUTION

```
10 PRINT CHR$(125)
20 GR. 4 + 16 : X = 0 : Y = 100 : REM USE FULL
   SCREEN GRAPHICS MODE 4
30 TOR = PEEK (106) - 8 : POKE 54279, TOR
40 PMB = 256 * TOR
50 RES = 559 : POKE RES, 62 : ENABLE = 53277 :
   POKE ENABLE,3 : REM CHANGE RES
   FROM 46 TO 62
60 HOR = 53248 : POKE HOR, X
70 P1 = 1024 : REM PLAYER 0 IN SINGLE
   LINE RESOLUTION
80 FOR I = PMB + P1 TO PMB + P1 + 256 : POKE
   I,0 : NEXT I : REM NOTE CHANGE
   FROM 128 TO 256
90 C1 = 704 : POKE C1, 3 * 16 + 6
100 PSIZE = 53256 : POKE PSIZE, 0
110 FOR I = PMB + P1 + Y TO PMB + P1 + Y + 6
    : READ D : POKE I,D : NEXT I
120 FOR X = 0 TO 255 : POKE HOR,X : NEXT X
130 GOTO 120
200 DATA 192, 224, 62, 127, 62, 224, 192
```

That's about it for player/missiles; whatever you want to do with them is left to your imagination. They are a bit more complicated than what we have dealt with previously, but if you remember to organize your programs into blocks, have recognizable variables, and pay attention to the sequence, there is a great deal you can do with player/missiles. You may have noticed that animation is actually simpler with player/missiles than with previous animation we studied. We did not have to follow our player/missiles with an erase, and you might notice that one player/missile can pass behind another. If you want, you can even control whether a player/missile passes in front of or behind another player or the background using register 623. The following parameters are used:

PRIORITY = 623

POKE PRIORITY, 1 : All the players have priority over the background.

POKE PRIORITY, 2 : Players Ø and 1 first, then the background, and then Players 2 and 4

POKE PRIORITY, 4 : The background has priority over all players.

POKE PRIORITY, 8 : Playfield registers Ø and 1, then all the players, and then Playfield registers 2 and 3.

Experiment with the priority registers. We did not use them in our examples simply to keep things as simple as possible. So, while there is a good deal of figuring to be done, there is more you can create with player/missiles than with other forms of animation.

SUMMARY

This chapter has taken us into the world of computer graphics. Beginning with screen graphics, we saw how we could mix graphics and text together to create graphs. Then we saw how we could animate screen figures by putting them in different screen locations, erasing them, and then re-entering them at another location. We also found out how to color our graphics both from the keyboard and from POKEing the color screen on top of the figures we had entered. By programming with "offsets" we were able to coordinate our figures and colors.

The final part of our exploration into graphics took us into the world of player/missiles. Beginning with a drawing on graph paper, we transferred our creations to the computer's memory by translating our figures into binary images. Then we learned how to store the information into memory and bring out an animated player/missile. Next, we added color and expanded both the size of our player/missiles and their placement on the screen. Finally, we saw how to create and animate multiple player/missiles simultaneously.

As a final note on graphics, it should be pointed out that besides being fun and artistic, computer graphics can be put to other practical uses as well. We saw, for example, how to create graphs with screen graphics, but you can also use player/missile graphics in programs to make them clearer and more interesting. We naturally think of games when working with player/missiles and animation, but do not limit your use of graphics to the obvious. Also, see how they can be employed to enhance information for your computer or used in some other creative manner.

CHAPTER 8

Data and Text Files with the Tape and Disk System

Introduction

In this chapter we are going to learn more about some advanced applications with the tape and disk system. First, we will look at some additional commands for saving information to tape and disk as well as doing other programming chores. These new forms of saving information will allow you to load different parts of a program from separate files. Secondly, we will be covering two types of files: (1) Data files, and (2) Sequential files. There are many similarities between data and sequential files, and once you've learned one, the other will be simple. Your disk system's data files are a type of sequential file, and we might even consider the way in which your cassette stores data to be a form of sequential text file. However, for the sake of clarity we will discuss each separately.

Before beginning, I want to point out that the ATARI 81Ø and 1Ø5Ø floppy disk systems are very sophisticated and smart devices. For beginners, it can be difficult to understand some of a disk drive's more advanced applications, and there is a very real risk of destroying programs and data on your disk. Therefore, in this section, we will take each step slowly and, even at the risk of redundancy, explain the various functions of commands dealing with your disk system. Also, we will not be dealing with the most advanced features of the disk operating system, for they are beyond the scope of this book. However, we will be going to a middle range of sophistication, and it is strongly advised for those of you with a disk system to use a blank formatted disk on which you have *not* accumulated programs. By doing so you will not inadvertently destroy valuable data and programs. (This comes from the voice of experience, having clobbered numerous disks myself!)

Listing and Entering Programs to Cassette and Disk

Up to this point, all we have used the LIST command for is to look at the contents of our programs. It is possible to use LIST to save programs to cassette or disk as well, and programs saved in this manner can be loaded with ENTER. The advantage of using this method is that you can save just a portion of your program and then ENTER it into memory without destroying the contents of memory. For example, let's say that you have labored long and hard on graph paper to create several player/missiles. Instead of having to key them in anew every time you want to use them in a program, wouldn't it be nice simply to tack them onto a program? Or even better, what if you have several routines you've created and you want to use these routines in various programs without having to key them in anew every time you use them. That's exactly what LIST and ENTER allow you to do.

To use these, let's load into memory the program we wrote in Chapter 7 to illustrate player/missiles. Now enter the following:

```
CASSETTE USERS
LIST "C:", 450 <RETURN> Press REC/PLAY
<RETURN>
DISK USERS
LIST "D1: PMDATA" , 45Ø
```

What we did was save only line 45Ø, the line with our player/missile DATA. If we had not entered any line numbers, the entire program would have been recorded on cassette or diskette, or if we had entered a range of lines (e.g., 4ØØ, 5ØØ) the specified range of line numbers would have been saved.

Now let's try a little experiment. Clear memory with NEW, and enter the following little program:

```
1Ø PRINT CHR$(125)
2Ø FOR I = 1 TO 7
3Ø READ D
4Ø PRINT D
5Ø NEXT I
```

Cassette users should rewind their tape and key in:

ENTER "C:" <RETURN> Press PLAY <RETURN>

Disk users key in:

ENTER "D1: PMDATA" <RETURN>

Once your READY prompt returns, enter RUN. Voila! Your program now has DATA to read, and it did not get clobbered when you used ENTER as it does with CLOAD or LOAD. LIST your program to make sure that line 45Ø has been added. Experiment with different program parts to see how you can use the LIST and ENTER commands with your program recorder and disk drive. As you begin writing often-used subroutines, you can save them with LIST and create all kinds of different programs simply by ENTERing different segments rather than keying them in over and over again.

OPEN, GET and PUT

There is another way to input data that we have not yet examined. Usually, when we have data to input, we use the INPUT statement in our programs. However, if we want only a single key to enter information without having to press RETURN, the GET statement is handy. We have not discussed it until now since it is necessary to use the OPEN command to access an "Input/Output Control Block" or IOCB. To use GET it is necessary to direct input to the keyboard with OPEN. We use the following format with OPEN:

OPEN, (Ref. number 1-5), (Code number), (Auxiliary code), ("File designation : title")

As we look further into files, we will provide the various parameters used with OPEN, but for now, we will see how to use GET with the keyboard and OPEN. Enter the following program:

```
1Ø PRINT CHR$(125)
2Ø OPEN #5, 4, Ø, "K:" : REM THE "K:" INDICATES
'KEYBOARD'
```

```
30 PRINT "PRESS ONE KEY"
40 GET #5, V
50 PRINT V
60 PRINT CHR$(V)
70 CLOSE #5
```

Let's go over this step by step so that you can see what happened:

Step 1 LINES 10-20. Clear the screen in line 10. In line 20, we used the Reference Number 5. We could have used any number between 1 and 5 (and sometimes 6 and 7). The second number, '4', is a code for an input operation. The third number is '0', indicating no special device dependent auxiliary is required. Finally, we used "K:" to indicate the keyboard, just as we have used "C:" for cassette and "D:" for disk drive.

Step 2 LINES 30-40. Line 30 prompts the user to press a key, and line 40 GETs the key in the variable 'V'. The value of GET is the ATASCII value of the key pressed. Note that we used the #5 reference we set up in the OPEN statement in line 20.

Step 3 LINES 50-70. First we printed out the value of V, and then to show that V was equal to the CHR$ value of V, we PRINTed CHR$(V). Finally, we CLOSEd the channel we had opened, #5.

Now that we can see how to use GET to input a single byte, let's look at PUT, which outputs a single byte. Try the following program, and note that the output device is "S:" for 'screen'. (We would not want *output* to the keyboard!)

```
10 PRINT CHR$(125)
20 OPEN #3, 8, 0, "S:"
30 FOR I = 0 TO 255
40 IF I = 125 THEN NEXT I
50 PUT #3, I
60 NEXT I
70 CLOSE #3
```

When you RUN this program, notice how the output was formatted. Usually when there is no semi-colon after a symbol output to the screen, there is a line feed. However, with the PUT statement, the output begins in the upper lefthand corner and each symbol is placed into the next location. To see something really interesting, delete line 1Ø. LIST the program so that there's something on the screen and RUN the program again. As you will see, the screen is still cleared, and the output begins in the upper left hand corner. Remember this when using PUT.

Data Files and Your Cassette

OPEN, INPUT#, PRINT# and CLOSE

In order to prepare your cassette for reading or writing information from within a program, the tape file must first be prepared with an OPEN statement, just as we saw with the GET and PUT commands. The format is as follows for 1) Writing and 2) Reading:

```
Write To Tape
OPEN #2, 8, Ø, "C:"

Read From Tape
OPEN #2, 4, Ø, "C:"
```

As you may have noted, the only difference is that an '8' is used to output data to tape and a '4' is used to input (read) data from tape.

To see how data files can be used, let's write a little program which stores batting averages in data files. We will create a program which first uses input from the keyboard and writes the information to tape and then a second program which reads the data from tape and figures out a batting average.

```
10 PRINT CHR$(125)
20 DIM BA(10) : REM BATTING AVERAGE
30 FOR I = 1 TO 10
40 PRINT "BATTING AVERAGE FOR GAME #"; I
50 INPUT AV
60 BA(I) = AV
70 NEXT I
80 PRINT CHR$(125) : REM CLEAR SCREEN
90 PRINT "PRESS PLAY & REC ON RECORDER"
   : PRINT : PRINT "PRESS <RETURN>
   ON COMPUTER"
100 REM
110 REM ****************
120 REM WRITE TO TAPE
130 REM ****************
140 REM
150 OPEN #2, 8, 0, "C:"
160 FOR I = 1 TO 10
170 PRINT #2; BA(I)
180 NEXT I
190 CLOSE #2
```

Before running this program, be sure to note the beginning position on your tape counter. We will use it in our program which reads from the tape. OK, now dream up some batting averages (or any numbers you'd like if you're not a baseball fan) and RUN the program. When you're finished entering and recording the information, press PLAY and REC on your program recorder and RETURN on your computer. Wait a while, and when the READY prompt comes up, press STOP on your recorder and rewind it. Now, we're ready to read the data from the cassette tape. To do so, we have to use a tape reading program:

```
10 REM BATTING AVERAGE STARTS AT
10 COUNTER #N (use the counter value for the
   beginning of the data from the program which
   wrote the data to tape.)
20 PRINT CHR$(125)
30 PRINT "PRESS PLAY ON RECORDER" : PRINT
   : PRINT "PRESS <RETURN> ON COMPUTER"
100 REM
110 REM *************************
120 REM READ DATA FROM TAPE
130 REM *************************
140 REM
150 OPEN #2, 4, 0, "C:"
160 FOR I = 1 TO 10
170 INPUT #2; AV
180 PRINT AV
190 AT = AT + AV : REM RUNNING TOTAL
    OF BATTING AVERAGES
200 NEXT I
210 CLOSE #2
300 REM
310 REM ***************************************
320 REM FIND AVERAGE FROM DATA ON TAPE
330 REM ***************************************
340 REM
350 PRINT "AVERAGE FOR 10 GAMES ="; AT/10
```

In the above two programs, we used two new commands, even though you may not have noticed it. We used PRINT # and INPUT #. When we write data to tape we PRINT # it to the cassette instead of to the screen. When we read data from a tape, we INPUT # it from the tape instead of the keyboard. Think of the PRINT # and INPUT # statements in the same way you would PRINT and INPUT, but going to or coming from different sources.

Now that we have seen all of the commands for reading and writing files from and to tape, let's take a look at an application. We might as well use a practical application, so we will make a list of our friends' phone numbers. Whenever we want to call a friend, all we have to do is read the list from tape. First, we must create a list to enter names and save them to tape. After we have done that, we will write a program to retrieve the names and numbers.

```
10 PRINT CHR$ (125) : DIM FN$(35), FP(6)
20 FOR I = 1 TO 6 : READ FN$
30 PRINT FN$; " 'S NUMBER";
40 INPUT FPH : REM ONLY ENTER NUMBER
   WITHOUT SPACES OR DASHES
50 FP(I) = FPH
60 NEXT I
70 RESTORE : REM RESET DATA POINTER
   TO BEGINNING
100 REM
110 REM ****************
120 REM WRITE TO TAPE
130 REM ****************
140 REM
150 PRINT CHR$(125) : PRINT "PRESS PLAY &
    REC ON RECORDER" : PRINT : PRINT "PRESS
    <RETURN> ON COMPUTER"
160 OPEN #5, 8, 0, "C:"
170 FOR I = 1 TO 6
180 READ FN$
190 PRINT #5;FN$
200 PRINT #5;FP(I)
210 NEXT I
220 CLOSE #5
300 REM
310 REM ************
320 REM NAME LIST
330 REM ************
340 REM
350 DATA ART, SALLY, BILL, NANCY, MARCIA, DAVE
```

To use this program, get a blank tape and rewind your cassette. RUN the program, and you will be prompted to PRESS PLAY and REC ON RECORDER when you have entered all the numbers from the NAME LIST from the DATA statements in line 350. As soon as you press the play and record buttons and RETURN on your computer, your tape recorder spindles will begin turning. When all the information is saved, the recorder will stop and the screen will display the READY prompt. All your data has been saved. (Tape storage is relatively slow compared to disks, so to save time it is suggested to use just a few names (six or so as in our example) at first.

Now let's see if everything worked out according to plan. To do that we need a program to read our data; we will use INPUT# to read the names and numbers. Since the names were saved as strings, and the phone numbers as numeric variables, we will have to alternate between string and numeric variables with our INPUT#. While we're at it, let's make a program which will read a list of any number of names. Since our example used six, we could use a FOR/NEXT loop to generate the INPUT#s, but sometimes we may have forgotten the number of names we used. Therefore, we will use the TRAP statement. Essentially the TRAP statements will branch to a line in the TRAP statement when an error is encountered. In this case the ERROR would be 136, indicating "End of File." So when we run out of data, instead of bombing, the program will branch to the CLOSE# routine at line 15Ø. (Remember to rewind your tape before RUNning this program!)

```
1Ø PRINT CHR$(125) : DIM FN$(35)
2Ø TRAP 15Ø
3Ø PRINT "PRESS PLAY ON RECORDER" : PRINT
   : PRINT "PRESS <RETURN> ON COMPUTER"
4Ø OPEN #5, 4, Ø, "C:"
5Ø INPUT #5; FN$
6Ø INPUT #5; FP
7Ø PRINT FN$; " ";FP
8Ø GOTO 5Ø
1ØØ REM
11Ø REM ******************************
12Ø REM CLOSE THE FILE ON TRAP
```

```
130 REM ******************************
140 REM
150 CLOSE #5
```

When you RUN this program, you will be prompted to PRESS PLAY on RECORDER and PRESS <RETURN> ON COMPUTER. When you do so, the screen will freeze, and after a bit your friends' names and phone numbers you entered will appear. After a little while your READY prompt will appear indicating the end of file has been reached and the file is closed.

Now let's go back to see how we can save player/missile information on tape. Also, we will see how we can load the information from tape and execute a program using the tape data. There is a word of caution in order, however. Sometimes there is more information on the tape then we want, and so it is important to load into memory just what we want and ignore everything else. This is a little inconvenient since we have to keep an eye on all of our data and know how many pieces of data make up our player/missiles. However, since that information is necessary anyway, our job is not too difficult.

To get started, we will create a player/missile and save it to tape. We'll use our "rocket" character again:

WRITE PLAYER/MISSILE DATA TO TAPE

```
10 PRINT CHR$(125) : DIM PMD(7)
20 FOR I = 1 TO 7
30 READ D
40 PMD(I) = D
50 NEXT I
100 REM
110 REM **********************
120 REM WRITE DATA TO TAPE
130 REM **********************
140 REM
150 PRINT "PRESS PLAY & REC ON RECORDER"
    : PRINT : PRINT "PRESS <RETURN>
    ON COMPUTER"
```

```
160 OPEN #1, 8, 0, "C:"
170 FOR I = 1 TO 7
180 PRINT #1; PMD(I)
190 NEXT I
200 CLOSE #1
300 REM
310 REM *************
320 REM READ DATA
330 REM *************
340 REM
350 DATA 192, 224, 62, 127, 62, 224, 192
```

We created the player/missile just as we would were it part of a program to make the character. We need only to change the DATA elements in line 350 whenever we want a different player/missile recorded on tape. For larger player/missiles, we simply DIM PMD to the appropriate size and adjust the size of the loop in line 170. The advantages of using this method over CLISTing player/missile data to tape in line numbers is that we can write programs which use player/missiles without having to worry about conflict with the CLISTed DATA's line numbers. For example, if we have a player/missile saved with CLIST in line numbers 400-500, and our program uses those same line numbers, we would run into a conflict. However, by just saving the data itself to tape, we don't have to be concerned about what line numbers we use.

Now let's load the player/missile from tape and run it in a program. Be sure to save the following program, for with it you can load any player/missile from tape you want and run it. This will save a good deal of time, since, rather than having to write a player/missile routine every time you want to have a different character, simply load the program, set your cassette tape at the beginning of a player/missile data storage area and run the program. You can do this with any player/missiles you want. However, you will have to adjust for the number of bytes that make up your player/missile. The following program is set for ones using seven bytes.

```
10 PRINT CHR$(125) : DIM D(7), PD (7)
20 X = 0 : Y = 50 : C = 0
30 TOR = PEEK (106) - 8
40 POKE 54279, TOR
```

```
50 PMB = 256 * TOR
60 RES = 559 : POKE RES, 46
70 ENABLE = 53277 : POKE ENABLE, 3
80 H0 = 53248
90 P0 = 512
100 REM
110 REM ********************************
120 REM CLEAR AND SET P/M COLOR
130 REM ********************************
140 REM
150 FOR I = PMB + P0 TO PMB + P0 + 128
    : POKE I, 0 : NEXT I
160 C0 = 704 : POKE C0, 3 * 16 + 6
200 REM
210 REM ***************************
220 REM READ DATA FROM TAPE
230 REM ***************************
240 REM
250 PRINT "PRESS PLAY ON RECORDER" : PRINT
    : PRINT "PRESS <RETURN> ON COMPUTER"
260 OPEN #1, 4, 0, "C:"
270 FOR I = 1 TO 7
280 INPUT #1;PV
290 D(I) = PV : REM CREATE AN ARRAY TO
    STORE P/M DATA
300 NEXT I
310 CLOSE #1
400 REM
410 REM ********************************
420 REM CREATE AND MOVE PLAYER
430 REM ********************************
440 REM
450 FOR I = PMB + P0 + Y TO PMB + 0 + 6 + Y
    : C = C + 1 : POKE I, D(C) : NEXT I
460 REM *** NOW MOVE PLAYER ***
470 FOR I = X TO 255 : POKE H0, I : NEXT I
```

Besides using this method to load a single player, it can be used for several. Remember, when the information is stored on tape, all you have is a set of values. These values are stored on a strip of tape, and as the cassette turns, it sequentially reads the information on tape. Think of the tape as entering the values in the same way you would from the keyboard or in

DATA statements in a program. Using the TRAP command and a "counter," it is possible to modify the program to take in any size of player/missile you may create. For practice, why not create several different players with seven bytes (e.g., seven values), and watch your program load them from tape and enter them into your program.

Sequential Files and the Disk System

If you do not have a disk system, you can skip this section and go on to the next chapter. However, if you are considering purchasing a disk drive for your ATARI, the following material will be of interest. In many respects storing data on disks is similar to storing it on tape except the storage and retrieval process is much quicker. In fact, all of our examples in the previous section can be operated with the disk system with only a few minor changes in the format. Therefore, to get started, we will see how we can store data to disks using a slightly different format than we did with tape. To do this we will examine the OPEN, CLOSE, INPUT#, PRINT# and GET# commands for disk.

OPEN

To open a disk channel, we access the device "D: <File Name>" instead of "C:" as we did with the cassette. It is very important to remember to include the *file name* when using the disk system. For example, we would enter the following to read a file named PMDATA:

```
OPEN #3, 4, Ø, "D : PMDATA"
```

Likewise, to write, we use Code 8, just as we did with the cassette. However, with the disk system, there are some very important additional codes we can use. If we enter a 9 in the second position, instead of overwriting a file, information will be appended to the file. Whenever a file is OPENed to write (Code 8), the exiting file is erased, but with Code 9, information is added to the file. We will examine this append code further on in this chapter. Finally, Code 12 allows both reading and writing to a file. This can be used to re-enter and correct data in files.

DISK CODES	**MEANING**
4	Read a file
8	Write a file
9	Append a file
12	Read & write a file (Used to correct/ change data)

Now to see how all of this goes together, we will re-do our original FRIENDS PHONES program we created for tape. The data entry block is identical, so we will do only the block which saves the information to disk:

```
10 PRINT CHR$ (125) : DIM FN$(35), FP(6)
20 FOR I = 1 TO 6 : READ FN$
30 PRINT FN$; " 'S NUMBER";
40 INPUT FPH : REM ENTER NUMBER
   WITHOUT SPACES OR DASHES
50 FP(I) = FPH
60 NEXT I
70 RESTORE : REM RESET DATA POINTER
```

```
    TO BEGINNING
100 REM
110 REM *****************
120 REM WRITE TO DISK
130 REM *****************
140 REM
150 OPEN #5, 8, Ø, "D1: FPHONES"
160 REM WITH 1 DISK DRIVE THE NUMBER
     AFTER 'D' IS OPTIONAL
170 FOR I = 1 TO 6
180 READ FN$
190 PRINT #5;FN$
200 PRINT #5;FP(I)
210 NEXT I
220 CLOSE #5
300 REM
310 REM *************
320 REM NAME LIST
330 REM *************
340 REM
350 DATA ART, SALLY, BILL, NANCY, MARCIA, DAVE
```

As can be seen, the main difference between tape and disk is in the format in line 15Ø. Otherwise, the disk and tape writing format is identical. Likewise, in retrieving information from disk, there are more similarities than differences between tape and disk.

```
10 PRINT CHR$(125) : DIM FN$(35)
20 TRAP 150
50 OPEN #5, 4, Ø, "D1: FPHONES"
60 INPUT #5; FN$
70 INPUT #5; FP
80 PRINT FN$; " ";FP
90 GOTO 60
100 REM
110 REM ****************************
120 REM CLOSE THE FILE ON TRAP
130 REM ****************************
140 REM
150 CLOSE #5
```

If you have both a program recorder and a disk drive, you may have noticed how much faster the information was retrieved. The TRAP command is even more important with disk than tape since we will be seeing how to append information to a file, and after a while we lose track of how many items are in our file.

Now let's see how the "append" works on the disk system. We will take our FRIENDS' PHONES program and simply change the code number from 8 to 9 and change the names in the DATA statement:

```
10 PRINT CHR$ (125) : DIM FN$(35), FP(6)
20 FOR I = 1 TO 6 : READ FN$
30 PRINT FN$; " 'S NUMBER";
40 INPUT FPH : REM ENTER NUMBER
   WITHOUT SPACES OR DASHES
50 FP(I) = FPH
60 NEXT I
70 RESTORE : REM RESET DATA POINTER
   TO BEGINNING
100 REM
110 REM ******************
120 REM APPEND TO DISK
130 REM ******************
140 REM
150 OPEN #5, 9, 0, "D1: FPHONES"
160 REM THE '8' WAS REPLACED WITH A '9'
    IN LINE 150
170 FOR I = 1 TO 6
180 READ FN$
190 PRINT #5;FN$
200 PRINT #5;FP(I)
210 NEXT I
220 CLOSE #5
300 REM
310 REM ******************
320 REM NEW NAME LIST
330 REM ******************
340 REM
350 DATA JANET, VAL, NORMAN, KARL, ERICA, PETE
```

Now we can see how to write a file, read the file and append a file. Next, we will look at the mode used for reading and writing to a file — Code 12. The first thing we'll use update for is to find a single name and telephone number. While we're at it, we should also do something about formatting the output. Everyone knows that telephone numbers have a dash after the first three numbers, so let's put in that dash. To do this, we will convert the telephone number to a string variable and then use substrings to make the output look correct. The following program does two things, then. It finds the name and number you enter, and it prints out the name and number in a nice way.

```
10 PRINT CHR$(125) : DIM FN$(35), FF$(35),
   NN$(12)
20 TRAP 290 : REM IF THE NAME IS NOT FOUND
   CLOSE THE FILE
30 PRINT "NAME TO FIND ";
40 INPUT FN$
100 REM
110 REM ****************************************
120 REM OPEN FILE AND SEARCH FOR NAME
130 REM ****************************************
140 REM
150 OPEN #3, 12, 0, "D1: FPHONES"
160 INPUT #3, FF$ : IF FF$ = FN$ THEN 200
170 GOTO 160
200 REM
210 REM ****************************************
220 REM FORMAT AND OUTPUT INFORMATION
230 REM ****************************************
240 REM
250 PRINT FF$ : REM PRINT NAME
260 INPUT #3, FN : REM GET PHONE NUMBER
270 NN$ = STR$ (FN)
280 PRINT NN$ (1,3); "-"; NN$(4)
290 CLOSE #3
```

As you probably know, you could have done the same thing using Code 4 that reads the files. However, I wanted to show you that Code 12 both reads and updates (writes to) files. Once the name in the file has been found, the pointer is at the next item. In the case of our file called FPHONES, we know that the next element will be a seven digit phone number. So, by changing our previous program a little, we can find any name we want and update (change) the phone number. Notice that we use both INPUT # for reading and PRINT # for writing information. With this file, you can look up a name, change the number and then have it printed out for you:

```
10 PRINT CHR$(125) : DIM FN$(35), FF$(35),
   NN$(12)
20 TRAP 290 : REM IF THE NAME IS NOT FOUND
   CLOSE THE FILE
30 PRINT "NAME TO FIND ";
40 INPUT FN$
50 PRINT "NEW NUMBER";
60 INPUT XN
100 REM
110 REM ************************************
120 REM OPEN FILE AND SEARCH FOR NAME
```

```
130 REM ***************************************
140 REM
150 OPEN #3, 12, 0, "D1: FPHONES"
160 INPUT #3, FF$ : IF FF$ = FN$ THEN 200
170 GOTO 160
200 REM
210 REM ******************************************
220 REM ENTER NEW NUMBER INTO FILE AND
             PRINT IT OUT WITH NAME
230 REM ******************************************
240 REM
250 PRINT FF$ : REM PRINT NAME
260 PRINT #3; XN : REM ENTER NEW NUMBER
    INTO FILE
270 NN$ = STR$ (XN)
280 PRINT NN$ (1,3); "–"; NN$(4)
290 CLOSE #3
```

That about does it for files. There are several more things you can do with your ATARI 810 disk drive and the filing system we have discussed. However, these are for more advanced applications. In the meantime, though, this information should give you plenty of file handling ability for your own needs.

Before we conclude this chapter, there is one last thing we should cover. It has to do with reading the contents of your disk. When you work with files, there are several occasions for you to access DOS. Whenever you do that, your program is wiped out, and if you forget to SAVE it, a lot of work can be ruined. There are two ways to access the disk directory without losing your program. The first method is using MEM.SAV. Whenever a diskette has MEM.SAV on it, your current program will be SAVEd automatically whenever you enter DOS. When you return to BASIC, your program will be there waiting for you. To initialize a diskette with MEM.SAV, simply enter:

```
SAVE "D1 : MEM.SAV"
```

Now there will be a MEM.SAV file on your diskette, and you do not have to worry about losing your program. However, when you do that it takes a lot more time for DOS to load and unload. (It seems like FOREVER!)

An alternative method that I like to use is a little utility subroutine I stick on the end of a file. When the program is completed, I delete the file. It lists the contents of your directory quickly without bothering your program in memory. In this way, either with or without MEM.SAV, it is possible to check your directory while working on a program. Code 6 is used when you OPEN a file:

```
5000 END : REM ** DELETE WHEN FINISHED **
5010 CLR : DIM DIR$(25)
5020 OPEN #5, 6, 0, "D1: *.*"
5030 TRAP 5000
5040 INPUT #5; DIR$
5050 PRINT DIR$ : GOTO 5040
```

Whenever you want to see the contents of the directory, simply enter GOTO 5010. Since this is such a handy utility, save it with the LIST command, and then ENTER it to the end of your program. If your program line numbers extend over 5000, simply use higher line numbers. Also note that it *begins* with an END statement in line 5000. This is so that it will not get in the way of testing programs during their development.

SUMMARY

In this chapter we learned how to save a lot of time by saving files to tape and disk. Data can be saved to your cassette tape for use later within a program. This is handy since it allows you to enter data at one time and then use it later without having to key in the data all over again. Using CLIST and LIST, it is possible to save DATA statements and then later append them to your program with ENTER. By storing data on tape, it is possible to use it in many different programs. This is especially handy with player/missiles you have created.

Using a disk system, it is possible to store data in sequential files much like saving data to tape. However, disks access the data much faster than tapes, and it is possible to have a single program do several different things with data files on disks. By combining the various programs we showed above, it is possible to jump to subroutines which will read, write, append or update files. Care has to be taken to keep everything straight with such a program, but using sequential files increases the power of your computer a great deal. The practical applications of such programs are immense.

CHAPTER 9

You and Your Printer

Introduction

By now you should be used to "outputting" information to your screen, cassette, or disk. When you write in PRINT "HELLO" you output to your screen. When you CSAVE, SAVE or PRINT# something, you "output" to your tape or disk. In the same way that you access your screen, tape or disk, you can access your printer. It is simply another output target. However, you cannot LOAD, INPUT, or in some other way get anything from your printer as you can from your keyboard, tape, or disk. (How are you going to get the ink off the paper and back into memory?)

The procedures for getting material out to your printer and using your printer's special capabilities require certain procedures not yet discussed. Therefore, while much of what we will examine in this chapter will not be new in terms of the language of commands, it will be new in terms of how to arrange those commands. Also, we will see how we can use the printer in ways which have been done poorly using the screen. For example, no matter how long a program listing is, it can be printed out to the printer, while long listings on the screen scrolled right off the top into Never-Never land. Likewise, in Chapter 8, we made a handy little program for storing friends' phone numbers. With a printer we can print out our phone numbers or run off mailing labels with commands which output information to the printer.

There are a lot of printers for computers on the market. The ones chosen for this book are the more popular ones, but if your printer interfacing is correct you can use just about any computer printer. Also, we will be working with examples from 8Ø column printers, and so if you have a 4Ø column printer, the examples will turn out a little different than what is described here. ATARI Inc. sells the ATARI 825 printer, along with all the appropriate cables you will need to hook it up to the ATARI 85Ø Interface Module (or some other ATARI compatible interface). With the new ATARI 1Ø25 printer, there is no need for the ATARI 85Ø interface, and you can plug it directly into any of the XL series models. If you have some other printer, such as an Epson, C. Itoh, IDS or NEC, you will need to purchase a special cable which hooks up to the interface and the printer. In fact, Microbits Peripheral Products makes the MPP-11ØØ Parallel Printer Interface that works without the ATARI 85Ø Interface Module. (MPP 434 W. First Street, Albany, OR 97321, (5Ø3) 967-9Ø75.) It costs only $99 and works with most parallel printers. If you have an ATARI 85Ø Interface module, Milford Null Modem (MNM, Phx'ville Pike and Chas'tn Road, Malvern, PA 19355, (215) 296-8467) sells cables which interface to several popular parallel printers through the ATARI 85Ø. If you have an XL model, you simply plug in your printer to the parallel interface on the computer.

BEFORE YOU BUY A PRINTER!!

The most important aspect in purchasing a printer is making certain it will interface with your ATARI. Many times over-enthusiastic salespersons will tell buyers all the qualities of a printer and naively believe they can be used on any computer. This is simply not true! In order for a printer to work with a computer, it must have the proper interface; the best printer in the world will not work with your ATARI without such an interface. Therefore, when you buy a printer other than one made specifically for your ATARI, make sure to buy the proper interface for it. The only *certain* way to insure the printer works with an ATARI is to have it demonstrated with your computer. The ATARI 822, 82Ø, 825 and 1Ø25 printers will work with the ATARI, but otherwise you should have the printer's ability to work with your computer shown to you. With the XL series, the problem of interfacing is not as troublesome, but still, test a printer on your model before purchase!

And another thing!

SET PRINTER LINE FEED

On some printers, you have a choice of having the printer automatically give a line feed when it encounters a CR (carriage return) or wait until it gets one from the computer. The ATARI is set up so that the printer provides the linefeed. Therefore, if your printer keeps running over the same line, flip the necessary switch that indicates auto-line feed. Your printer manual will describe how to do this.

Printing Text on Your Printer

The first thing you will want to do with your printer is to print some text in hardcopy. (Hardcopy is a really impressive term computer people use to talk about print outs on paper. Use the term and your friends will be amazed.) Like your cassette tape and disk drive, it is necessary to first go through a number of steps to channel information to your printer. There are several different ways to send output to your printers. Let's review those ways now.

LPRINT The most direct and simple way to send output to your printer is with the LPRINT command. It can be used from either the Immediate or the Program mode. For example:

```
LPRINT "This will come from my printer"
```

or

```
10 DIM A$(22) : A$ = "This should be printed on
   the printer"
20 LPRINT A$
```

RUN the program, and it will print to your printer in the same way as it would to the screen. Think of LPRINT as a substitute for PRINT with the former going to the printer instead of the screen.

LIST "P:" One of the best ways to debug a long program is to list it to the printer. Once your program is about 22 lines long, things start scrolling off the screen. (Using long multiple lines, it'll scroll much sooner!) If you want to examine an entire program, instead of entering LIST, use LIST "P:". You can also list a range of lines, using, for example, LIST "P:", 40,100. That is easy!

```
LIST "P:"
```

or

```
LIST "P:", 50, 70
```

PRINT# If a channel is OPENed to the printer, all PRINT# statements will go to the printer. The following command sequence is used:

```
OPEN #3, 5, Ø, "P:"
```

Any PRINT# command will now send information to the printer.

With what we've see so far, there would not seem to be any reason to have more printer commands, but as you will see, there is. Enter and RUN the following program:

```
10 FOR I = 1 TO 20
20 LPRINT "X";
30 PRINT "X";
40 NEXT I
```

There is an important output difference between your printer and your screen. Twenty X's lined up on your screen, but the X's to the printer went all over the place. Now try the following program:

```
10 OPEN #3, 3, 0, "P:"
20 FOR I = 1 TO 20
30 PRINT #3; "X"; : REM NOTE FORMAT
40 PRINT "X";
50 NEXT I
60 PRINT #3
70 CLOSE #3
```

When you RUN the program, your X's on the printer will line up on your printer paper as they did on the screen. Thus, when you have formatted output, it is better to use the OPEN . . . "P:" and PRINT# sequence than LPRINT. *NOTE: Line 60 is necessary to initiate an End Of Line <EOL> to the printer buffer. Take that line out and see what happens. Enter* RUN *several times and you will see that the program outputs to the printer only every* other RUN. *That's because it takes a second RUN to kick it out to the printer from the buffer. Also note the different printer output without line 60.)*

Formats for PRINT# include the following:

```
PRINT#7; NA$ (String variables)
```

or:

```
PRINT#7; "Charlie Tuna" (Strings)
```

or:

```
PRINT#7; 12345 (Numbers)
```

Let's try a little program to print names to the printer to show how PRINT# can be used in programs where you want to use both the screen and the printer.

```
10 PRINT CHR$(125) : DIM A$(1), AN$ (1), NA$(20)
20 PRINT : PRINT : PRINT "{ATARI KEY} TURN
   ON PRINTER {ATARI KEY}"
30 PRINT : PRINT : PRINT "PRESS RETURN
   TO CONTINUE";
40 INPUT A$
50 PRINT CHR$(125)
60 OPEN #1, 1, 0, "P:"
```

```
70 PRINT "NAME TO PRINT";
80 INPUT NA$
90 PRINT #1; NA$
100 PRINT #1 : REM KICK IT OUT OF THE BUFFER
110 PRINT "ANOTHER(Y/N)";
120 INPUT AN$
130 IF AN$="Y" THEN 70
140 CLOSE #1
150 END
```

CLOSE The final command in accessing your printer is CLOSE. As we can see in the above program, it closes the channel to the printer and turns it off. For the most part CLOSE works pretty much the same way as it does with the tape and disk systems; however, there is an important protocol involved.

CHR$ to the Rescue

The secret to using printers is in understanding what their control codes mean and how to use those codes. For example, the following is a partial list of codes provided with a CENTRONICS 737 printer (which just so happens to be identical to the ATARI 825):

Mnemonic	Decimal	Octal	Hex	Function
ESC,SO	27,14	Ø33,Ø16	1B,ØE	Elongated Print
ESC,DC4	27,2Ø	Ø33,Ø34	1B,13	Select 16.7 cpi
ESC,DC1	27,17	Ø33,Ø21	1B,11	Proportional Print

Now, for most first-time computer owners, that could have been written by a visitor from another planet for all the good it does. However, there is important information in those codes and, once you get to know how, it is relatively easy to use them.

To get started, forget everything except the Decimal and Function columns. Now, taking the first row, we have decimal codes 27 and 14 to get elongated print. To tell your printer you want elongated print you would use CHR$(27) and CHR$(14). To kick that into your printer you would do the following:

2. LPRINT CHR$(27); CHR$(14); "FAT MESSAGE"

If you have a Centronics 737 or 739 printer (or ATARI 825), that would have printed the string FAT MESSAGE in an elongated print. Likewise, for the condensed printing 16.7 cpi (characters per inch), you would have entered CHR$(27); CHR$(20) and for the proportional type face, CHR$(27); CHR$(17). Once you get the decimal code, enter that code to the printer and it will do anything from changing the type-face to performing a backspace function. So, taking the same information, we can make a more useful chart:

PRINTER OUTPUT	CHR$ CODE
Elongated	CHR$(27); CHR$(14)
Condensed	CHR$(27); CHR$(2Ø)
Proportional	CHR$(27); CHR$(17)

To see how the CHR$ functions work, we will use a simple program which will print out your name. Since we already know how to print out normal text, we will being with expanded text. Looking at our chart, we see that CHR$(14) will expand our print out; so we will use it in our program:

```
10 PRINT CHR$(125) : DIM NA$(20)
20 OPEN #7, 7, 0, "P:"
30 PRINT "YOUR NAME";
40 INPUT NA$
50 PRINT#7 CHR$(27); CHR$(14); NA$
60 PRINT#7
70 CLOSE #7
```

RUN the program, print out some names, and note the expanded characters. (Try that on your typewriter!) On some printers, such as the ATARI 1025 (essentially the same as a C. ITOH 8510), EPSON MX-80FT with GRAFTRAX PLUS and GEMINI, it is possible to have not only expanded print but also italicized, condensed, double strike, emphasized, and super/subscript type faces and any combination of them together. Using CHR$, all of the different type styles can be used separately or in combination with one another.

POSSIBLE SHORT-CUT

Instead of using CHR$ commands, you can get different type styles on your printer using your keyboard. For example, LPRINT CHR$(27); CHR$(14); "WIDE PRINT" can be produced with LPRINT "{ESC} {ESC} {CTRL-N} WIDE PRINT". This is a way to save keystrokes, but it may not be clear to you in a program listing. Look up the decimal control values, using {ESC} {ESC} for CHR$(27), and then look up the character associated with the CHR$ of that value. For a good article on how to do this with Epson printers, see "Epson Printing Modes Simplified" by Thomas M. Krischan in A.N.A.L.O.G., No. 10, pp 61-62.

Now that we have seen different ways to operate the type faces on the printer, let's do something practical. We will make a mailing label program for your printer. Various label manufacturers make adhesive labels with tractor-feed margins so that you can put them into your printer just like your paper. Our program will make labels which will print the addressee's name in expanded type, the address, city, state, and zip code in normal. (This program will work with the ATARI 825 and 1Ø25, Centronics 737 & 739, Epson and Gemini printers. If you have a different printer, check to see if the code for expanded print is the same.

```
10 PRINT CHR$(125) : CLR : DIM AN$(1), NA$(20),
   AD$(20), CT$(20), SA$(2), ZI$(6)
20 REM ** ENTER INFORMATION **
30 PRINT "NAME "; : INPUT NA$
40 PRINT "ADDRESS "; : INPUT AD$
50 PRINT "CITY "; : INPUT CT$
60 PRINT "STATE "; : INPUT SA$
70 PRINT "ZIP CODE " ; : INPUT ZI$
100 REM
110 REM **********************************
120 REM FORMAT AND PRINT TO PRINTER
130 REM **********************************
140 REM
150 OPEN #7, 7, 0, "P:"
160 PRINT#7; CHR$(27); CHR$(14); NA$
170 PRINT#7; AD$
180 PRINT#7; CT$; ", "; SA$; " "; ZI$
190 PRINT #7
200 CLOSE #7
210 PRINT "{ATARI KEY} ANOTHER(Y/N)
    {ATARI KEY}"; : INPUT AN$
220 IF AN$ = "Y" THEN 10
230 END
```

In order for the program to be more practical, we will need a few line feeds at the end of the printing so that your labels can be properly aligned. Depending on the size of your mailing labels, you will need a greater or fewer number of line feeds. Change line 19Ø in your program and adjust the size of the loop to align your labels properly:

```
190 FOR I = 1 TO 3 : PRINT #7 : NEXT I: REM
CHANGE "3" TO THE CORRECT NUMBER OF LINE
FEEDS FOR YOUR LABELS
```

Instead of having to enter all of your typefaces individually, why not have a program that selects the typeface for you? On Epson printers with GRAFTRAX PLUS, there are several different typefaces and combinations of typefaces. The basic typefaces include:

1. Expanded (Shift-out)
2. Condensed (Shift-in)
3. Emphasized
4. Double Strike
5. Italics

Each of these typefaces, with the exception of the Expanded, remains the typeface until you enter the code to remove it. Therefore, if you have the Condensed typeface working, and you enter the code for Italics, you will have Condensed-Italic typeface. The following program works on Epson printers. If you have a different type of printer, simply change the code and typeface designations to work with your printer.

EPSON TYPEFACE CONTROLLER

```
10 PRINT CHR$(125) : DIM T$(25), UL$(25), D$(15)
20 FOR I = 1 TO 35 : PRINT "{ATARI KEY} {SPACE}
   {ATARI KEY}"; : NEXT I
30 T$ = "EPSON TYPEFACE CONTROLLER"
   : L = 19 - LEN(T$)/2 : POSITION L, 4 : PRINT T$
40 UL$ = "          " : REM 25 CTRL-R'S
50 POSITION L,5 : PRINT UL$
60 FOR I = 2 TO 15 : POSITION 2,I : PRINT
   "{ATARI KEY}{SPACE}{ATARI KEY}" : POSITION 36,I
   : PRINT "{ATARI KEY} {SPACE} {ATARI KEY}"
70 NEXT I
80 FOR I = 1 TO 6 : READ D$ : POSITION 9, I+6
   : PRINT I; ".";D$ : NEXT I
90 FOR I = 2 TO 36 : POSITION I,15 : PRINT
   "{ATARI KEY} {SPACE} {ATARI KEY}" : NEXT I
100 POSITION 5,20 : PRINT "CHOOSE BY
    NUMBER "; : INPUT CHOICE
110 GOSUB 200
120 ON CHOICE GOSUB 300, 400, 500, 600, 700, 800
130 CLOSE #5
140 GOTO 100
200 REM
210 REM ******************************
220 REM OPEN PRINTER CHANNEL
230 REM ******************************
240 REM
250 OPEN #5, 5, 0, "P:"
```

```
260 RETURN
300 REM
310 REM *************
320 REM EXPANDED
330 REM *************
340 REM
350 PRINT#5; CHR$(27); CHR$(14); "HERE IS
     YOUR TYPE FACE"
360 PRINT# 5
370 RETURN
400 REM
410 REM **************
420 REM CONDENSED
430 REM **************
440 REM
450 PRINT#5; CHR$(27); CHR$(15); "HERE IS
     YOUR TYPE FACE"
460 PRINT #5
470 RETURN
500 REM
510 REM ***************
520 REM EMPHASIZED
530 REM ***************
540 REM
550 PRINT#5; CHR$(27); CHR$(69); "HERE IS
     YOUR TYPE FACE"
560 PRINT #5
570 RETURN
600 REM
610 REM ******************
620 REM DOUBLE STRIKE
630 REM ******************
640 REM
650 PRINT#5; CHR$(27); CHR$(71); "HERE IS
     YOUR TYPE FACE"
660 PRINT #5
670 RETURN
700 REM
710 REM *********
720 REM ITALICS
730 REM *********
740 REM
750 PRINT#5; CHR$(27); CHR$(52); "HERE IS
     YOUR TYPE FACE"
```

```
760 PRINT #5
770 RETURN
800 REM
810 REM ******
820 REM EXIT
830 REM ******
840 END
1000 REM
1010 REM *************
1020 REM MENU DATA
1030 REM *************
1040 REM
1050 DATA EXPANDED, CONDENSED, EMPHASIZED
1060 DATA DOUBLE STRIKE, ITALICS, EXIT
```

The above program ought to give you a pretty handy utility for setting up typestyles on your Epson printer. Now, the next program is the world's most primitive word processor, PRIMO-WRITER. With it, you can actually write and edit text, but it prints out whatever you write as soon as you press RETURN. However, using the built-in editor on your ATARI, if you change the text before you press RETURN, it will edit it just fine. Otherwise, it has none of the properties of a real word processor, but it is a lot of fun and the price is right. (It will also work with any printer.)

PRIMO-WRITER

```
10 PRINT CHR$(125)
20 DIM S$(70) : REM SETS MAXIMUM LINE
   LENGTH TO 70. CHANGE IF DESIRED.
30 OPEN #1, 1, 0, "P:"
40 PRINT ">"; : INPUT S$
50 PRINT #1; " "; S$ : REM LEFT MARGIN SET
   WITH SPACES BETWEEN QUOTES
60 PRINT #1 : REM GIVES DOUBLE SPACE.
   REMOVE LINE FOR SINGLE SPACE
70 CLOSE #1
80 GOTO 30
100 REM
110 REM ************************************
120 REM USE ONLY PRIMO-WRITER TO
130 REM WRITE TO AUTHOR WITH YOUR
```

```
140 REM COMMENTS ON THE BOOK.
150 REM   TO:
160 REM      WILLIAM B. SANDERS
170 REM      C/O DATAMOST
180 REM      8943 FULLBRIGHT
190 REM      CHATSWORTH, CA 91311
200 REM ***********************************
210 REM
```

SAVE THE WORLD FROM PRIMO-WRITER!

PRIMO-WRITER is so dumb, it is a pleasure to take credit for it. However, by this time, you ought to be smarter than the author; so why not improve on PRIMO-WRITER. Enhance it so that it can change typefaces, save text to tape or disk and do other neat things. Send your *original* entry to:

PRIMO-WRITER CONTEST
DATAMOST
8943 FULLBRIGHT
CHATSWORTH, CA 91311

If your enhancement of PRIMO-WRITER is judged to be the best and weirdest, you will win $1ØØ. (Donated by the Dave Gordon Lunch Money Fund.) In future editions of THE ELEMENTARY ATARI, your program will be published. The only rules are:

1. The program must be original.
2. All documentation must be written on your version of PRIMO-WRITER.

Printer Graphics

If you want to dump graphics from the screen to your printer, you will need a special program to do so. For example, GRAPHICS HARDCOPY by Macrotronics, Inc. dumps graphics to most popular brands of printers. (The ATARI 825 does *not* have graphics capabilities, but the ATARI 1Ø25 does.) Also check with your club's public domain software library. It will probably have some kind of program for dumping graphics to your printer, but it will almost undoubtedly be for only a single printer type.

PSEUDO-GRAPHICS

One way to print graphics to your printer is with pseudo-graphics. Early graphics from computers were produced by programming various ASCII characters and then dumping them to the printer. For example, the following program makes a diamond:

```
10 PRINT CHR$(125)
20 OPEN #1, 1, Ø, "P:"
30 PRINT #1; "    *"
40 PRINT #1; "   ***"
50 PRINT #1; "  *****"
60 PRINT #1; "   ***"
70 PRINT #1; "    *"
80 PRINT #1
90 CLOSE #1
```

That should give you an idea of how to create pseudo-graphics. Using different combinations of characters, it is possible to create many different low resolution graphics with the ASCII characters.

Now, let's do something a little more practical. Remember how we needed graph paper to make our graphic PLAYERS in Chapter 7? Instead of using graph paper, we can use our printer to make the graph paper for us. The following program makes an 8 by 8 PLAYER/MISSILE TABLE you can use in designing players. If you want a longer table, increase the value in the "I" loop.

```
10 PRINT CHR$(125)
20 OPEN #1, 1, Ø, "P:"
30 PRINT #1; "PLAYER/MISSILE TABLE"
40 PRINT #1
50 FOR I = 1 TO 8
60 PRINT #1; I; " ";
70 PRINT #1; CHR$(124); CHR$(95);
```

```
80 NEXT J
90 PRINT #1; CHR$(124)
100 NEXT I
110 CLOSE #1
```

PLAYER/MISSILE TABLE

1								
2								
3								
4								
5								
6								
7								
8								

SUMMARY

The ATARI computer has several built-in words which can be used with a printer. Combined with the ATARI 85Ø interface, or another ATARI compatible interface, it is a simple matter to send information to the printer. Using LIST "P:", programs can be dumped to the printer for debugging or for sending to a friend in the mail. The LPRINT command, in both the Immediate and the Program modes will output to the printer instead of to the screen. It is almost like using PRINT except, instead of sending the information to the screen, it goes to the printer.

Using a similar format as employed for outputting to a cassette tape or disk, it is also possible to vector output to the printer. Instead of using OPEN to prepare a channel to tape, disk, or screen, you can also OPEN a channel to the printer. Then when you PRINT #, your formatted messages or characters will be sent to the printer. Using the OPEN/PRINT # sequence, it is possible to exercise more control over the manner in which material is printed.

Dumping graphics to the screen requires special utility programs which are too advanced for this book, but it is possible to obtain such programs from commercial vendors or public domain sources. However, using ASCII characters, we saw how we could produce pseudo-graphics with the knowledge we now have of programming. With some practice, you will be able to do just about anything you want with your printer and the ATARI.

CHAPTER 10

Program Hints and Help

Introduction

Well, here we are at the last chapter. We've covered most of the commands used for programming in BASIC on the ATARI and many tricks of the trade. However, if you are seriously interested in learning more about your computer and using it to its full capacity, there's more to learn. In fact, this last chapter is intended to give you some direction beyond the scope of this book.

First, we will introduce you to the best thing since silicon — ATARI Users Groups. These are groups who have interests in maximizing their computer's use. Second, I would like to suggest some periodicals with which you can learn more about your ATARI computer. Third, we will examine some languages other than BASIC which you can use on your ATARI. BASIC has many advantages, but like all computer languages it has its limitations, and you should know what else is available.

Next, we will examine some more programs. First, there will be listings of programs which you may find useful, fun, or both. The ones included were chosen to show you some applications of what we have learned in the previous nine chapters, enhancing what you already know. Then we will look at different types of programs you can purchase. These are programs written by professional programmers to do everything from making your own programming simpler to keeping track of your taxes. Finally, we will examine some hardware peripherals to enhance your ATARI.

ATARI User Groups

Of all the things you can do when you get your ATARI, the most helpful, economical, and useful is joining an ATARI User Group. Not only will you meet a great group of people with ATARI computers, but you will learn how to program and generally what to do and not to do with your computer. My club, The San Diego Atari Computer Enthusiasts (ACE), is made up of people who have ATARI 400s, 600XLs, 800s, 800 XLs, 1200XLs, 1400XLs, 1450XLs and every kind of adaptation of those models imaginable. Various club members helped me a great deal in learning about all the ins and outs of my ATARI. On top of all that, clubs have libraries of Public Domain software (FREE!) for their members and special discount rates for commercial software from stores.

Usually the best way to contact your ATARI User Group is through local computer or software stores. Often stores selling ATARI computers and/or software will have membership application forms, and some even serve as the meeting site for the clubs. Other microcomputer clubs in your area may also have ATARI users in them, so if there is not an ATARI club, join a general computer group. The help you get will be worth it.

To start your own ATARI Users group, post a notice and meeting time and site in your local computer store. Fellow ATARI users will get in touch with you, and before you know it, you'll have a club. Another way to get in touch with fellow ATARI users is via a modem. Using the ATARI 850 Interface Module and either an ATARI 830 Acoustic Modem or an ATARI 835 Direct Connect Modem, dial up the computer bulletin boards in your area and look for messages pertaining to ATARIs. Usually, you can get in contact with other users very quickly this way. (Ask for the PMS (Public Message System) numbers at your local computer store.) If you don't see any references to the ATARI, leave a message for people to get in touch with you.

ATARI Magazines

There are several periodicals with information about the ATARI. Some microcomputer magazines are general and others are for the ATARI only. When you're first starting, it is a good idea to stick with the ones dedicated to the ATARI since there are different versions of BASIC for non-ATARI computers. When you become more experienced, you can choose your own, but to get started there are several good ones with articles exclusively on the ATARI. These are as follows:

A.N.A.L.O.G. COMPUTING: The Magazine for ATARI Computer Owners
A.N.A.L.O.G., 565 Main Street, Cherry Valley, MA Ø1611, PH. (617) 892-3488.

A.N.A.L.O.G. is a bi-monthly publication with a wide variety of articles and programs for the ATARI. Here you will find programming techniques, tips for beginners, reviews of new hardware and software available, and various applications. Articles range from the simple to the technical, so regardless of your level of expertise, you will find this extremely useful. Subscriptions are $14.ØØ per year for 6 issues.

ANTIC: The ATARI Resource
Antic, 6ØØ 18th Street, San Francisco, CA 941Ø7, PH. (415) 864-Ø886

A second magazine for your ATARI is ANTIC, a monthly publication, which covers a broad range of ATARI applications, software and hardware, and has several programs for you to key in. There are plenty of articles for beginners, and each issue has a list of Public Domain software available. Subscriptions are $12.ØØ per year for 12 issues.

Compute!
P.O Box 54Ø6, Greensboro, NC 274Ø3

Compute! is not dedicated to the ATARI, but it generally has one or more articles on the ATARI in each issue. More than most other general computer magazines, Compute! will provide you with programs and programming techniques which can be applied to your computer. Additionally, it has several general articles on programming, hardware, and software which you will find useful. Finally, there are many bargains on software and peripherals to be found in the magazine. Subscriptions are $2Ø for 12 issues.

OTHER USEFUL PUBLICATIONS

In addition to the above three magazines, there are several others that you may find useful. Publications such as *Creative Computing, Byte, Interface Age, Popular Computing* and *Personal Computing* all have had articles about the ATARI. The best thing to do is to go through the table of contents in the various computer magazines in your local computer store. This will tell you at a glance if there are any articles or programs for the ATARI. As more and more clubs begin springing up, club newsletters can often be an invaluable source of good tips and programs for your computer, and they are a resource that should not be overlooked.

ATARI Speaks Many Languages

Besides BASIC, your computer can be programmed and can run programs in several other languages. In some cases, special hardware devices are required to run the languages, and there is special software required as well. Now let's look at some of these other languages.

Assembly Language

Assembly language is a "low level" language, close to the heart of your computer. It is quite a bit faster than BASIC or virtually any other language we will discuss. To write in assembly language, it is necessary to have a monitor or assembler to enter code. This language gives you far more control over your ATARI than BASIC, but it is more difficult to learn, and a program takes more instructions to operate than BASIC. (However, the object code is more compact, taking up fewer sectors on your disk.) For the ATARI, ATARI makes an Assembler Editor cartridge you can install for entering assembly/machine code. Also, for users with a disk drive, the ATARI Macro Assembler and Program-Text Editor is available on disk. If you are not sure you will like assembly language, you can try the public domain version written in BASIC. It is slow, but since it is free from your club library, or available for $1Ø from ANTIC Magazine (see above for address) on *ANTIC* Utility Disk #1, it might be a useful preview of what you can do with this very fast language. Several other commercial assembler/editors are available. Check the reviews and advertisements of the different magazines to see what best fits your needs.

To learn how to program in assembly language, the following were found to be the most useful:

1. *The ATARI Assembler* by Don Inman and Kurt Inman. (Reston, VA. : Reston Publishing Co., 1981.)

   This book was written for the ATARI Assembler Editor Cartridge. However, it can be used with other assembler editors since it uses general 65Ø2 Opcodes and machine code listings. It is strictly for beginners in assembly language, and while you can't expect to learn everything about machine/assembly language from it, it will get you well on your way.

2. *HOW TO PROGRAM YOUR ATARI IN 65Ø2 MACHINE LANGUAGE* (Upland, CA : IJG, Inc.) $9.95.

   While learning assembly language, this book will be of great assistance, especially as a reference guide to the functions of the various machine codes on your ATARI. However, it is best used in conjunction with the ATARI TECHNICAL REFERENCE NOTES. (See below.)

3. *ATARI TECHNICAL REFERENCE NOTES.* (ATARI, Inc., 1982).

   This collection has everything you need to find by way of machine level subroutines, special registers, and all the rest you need to know about your ATARI 4ØØ/8ØØ. (Most of it applies to the XL series machines as well, but there are some differences in the XL's not found in the NOTES.) Included in the NOTES are the OPERATING SYSTEM USER'S MANUAL, HARDWARE MANUAL, and the OPERATING SYSTEM SOURCE LISTING. The last of these three manuals in the NOTES is the most useful for beginners in assembly programming since it provides the addresses of the built-in machine language subroutines.

Other books are available for learning assembly level programming, and you will find books for other 65Ø2 computers, such as the Apple II, to be of some value.

HIGH AND LOW LEVEL LANGUAGES

When computer people talk of high and low level languages, think of high level as being close to talking in normal English and low level in terms of machine language, e.g., binary and hexadecimal. Assembly language is a low level language, one notch above machine level. The other languages we will discuss are high-level.

Forth

FORTH is a very fast high-level language, developed to create programs which are almost as fast as assembly language but take less time to program. Faster than Pascal, BASIC, Fortran, COBOL and virtually every other high-level language, FORTH is programmed by defining words which execute routines. New words incorporate previously defined words into FORTH programs. The best part of FORTH is that several versions are public domain. The Fig (FORTH Interest Group) FORTH version is in the public domain, available from your user group. If you are handy with assembly programming, you might even be able to install your own. However, there are FORTH vendors who have FORTH for the ATARI. One version recommended is:

valFORTH (24K RAM minimum required) $45.ØØ
Valpar International
38Ø1 E. 34th Street
Tucson, AZ 85713
Ph. (8ØØ) 528-7Ø7Ø

The nice thing about valFORTH is that it is supported by several other valFORTH utility packages allowing the user to enhance graphics (e.g., create and speed up vertical movement of player/missiles, etc.), manipulate text, and other useful applications.

The best source to learn about what is available is through the publication, *FORTH Dimensions* (see below) and your magazines where ATARI products are advertised.

Good books on learning FORTH are only just now becoming available. For learning FORTH, the following are recommended:

1. *FORTH PROGRAMMING* by Leo J. Scanlon (Indianapolis: Howard S. Sams & Co., 1982). This book uses the FORTH-79 and fig-FORTH models as standards, thereby providing the user with the most widely distributed versions of FORTH. This is a well organized and clear presentation of FORTH.

2. *STARTING FORTH* by Leo Brodie (Englewood Cliffs: Prentice-Hall, 1981). Well written and illustrated work on FORTH for beginners. Uses a combination of words from Fig, 79-Standard and polyFORTH.

3. *FORTH Dimensions*. Journal of FORTH INTEREST GROUP. P.O. Box 11Ø5, San Carlos, CA 94Ø7Ø. This periodical has numerous articles on FORTH and tutorial columns for persons seriously interested in learning the language.

Pascal

Pascal is a high-level language originally developed for teaching students structured programming. It is faster than BASIC, but is not as difficult to master as assembly language. It is probably the most popular high level language next to BASIC. You will find different versions of Pascal, but the language is fairly well standardized so that whatever version of Pascal you purchase will work with just about any Pascal program. Currently, ATARI PASCAL is available through the ATARI Program exchange (APX). It requires two drives, and an 8Ø column cartridge is useful but not required. To learn how to program in Pascal, there are several books available, the following having been found to be among the best:

1. *ELEMENTARY PASCAL: LEARNING TO PROGRAM YOUR COMPUTER IN PASCAL WITH SHERLOCK HOLMES.* By Henry Ledgard and Andrew Singer. (New York: Vintage Books.) This is a fun way to learn Pascal since the authors use Sherlock Holmes type mysteries to be solved with Pascal. It is based on the draft standard version for Pascal called X3J9/81-ØØ3 and may be slightly different from the version you have, but only slightly so.

2. *PASCAL FROM BASIC.* By Peter Brown. (Reading, MA: Addison-Wesley, 1982). If you understand BASIC, this book will help you make the transition from BASIC to PASCAL. It is written with the PASCAL novice in mind but assumes the reader understands BASIC.

Pilot

This language is for children. It was developed primarily as a teaching tool and is very simple to use, especially with turtle graphics. One version of this language available for the ATARI is available from ATARI, Inc. in both an Educator's Package and a Home Package. The Educator's Package requires an ATARI 41Ø Program Recorder, while the Home Package is on a cartridge. For a first programming language for children, PILOT is highly recommended.

Finally, if you find that programming in BASIC is most suitable for you, but you would like to speed up your programs, a simple way to do that is with a compiler. Essentially, a compiler is a program which transforms your code into a binary file which will run four to five times faster than ATARI BASIC. All you do is write the program in BASIC, compile it, and then save the compiled program. From then on, you run your compiled program as a machine language program. Two compilers available for your ATARI are

> ATACOMP (4ØK Disk System required) $34.ØØ
> ATACOMP, RR 3, P.O. Box 21
> Coggon, IA 52218 PH. (319) 435-2Ø31.
>
> BASM BASIC COMPILER and ASSEMBLER (32K Disk System required.) $99.95.
> 21115 Devonshire St. #132
> Chatsworth, CA 91311 PH. (213) 368-4Ø89.

The BASM compiler is actually a combination compiler and assembler/editor. It can be used as a transition between BASIC and assembly language programming as well as a compiler.

Sort Routines

These programs will sort numbers for you. The first program uses the "Bubble Sort" algorithm, which is simple but relatively slow. A random set of numbers is generated, and then they are printed out to the screen, first in random order and then in sorted order. Note how long it takes. The second program, using the "Shell Sort" algorithm, does something a little more useful. It sorts ZIP codes for you, but for purposes of comparison, RUN it with the random number routine. (Just substitute the first part of the "Bubble Sort" program before the "Shell Sort" routine.) By choosing the correct algorithm, you can save a lot of time.

BUBBLE SORT

```
10 PRINT CHR$(125)
20 PRINT "NUMBER OF NUMBERS TO SORT";
30 INPUT TN
40 DIM A(TN)
50 FOR I = 1 TO TN
60 X = RND (0)
70 A(I) = INT (1000 * X)
80 NEXT I
90 FOR I = 1 TO TN : PRINT A(I) : NEXT I : PRINT
100 REM
110 REM ****************
120 REM BUBBLE SORT
130 REM ****************
140 REM
150 FOR J = 1 TO TN-1
160 FOR I = 1 TO TN-1
170 IF A (I) <= A(I+1) THEN 210
180 T = A(I)
190 A(I) = A(I+1)
200 A(I+1) = T
210 NEXT I
220 NEXT J
300 REM
310 REM ********************
320 REM ORDERED OUTPUT
330 REM ********************
340 REM
350 FOR I = 1 TO TN
360 PRINT A(I)
370 NEXT I
```

SHELL SORT

```
10 PRINT CHR$(125)
20 PRINT "NUMBER OF ZIP CODES TO ENTER";
30 INPUT TZ : DIM A(TZ+1), L(TZ), R(TZ)
40 FOR N =1 TO TZ
50 PRINT "ENTER ZIP CODE ";
60 INPUT ZIP : A(N) = INT (ZIP)
70 NEXT N
100 REM *** SHELL SORT ***
110 L = (2 ^ INT (LOG (TZ) / LOG (2))) -1
120 L = INT (L/2)
130 IF L < 1 THEN 300
140 FOR J = 1 TO L
150 FOR K = J + L TO TZ STEP L
160 I = K
170 T = A(I)
180 IF A(I-L) <= T THEN 220
190 A(I) = A(I-L)
200 I = I-L
210 IF I > L THEN 180
220 A(I) = T
230 NEXT K
240 NEXT J
250 GOTO 120
300 REM
310 REM ********************
320 REM ORDERED OUTPUT
330 REM ********************
340 REM
350 PRINT
360 FOR I = 1 TO TZ
370 PRINT A(I)
380 NEXT I
```

Key Tricks

Before you read this, promise not to get angry. OK? All right, now you can read on. Up to this point we have not used a number of short-cuts available on your keys. This is because it was important for you to first get used to the commands and how to use them correctly. Also, as we will see, the short-cuts do not clearly show you what is happening on your computer as fully as writing out the commands.

In Appendix A of your BASIC REFERENCE MANUAL there is a chart which shows how to enter the first one or two letters of a command and a period (.) to get the whole command into your program. This will save you some time in programming, but it is difficult to read the command until you get used to it. For example, put a program into memory and enter L. and RETURN. The command is the same as entering LIST except you have to make only two key presses instead of four. Now, clear memory and enter the following:

```
10 ? CHR$ (125) : DIM A$(8) : A$= "ALL RIGHT"
20 F. I = 1 TO 10 : ? A$ : N. I
```

Before you RUN the program, can you guess what will happen? If you cannot, don't feel bad since it is confusing, especially the way it appears on the screen. When you RUN the program, it will clear the screen and print the message ALL RIGHT 10 times. Now LIST your program, and all the commands are clear except for the PRINT statement remaining as a question mark. These key short-cuts are handy in some cases and confusing in others. The L. for LIST command is usually from the Immediate mode and is handy to use in the abbreviated fashion. But until you become better acquainted with programming, these short-cuts may be more confusing than helpful. Use the ones with which you feel comfortable, and introduce them gradually.

Console Keys

To the right of your keyboard are four keys we have not mentioned yet. They are called the Console Keys and are accessed by PEEKing location 53279. To use them, a keyboard scan is set up, and when one of the four keys is pressed, the program branches to a subroutine. They have applications where the user is expected to interact with the program from the keyboard, but the other keys are used for INPUT of characters and keyboard graphics. For example, let's say you wanted to have a program that would enter names until a certain key was pressed. Since you would not want the key to be one with which you entered characters for the name you are entering, you could use the Console Keys. The values 3, 5, and 6 returned from location 53279 mean that the START, SELECT or

OPTION key is being pressed, respectively. By scanning address 53279, it is possible to branch to a subroutine when a specified key is pressed. The following program illustrates how this is done:

```
10 PRINT CHR$(125) : PRINT "CHOOSE
   CONSOLE KEY"
20 CONSOLE = 53279
30 START = 6
40 SELECT = 5
50 OPTION = 3
60 IF PEEK (CONSOLE) = START THEN GOSUB 100
70 IF PEEK (CONSOLE) = SELECT THEN GOSUB 200
80 IF PEEK (CONSOLE) = OPTION THEN GOSUB 300
90 GOTO 60
100 PRINT "START KEY PRESSED" : RETURN
200 PRINT "SELECT KEY PRESSED" : RETURN
300 PRINT "OPTION KEY PRESSED" : RETURN
```

You probably noticed that if you held the key down there were repeat messages. You have to be nimble with this program!

Function Keys on the 1200XL, 1400/1450 XL Series Computers

If you have the ATARI 12ØØXL, 14ØØXL, or 145ØXL you may have discovered the use of the four "function keys" at the top of the keyboard. These keys, numbered F1, F2, F3, and F4 are primarily for moving the cursor. In the normal or shifted mode, the function keys will move the cursor one step or a screen jump. With the CTRL and function keys you can do special things. The following summarizes their uses:

KEY	NORMAL	SHIFTED	CTRL
F1	Cursor up 1	Cursor to top	Toggle keyboard
F2	Cursor down 1	Cursor to bottom	Toggle screen
F3	Cursor left 1	Cursor far left	Toggle key click
F4	Cursor right 1	Cursor far right	Toggle European Character set

The normal and shifted modes are fairly self-explanatory, but the CTRL modes need some elaboration. First, by toggle we refer to setting one state by pressing the CTRL and function keys and then setting the opposite state by pressing that combination a second time. When CTRL-F1 is pressed, the keyboard locks up so that no one can use it. This might be handy when you're in the middle of a program and the phone rings and you don't want anyone goofing up your program while you're on the phone. The CTRL-F2 disables the screen. This can be useful in the middle of a program since computations can be done faster with the screen off. To get the screen back, just press CTRL-F2 a second time. If the keyboard click bothers you, the CTRL-F3 disables it. Finally, if you want to enter European characters, use the CTRL-F4 combinations. (Give your programs the continental look.)

Utility Programs

What's a Utility?

Utility programs are programs which help you program or access different parts of your computer. In this section we will review some of the more useful utility programs available at this time.

Currently, ATARI does not make utilities, other than tutorial cartridges and MICROSOFT BASIC. However, MICROSOFT BASIC is an excellent language compared to the standard ATARI BASIC. It does require a disk drive system, 32K RAM configuration, and is designed for the ATARI 8ØØ. However, if you want a more powerful language to develop and speed up your programs, as well as a form of BASIC which is becoming the standard in microcomputers, it would be worth having a look at MICROSOFT BASIC.

For ATARI 8ØØ owners only, one of the few cartridges available for the right hand cartridge slot is a general utility called MONKEY WRENCH II. This is a true programming utility providing automatic line numbering, renumbering, search and find strings within a program, search and replace and several other handy utilities. In addition it has a 65Ø2 monitor

for examining and changing memory contents. Unfortunately, this works only on the ATARI 8ØØ since it is the only model with dual cartridge slots.

More universal utilities are available. Probably the best place to start looking for what you need is in your ATARI club's library of public domain utilities on tape and disk. Two public domain utility disks are available through ANTIC magazine, so you should check them as well.

Word Processors

Your ATARI computer can be turned into a first class word processor with a word processing program. Word processors turn your computer into a super typewriter. They can do everything from moving blocks of text to finding spelling mistakes. Editing and making changes is a snap, and once you get used to writing with a word processor, you'll never go back to a typewriter again. This book was written with a word processor, and it took a fraction of the time a typewriter would have taken. (Believe me, I've written 1Ø books with a typewriter!)

There are some limitations with word processors. First, the ATARI screen displays only 4Ø columns. Since the standard page size is 8Ø columns, this bothers some people since what appears on the written page is different from what appears on the screen. However, since I write material which will be printed out in everything from 2Ø to 132 columns, the 4Ø columns do not bother me. If you want 8Ø columns for your screen, though, you can purchase adaptors which will provide 8Ø columns on the screen for you. Using an 8Ø column adaptor, you can see exactly what you will get when you print out your material. To give you some help in making up your mind, the following are some features you might want to look for:

1. Find/Replace.
   Will find any string in your text and/or find and replace any one string with another string. Good for correcting spelling errors and locating sections of text to be repaired.

2. Block Moves.
   Will move blocks of text from one place to another (e.g., move a paragraph from the middle to end of document). Extremely valuable editing tool.

3. Link Files.
   Automatically links files on disks. Very important for longer documents and for linking standardized shorter documents.

4. Line/Screen Oriented Editing.
   Line oriented editing requires locating beginning of line of text and then editing from that point. Screen oriented editing allows beginning editing from anywhere on the screen. The latter form of editing is important for large documents and where a lot of editing is normally required.

5. Automatic Page Numbering.
   Pages are automatically numbered without having to determine page breaks in writing text.

6. Embedded Code.
   In word processors, this enables the user to send special instructions directly to the printer for changing tabs,

printing special characters on the printer, and doing other things to the printed text without having to set the parameters beforehand and/or having the ability to override set parameters.

These are just a few of the things to look for in word processors. As a rule of thumb, the more a word processor can do, the more it costs. If you want to write only letters and short documents, there is little need to buy an expensive word processor. However, if you are writing longer, more complex, and a wider variety of documents, the investment in a more sophisticated word processor is well worth the added cost. If you have specialized needs (e.g., producing billing forms), you will want to look for those features in a word processor which meet those needs. Therefore, while a particular word processor may not do certain things, it may be just what you want for your special applications. As with other software, get a thorough demonstration of any word processor on an ATARI before laying out your hard earned cash. The ATARI WORD PROCESSOR (for the 8ØØ only) and the newer ATARI-WRITER, for the 4ØØ, 8ØØ and 12ØØXL, are available directly from ATARI dealers. The newer ATARIWRITER is an excellent word processor with most of the features listed above. It comes on a 16K cartridge. The following are some other word processors you might consider:

1. BANK STREET WRITER (48K RAM and Disk Drive required.)
   $69.95
   Broderbund Software
   1938 Fourth Street
   San Rafael, CA 949Ø1
   (415) 456-6424

Bank Street Writer is an excellent word processor, especially for younger writers. It is very "user friendly," and was used in educational programs to encourage and help students to learn writing skills.

2. LETTER PERFECT (16K RAM.$149.95 disk/ $199 cartridge)
   LJK Enterprises, Inc.
   P.O. Box 1Ø827
   St. Louis, MO. 63129

This word processor comes in 8Ø or 4Ø column versions. It is configured to use any printer, an important feature of any word processor. It is also compatible with Data Perfect, a data base program by the same company.

3. ACCU/WRITE. (16K Cassette). $2Ø.ØØ
   DPH, Inc.
   1700 Stumph Blvd. Suite 7Ø5
   Gretna, LA 7ØØ53
   (5Ø4) 361-8594

For those who have limited memory and uses for a word processor, ACCU/WRITE might be just the thing. It takes up little room, is cassette based and is inexpensive. Also, it requires the use of an Epson printer.

As a cautionary note, word processors take a bit of time to learn to use effectively. It is possible to start writing text immediately with most word processors, but in order to use all of their features, some practice is required. One of the strange outcomes of this is that once a user learns all of the techniques of a certain word processor, he or she will swear it is the best there is! Therefore, avoid arguments about the best word processor. It's like arguing politics and religion.

If you want to write text in more than 8Ø columns, you will need an adaptor. The following cartridge will do that for you:

1. 4Ø/8Ø VIDEO CARTRIDGE $219.95
   FULL-VIEW 80. $349.ØØ (Cartridge)
   Bit-3 Computer Corp.
   812Ø Penn Ave. South, Suite 548
   Minneapolis, MN 55431.

This cartridge can be used with or without a word processor, providing both 4Ø and 8Ø columns of text. It fits into the "back slots" (slot 3) of your computer. Compatible with Letter Perfect as well as other word processors.

Also for 8Ø columns, you might want to look at:

2. CM-1ØØØ/V $489.ØØ
   Compu-Mate Corp.
   63Ø5 Arizona Ave.
   Los Angeles, CA 9ØØ45.

The Compu-Mate CM-1ØØØ/V serves as both an 8Ø column screen display and a peripheral interface (like the ATARI 85Ø interface). It serves as an "all-in-one" device for printer interface and 8Ø columns on the screen.

Keyboards for the ATARI 4ØØ

As much as you might love your ATARI 4ØØ, it would be nice to have a movable keyboard like the 8ØØ or XL models. Well, there are plenty available for you. The following are a sampling:

1. JOYTYPER-4ØØ $129.95
   Microtronics, Inc.
   P.O. Box 8894
   Ft. Collins, CO 8Ø525
   (3Ø3) 226-Ø1Ø8

The JOYTYPER-4ØØ plugs into the ATARI 4ØØ with no soldering necessary.

2. COMMANDER 24ØØ $1Ø9.ØØ - $199.ØØ
   RCE
   536 N.E. "E" Street
   Grants Pass, OR 97526
   (8ØØ) 547-2492

The Commander 24ØØ keyboard comes with or without a numeric keypad. It plugs into either the 4ØØ or 8ØØ and does not require soldering. Both your regular keyboard and the Commander 24ØØ can be used simultaneously if you want. Easily detachable if you don't want the kids (or their parents!) playing on it.

Data Base Programs

When you need a program for creating and storing information, a "data base" program is required. Essentially, professionally designed data base programs use either sequential or random access files. When you use one, you just use the predefined fields provided or create fields. For example, a user may want to keep a data base of customers. In addition to having fields for name and address, the user may want fields for the specific type of product the customer buys, dates of last purchase, how much money is owed, date of last payment, etc.

Probably more than most other packages, data base programs should be examined carefully before purchasing. Some of the more expensive data bases can be used with virtually any kind of application, but if you're going to be using your data base only to keep a list of names and addresses to print out mailing labels, for example, a data base program designed to do that one thing will usually do it better and for a lot less money. On the other hand if your needs are varied and involve sophisticated report generation and changing record fields, then do not expect a simple, specialized program to do the job. ATARI, Inc. has a nice data base program, MAILING LIST, which can be used for several general purpose lists, such as names and addresses, client names, and similar files requiring names. For bigger and more varied jobs, ATARI also has THE HOME FILING MANAGER, which has more general database uses. It can organize everything from small inventories to people on your Christmas list. For a really powerful database, you might want to look at DATA PERFECT from LJK Enterprises or FileManager 8ØØ or FileManager+ from Synapse Software. These database programs are for complex applications which require storing and retrieving large amounts of diverse information. As a cautionary note, before you get a sophisticated database program, check the RAM requirements. You can add up to 64K of RAM on your 4ØØ/6ØØXL/8ØØ. (For 8ØØXL, 12ØØXL, 14ØØXL, and 145ØXL users, you probably have the RAM, but check for compatibility!)

Business Programs

If you think that the ATARI is primarily for games, you will be amazed by the number of business programs there are on the market for ATARI. Business programs have such a wide variety of functions that it is best to start with a specific business need and see if there is a program which will meet that need. On the other hand there are general business programs which are applicable to many different businesses. Specific business programs include ones which deal only with real estate, stock transactions, and inventory planning. More general programs include "General Ledgers," "Financial Planning," and, as discussed above, data base programs.

Unfortunately, business people often spend far too much for systems which do not work. They believe that if one spends a lot of money on software and hardware, it must be better than a less expensive simpler system. This thinking is based upon a "You Get What You Pay For" mentality, and it leads to systems which are not used at all. Here is where a good dealer or consultant comes in handy. First, since computers are getting more sophisticated and less expensive, often you do not "Get What You Pay For" when purchasing a big expensive one. Often all the business person ends up with is a dinosaur system which is outmoded, too big, and too expensive for the needs. Some computer dealers specialize in helping the business person. They will help set up the needed system in your place of business, help train office personnel, and provide ongoing support. These dealers will charge top dollar for your system and supporting software, as opposed to the discount stores and mail order firms; however, if you have any problems you will have someone who will come and help you out. Since the ATARI is so inexpensive to begin with, the extra money spent on buying from a business supportive dealer is well worth the little extra cost. Alternatively, there are consultants for setting up your system. If you use a consultant, get one who is an independent without any connection to a vested interest in selling computers. Contact one through your phone book and tell him you want to set up an ATARI system in your office and let him know exactly what your needs are. If he is familiar with your system, he will know the available software and peripherals you need. If he tries to sell you another computer, that probably means he is unfamiliar with your system, and it would be a good idea to try another consultant.

I do not mean to sound cynical, but I have encountered too many unhappy business people who bought the wrong system for their needs. One businessman said he paid $14,ØØØ for a computer system which never did work for his requirements and finally bought a microcomputer system for about a tenth of the price and everything worked out fine. This does not mean that a business may not require an expensive computer to handle certain business functions, and the ATARI certainly has limitations. However, before you buy any system, make sure it does what you want and have it shown to you working in the manner that fits your needs. Often you will find that the less expensive new micros like the ATARI will actually work better than costly big machines.

A good start for business programs is some kind of spreadsheet or general ledger. These programs are excellent for keeping track of complicated accounting. The best known spreadsheet is VisiCalc, used for column/row tabulations with user produced formulas. It is the best general purpose financial calculator on the market and consistently a bestseller. ATARI, Inc. has THE BOOKKEEPER which has a general ledger, accounts receivable, and accounts payable along with commands for dumping output to the printer. Another general business program is the COLOR ACCOUNTANT from Programmer's Institute. It includes, among other features, a checkbook manager, check search, mailing list, decision maker and a color graph design package. It comes on both cassette and disk. Finally, Computari has a disk based program, A FINANCIAL WIZARD 1.5. This program has several utilities for creating custom business applications, tabulations, budget forecasts, and several other useful business features. It is also configured for printing out the results to several different brands of printers.

The above programs are a sampling of what is available, and I have touched only on the more general ones. For more specific applications, your ATARI software dealer can show you a lot more. And remember, before buying, get a demonstration to make sure what you buy is what you need.

Graphics Packages

In our chapter on graphics we discussed some of the ATARI's capabilities with graphics. However, certain uses require either highly advanced programming skills or a good graphics package. Using graphics utilities and/or hardware, it is possible to create pictures easily. The pictures produced can then be saved to disk or tape or printed out to your printer. Also, character editors, for producing different characters for your keys are available. These programs allow you to concentrate on the graphics themselves rather than the programming techniques necessary to produce them.

Probably the best bet for serious graphics work are the various packages which operate under valFORTH. Two programs highly recommended are the PLAYER MISSILE GRAPHICS, CHARACTER EDITOR AND SOUND EDITOR, and TURTLE AND VALGRAPHICS AND FLOATING POINT ROUTINES from Valpar. These programs will require purchasing valFORTH; but in addition to being able to create all kinds of interesting graphics (including professional quality graphics) you will learn how to program in FORTH. If you're on a budget, there are several public domain programs for doing graphics in your club library, or for $1Ø you can get ANTIC's public domain disk, ANTIC GRAPHICS AND SOUND DEMO #1. Don't expect to do anything of professional quality, but the price is right!

If you are not inclined to spend time programming graphics, you can purchase hardware devices which allow you to "draw" your graphics. One way is with a "light pen." Programmer's Institute has one for only $29.95. It requires software, also available from Programmer's Institute, but with it you simply draw on the screen, and your pictures can be saved to disk or dumped to a printer.

Finally, to dump your programs to a printer, you need, in addition to a printer, special hardware/software. Your club's public domain library probably has several programs for dumping graphics to various printers. One useful hardware/software package is GRAPHICS HARDCOPY for $79.95 from Macrotronics, Inc. It dumps text and graphics to your printer. If you get one, be sure to specify whether you are using the 4ØØ or 8ØØ and the type of printer you have so that you get the correct cable and software.

Expanded Memory

The ATARI's memory is "expandable." With an ATARI 8ØØXL, 12ØØXL, 14ØØXL or 145ØXL you don't have to worry too much about expanded memory since it comes with a lot, but your ATARI 4ØØ, 6ØØXL and 8ØØ might need more memory. ATARI Inc. makes RAM expansion modules that increase memory in the 4ØØ and 8ØØ up to 48K and up to 64K for the 6ØØ XL. Other companies also have up to 64K of RAM which can be added to the 4ØØ or 8ØØ models. One popular board is the Mosaic 64K RAM SELECT. If you are handy with hardware and on a budget, you can get kits for 16-32K upgrades for $49.95-$64.95 from Bontek, MPO Box 547, Niagara Falls, NY 143Ø2 (416) 245-9758. For the ATARI 4ØØ, Austin Franklin Associate makes a 48K board for $149.95 that is all set to install. If you join a club, ask other members what they recommend and their experiences with different memory upgrades.

Like software, before you purchase an interface or peripheral, make sure it works with your computer! Unfortunately, many hardware attachments come with such poor documentation that without someone to show you how to work them, it is almost impossible to get them to operate properly.

SUMMARY

The most important thing to understand from this last chapter is that we have only scratched the surface of what is available for the ATARI computer. There is much, much more than a single chapter could possibly cover, and, as you come to know your ATARI, you will find that the choice of software and peripherals is limited only by the confusion in making up your mind. There were other items for the ATARI that came to mind, but this chapter and book would have never ended were I to indulge myself and keep prattling on. The software and hardware I suggested were based on personal preferences; I would suggest that you choose on the basis of your own needs and preferences and not mine. Think of the items mentioned as a random sampling of what one user found to be useful and then, after your own sampling, examination and testing, get exactly what you need.

As you end this book, you should have a beginning level understanding of your computer's ability. Whether you use it for a single function or are a dedicated hacker, it is important that you understand the scope of its capacity to help you in your work, education and play. It is not a monstrous electronic mystery, but rather a tool to help you in various ways. You may not understand exactly how it operates, but you probably do not understand everything about how your TV set operates either, but that never prevented you from watching the evening news. With your computer, though, you make the "news" on your TV.

Farewell and Good Luck!!

ATARI COMMAND EXAMPLES

This glossary is arranged in *alphabetical* order. The examples are set up to show you how to use the commands and their proper syntax. In some cases when a command has different contexts of usage, more than a single example will be used. Some examples are given in the Immediate mode and some in the Program mode <those with line numbers> and some with both. Results are given to show what a particular configuration would create in some examples for clarification. Some commands of specialized use that were not covered in the text have been included here for a more complete glossary.

ABS( ) Gives the absolute value of a number or variable.

```
PRINT ABS(-123.45)
<RESULT> 123.45
```

ADR Returns memory address of string.

```
10 DIM A$(14)
20 A$ = "ATARI COMPUTER"
30 PRINT ADR(A$)
<RESULT> 7743 (Depends on memory size.)
```

AND Logical operator used in IF/THEN statement.

```
140 IF A$ < > "Y" AND A$ < > "N" THEN GOTO 10
 0
```

ASC( ) Returns ASCII value of first character in string.

```
PRINT ASC ("W") or A$ = "ATARI" : PRINT ASC(A$)
```

ATN( ) Returns arctangent of number or variable.

```
PRINT ATN (123)
<RESULT> 1.56266643
```

BYE Exits from BASIC to scratchpad.

```
BYE
```

CHR$( ) Returns the character with a given decimal value.

```
PRINT CHR$(65)
<RESULT> A
```

CLOAD Loads program from cassette tape into memory.

```
CLOAD
```

CLOSE #N Closes channel to device or file.

```
21Ø CLOSE #7 : REM 7 IS FILE NUMBER OF DEVICE
OR FILE BEING CLOSED.
```

CLOG Returns common logarithm of argument.

```
PRINT CLOG(123)
<RESULT> 2.Ø899Ø511
```

CLR All variables are reset to zero.

```
12Ø CLR
```

COLOR Sets color register with DRAWTO and PLOT and/or in GRAPHICS Ø, 1 or 2, the next character to be plotted.

```
2Ø COLOR 122
```

CONT Continues program after a STOP or <BREAK> in program

```
CONT
```

COS( ) Returns the cosine of variable or number.

```
PRINT COS(123)
<RESULT> -.887968907 4
```

CSAVE Saves program to cassette tape.

```
CSAVE
```

DATA Strings or numbers to be read with READ statement.

```
1000 DATA 2, 345, HELLO
```

DEG Sets up trigonometric functions to be expressed in degrees instead of radians.

```
10 DEG
20 PRINT COS(7)
<RESULT when RUN> 0.992546157
<RESULT without DEG> 0.7539026737
```

DIM Allocates maximum range of array OR string variable.

```
130 DIM A$ (20)
10 DIM JK (100)
```

DOS Accesses disk directory and menu.

```
DOS
```

DRAWTO C,R Draws a line between last point PLOTted and specified Column and Row.

```
10 GRAPHICS 7
20 COLOR 2 : PLOT 0,0
30 DRAWTO 50,50
```

END Terminates running of program.

```
200 END
```

ENTER Loads a LISTed program (saved to disk with "D:LIST") into memory without erasing current program.

```
ENTER
```

EXP( ) Returns e=2.71828179 to indicated power.

```
PRINT EXP (5)
<RESULT> 148.413155
```

FOR Set ups beginning of FOR/NEXT loop and top limit of loop.

```
40 FOR I = 1 TO 100
```

FRE( ) Returns available memory.

```
PRINT FRE(0)
```

GET #N Used to input single byte of information to disk or can be used to input single byte of information from keyboard. In latter application, it is used to halt program until number is pressed.

<KEYBOARD>

```
30 OPEN #5,4,0,"K:"
40 GET #5, A
```

<DISK>

```
10 OPEN #2, 4, 9, "D1: FILENAME"
20 GET #2; FV
```

GOSUB Branches to subroutine at given line number.

```
100 GOSUB 200
```

GOTO (or **GO TO**) Branches to given line number.

```
100 GOTO 200
```

GRAPHICS Sets graphics modes 0-8.

```
30 GRAPHICS 4
```

IF/THEN Sets up conditional logic for execution.

```
60 IF A$ = "Q" THEN END
```

INPUT Halts program execution until string or numbers entered and RETURN key is pressed. May enter message within INPUT statement.

```
90 INPUT "ENTER WORD-> "; W$(I)
100 INPUT "ENTER NUMBER -> "; A
110 INPUT "ENTER INTEGER NUMBER -> "; N%
120 PRINT "HIT 'RETURN' TO CONTINUE ";
130 INPUT R$
```

INPUT# Takes data from a previously OPENed file or device.

```
200 INPUT#1, R$
```

INT( ) Returns the integer value of real variable or number.

```
PRINT INT (123.45)
<RESULT> 123
```

LEN Returns the length in terms of number of characters for a specified string.

```
A$ = "COMPUTER AWAY"
PRINT LEN(A$)
<RESULTS> 12
```

LET Optionally used in defining value of variable or string.

```
20 LET A = 10
30 LET A$ = "ATARI"
```

LIST (Dos) Save a program to disk as ATASCII file.

```
LIST "D:GRAPH"
```

LOAD Loads program from disk.

```
LOAD "D: PROG1"
```

LOCATE C,R,V Store in variable V, the Column and Row data.

```
10 GRAPHICS 3
20 COLOR 2
30 SETCOLOR 2, 13, 6
40 PLOT 5,5
50 DRAWTO 20,20
60 LOCATE 19, 19, L
70 PRINT L
<RESULT when RUN> 2
```

LOG( ) Returns logarithm of specified number or variable.

```
PRINT LOG (123)
<RETURNS> 4.81218436
```

or

```
G = 123 : PRINT LOG (G)
```

LPRINT Sends output to printer.

```
LPRINT "Atari on my printer"
```

NEW Clears program in memory.

```
NEW
```

NEXT Sets the bottom of the loop begun with FOR statement.

```
10 FOR I = 1 TO 100
20 PRINT "THIS",
30 NEXT I
```

NOT Logical negation in IF/THEN statement.

```
60 IF A NOT B THEN GOTO 100
```

NOTE S,C Used in advanced disk file handling operations to find position of file pointer, indicating last Sector and Character.

```
NOTE #5, SEC, CHR
```

ON Sets up computed GOTO and GOSUB.

```
190 ON A GOSUB 1000,2000,3000
```

OPEN #R,CN,AC,"FD: TITLE" Opens channel to Reference number, Code Number, Auxiliary Code device or file.

```
4= READ    8= WRITE    12= READ/WRITE
6= READ DISK DIRECTORY
C:= CASSETTE    D:= DISK DRIVE    S:= SCREEN
  P:= PRINTER    K:= KEYBOARD    E:= EDITOR
```

500 OPEN #5,4,0, "D1: PMDATA" (Opens channel to disk drive for reading file.)

OR Logical OR in IF/THEN statement.

```
130 IF A=10 OR B = 20 THEN GOTO 190
```

PADDLE( ) Get information from paddle value.

```
140 A = PADDLE(1)
150 PRINT A
```

PEEK Returns memory contents of given decimal location.

```
170 PRINT PEEK (768)
180 IF PEEK(768) = 5 THEN GOTO 200
```

PLOT C,R Plots a point in graphics at Column, Row designated.

```
10 GRAPHICS 3
20 PLOT 5, 10
```

POINT #N,S,C Used in disk file handling operations to move position of file pointer, to Sector and Character of OPENed file, channel N. Used in advanced file handling.

```
20 POINT #5, 200, 20
```

POKE Inserts given value in specified memory location.

```
POKE 768,10 (Sets memory location 768 to decimal
value 10)
```

POP Used to exit GOSUB rather than using RETURN.

```
10 GOSUB 100
20 PRINT "HERE"
30 END
100 PRINT "NOW"
110 POP
<RESULT> NOW
```

POSITION C,R Places cursor at specified Column, Row.

```
10 PRINT CHR$(125)
20 POSITION 10,20
30 PRINT "THIS LINE"
```

PRINT Outputs string, number or variable to screen or printer. (Can substitute "?" for PRINT.)

```
PRINT 1;2;3; "GO"; F$; A; N%
```

PRINT# Sends output to specified OPENed device or file. (The question mark (?) cannot be substituted when using PRINT#.)

```
OPEN #5,8,Ø, "P:"
PRINT#5; "HELLO ATARI"
```

<RESULT> Prints message HELLO ATARI to printer.

PTRIG( ) Get information from paddle button - Ø if being pressed.

```
40 A = PTRIG(Ø)
50 IF A = Ø THEN GOSUB 1ØØ
```

RAD Default condition of trigonometric functions specifying radians rather than degrees. Used to restore to default after DEG is used.

```
1Ø DEG
2Ø PRINT COS(6)
3Ø RAD
4Ø PRINT COS(6)
```

<RESULTS when RUN> Ø.9945218991
Ø.96Ø17ØØ149

READ Enters DATA contents into variable.

```
1Ø READ A : READ B$
2Ø DATA 5, "BATS"
```

REM Non-executable command. Allows remarks in program lines.

```
1Ø DIM A$(122) : REM DIMENSIONS STRING
ARRAY "A$" TO 122
```

RESTORE Resets position of READ to first DATA statement.

```
1Ø FOR I = 1 TO 5 : READ A$(I) : NEXT
2Ø RESTORE
```

RETURN Returns program to next line after GOSUB command.

```
5ØØ RETURN
```

RND( ) Generates a random number less than 1 and greater than or equal to Ø.

```
PRINT RND(5)
```

INT (RND (1) * (N) + 1) Generates whole random numbers from 1 to N, with N being the upper limit of desired numbers.

```
1Ø N = 1Ø
2Ø R = INT (RND (1) * (N) + 1)
3Ø PRINT R
```

<RESULT> Random number between 1 and 1Ø

RUN Executes program in memory.

```
RUN
```

SAVE Records program on disk.

```
SAVE "D: GRAPH PLOT"
```

SETCOLOR CR,H,L Sets color of Color Register (CR) to Hue and Luminance. Color register is dependent on Graphics mode.

```
SETCOLOR 2, 16, 6
```

SGN( ) Returns value for sign. If positive number then 1, if Ø then Ø and if negative then -1.

```
PRINT SGN(123)
```

<RESULT> 1

SIN( ) Returns the sine of variable or number.

```
PRINT SIN(123)
<RESULT> -Ø.4599Ø3894
```

SQR( ) Returns the square root of variable or number.

```
PRINT SQR(64)
```

STEP Sets the increment/decrement of FOR/NEXT loop.

```
1Ø FOR X = 1 TO 1ØØ STEP 1Ø
2Ø FOR Y = 1ØØ TO 1Ø STEP -1Ø
```

STICK( ) Get information from joystick value. Values from 5-15.

```
1Ø S1 = STICK(1)
2Ø PRINT S1
3Ø IF S1 = 14 THEN R = R + 1
```

STRIG( ) Get information from joystick button - Ø if being pressed.

```
1Ø FIRE = STRIG(Ø)
2Ø IF FIRE = Ø THEN GOSUB 1ØØ
```

STOP Halts execution and prints line number where break occurs. (CONT command will re-start program at next instruction after STOP command.)

```
1ØØ STOP
```

STR$( ) Converts number/variable into string variable.

```
2Ø DIM T$(3) : T= 123 : T$= STR$(T) : TT$= "$" + T$
+ ".ØØ"
```

THEN Used in conjunction with IF. See IF/THEN above.

TO Used in conjunction with FOR/NEXT. See FOR/NEXT above.

TRAP Primarily used in detecting end of file in file programming. When INPUT to OPENed file is error, TRAP is used to branch to out of sequence line.

```
10 TRAP 150
.
.
150 CLOSE #5
```

VAL( ) Used to convert string to numeric value.

```
30 H$ = "123" : PRINT VAL(H$)
```

XIO (1) Used as "fill" and DRAWTO statement with graphics. (2) Advanced multi-function I/O.

```
(1) 60 XIO 18, #6, 0, 0, "S:" : REM FILL
(2) 200 XIO 5, #5, 0, 0, "PROG1.LST"
```

INDEX